The Financial Times Guide to Leadership

The Financial Times Guide to Leadership

How to lead effectively and get results

Marianne Abib-Pech

Harlow, England • London • New York • Boston • San Francisco • Toronto • Sydney • Auckland • Singapore • Hong Kong
Tokyo • Seoul • Taipei • New Delhi • Cape Town • São Paulo • Mexico City • Madrid • Amsterdam • Munich • Paris • Milan

PEARSON EDUCATION LIMITED

Edinburgh Gate
Harlow CM20 2JE
Tel: +44 (0)1279 623623
Fax: +44 (0)1279 431059
Website: www.pearson.com/uk

First published 2013 (print and electronic)

© Pearson Education Limited 2013 (print and electronic)

The right of Marianne Abib-Pech to be identified as author of this work has been asserted by her in accordance with the Copyright, Designs and Patents Act 1988.

Pearson Education is not responsible for the content of third-party Internet sites.

ISBN: 978-0-273-77602-4 (print)
    978-0-273-77914-8 (PDF)
    978-0-273-77915-5 (ePub)

British Library Cataloguing-in-Publication Data
A catalogue record for this book is available from the British Library

Library of Congress Cataloging-in-Publication Data
Abib-Pech, Marianne.
 The Financial times guide to leadership: how to lead effectively and get results /
Marianne Abib-Pech.
    p. cm.
Includes index.
ISBN 978-0-273-77602-4 (pbk.)
1. Leadership. I. Financial times (London, England) II. Title.
HD57.7.A225 2013
658.4'092--dc23
                2012047343

The Financial Times. With a worldwide network of highly respected journalists, *The Financial Times* provides global business news, insightful opinion and expert analysis of business, finance and politics. With over 500 journalists reporting from 50 countries worldwide, our in-depth coverage of international news is objectively reported and analysed from an independent, global perspective. To find out more, visit www.ft.com/pearsonoffer

10 9 8 7 6 5 4 3
16 15 14

Cover Image (c) Getty Images
Typeset in 9pt Stone Serif by 30
Printed and bound in Malaysia (CTP-PPSB)
NOTE THAT ANY PAGE CROSS-REFERENCES REFER TO THE PRINT EDITION

To José-Clément
To Xavier

Contents

About the author

Marianne Abib-Pech has led a highly successful international career in finance. She left France, her home country, in her twenties to study Finance and Business Organisation at Heriot-Watt University in Edinburgh. She then worked for some of the most admired corporations of the past twenty years, from Arthur Andersen and Motorola to General Electric and finally Shell, as Global CFO of one of their downstream divisions. She was the only woman ever hired externally at this level of the finance organisation in Shell.

Throughout her career, she has been exposed to the best leadership training possible and always demonstrated a keen interest in developing leaders within and outside her own teams.

Marianne is the Founder of Leaders!, a global leadership consultancy and think tank operating in Europe and Asia. Leaders! specifically focuses on leadership emergence, leadership transformation and cognitive diversity – gender, cultural and generational – to create business value.

Marianne is a regular columnist in *The Huffington Post, The Independent* and *Global Corporate Venturing. The Financial Times Guide to Leadership* is her first book.

She currently splits her time between Hong Kong, London and Paris.

Author's acknowledgements

This book would not have been possible without the help – conscious or not – of all the fantastic leaders and individuals listed below. I had the great pleasure of working with and learning from them. Some of them very kindly agreed to be interviewed, to share their journey or simply to brainstorm their views of leadership with me and some have acted as role models or mentors over the years.

Jeremy Bentham	Vice President, Global Business Environment, Head of Scenarios Team, Royal Dutch Shell
Alain Bloch	Director, HEC Entrepreneurs
Jeff Bornstein	Senior Vice President, General Electric, Chief Financial Officer, GE Capital
Ruth Cairnie	Executive Vice President Strategy and Planning, Royal Dutch Shell
Estelle Clark	Group Business Assurance Director, Lloyd's Register
Andrew L. Cohen	Chief Executive Officer, JP Morgan Private Bank, Asia
Fred Crognale	Downstream Controller, Royal Dutch Shell
Rachel Denoon	Director, Compliance, Barclays
Stéphane Distinguin	Founder, faberNovel
Michael Drexler	Senior Director, Head of Investors Industries, World Economic Forum, USA
Patrick Dunne	Director Marketing and Communication and Marketing, 3i

Mercédes Erra	Fondatrice, BETC, Directrice Générale, Havas, Présidente Exécutive d'Euro, RSCG Worldwide
Antoine Firmenich	PhD, Co-Founder, Alatus SA, Managing Director, Aquilus Pte Ltd
Emma Fitzgerald	Vice President Retail Network, Royal Dutch Shell
Guillaume Gauthereau	Founder, Totsy
Clara Gaymard	Présidente Général Electric France
Wolfgang Hafenmayer	Managing Partner, LGT Venture Philanthropy
Camilla Hartvig	Country President, Spain, AstraZeneca
Simon Hill	Founder and CEO, Wazoku
Venetia Howes	Past Master, Worshipful Company of Marketors
Richard Jory	General Manager, Shell Markets (Middle East) Limited
Nigel Kershaw	OBE, Chief Executive, Big Issue Invest, Group Chairman, The Big Issue Company
Philippe Kalmbach	Founder, Wine Source Group
Linda Kromjong	Vice President, Labor Relations, International Deutsche Post DHL
Hervé Latard-Baton	Financial Services, Global Business Unit, Cap Gemini
Scott Lawson	Founder, Sow Asia
Ning Li	Founder, Made.com
Eric Lim Yew Tou	Executive Director, Business Development Chemicals Limited, Far East

Gérard Lopez	Founder, Mangrove Capital, Partner-Owner, Lotus Formula One
Ruth Marshall-Johnson	Future Consumer and Trend Development Consultant, WGNS
Alison Maitland	Former *Financial Times* journalist and co-author of *Future Work* (2011, Palgrave Macmillan)
Sherene Metwally	Downstream LNG Finance Manager, Europe, Global Support, Royal Dutch Shell
Vincent Moge	Partner, Chief Executive Office, StormHarbour Securities, Singapore
Tobias Nevin	Founder, Everfeel
Sjoerd Post	Executive, Vice President Strategy, Downstream, Royal Dutch Shell
Alexandre de Rothschild	Member of Management Committee, Rothschild Merchant Banking
Tina Revsbech	Senior Vice President, Torm A/S
Adam Ritchie	Chief Economist, Royal Dutch Shell Trading and Shipping Company
Mary-Sue Rogers	Former General Manager, Global Human Resources, Learning and Recruiting, IBM, currently General Manager, Talent2
Robert Rozek	Executive Vice President and Chief Financial Officer, Korn Ferry International
Farid Salem	Directeur Général, Delegue CMA-CGM
Scott Schenkel	Senior Vice President Chief Financial Officer, eBay MarketPlaces
Marc Simoncini	Founder, Meetic

Murray Steele	Senior Lecturer, Strategic Management, Cranfield School of Management
Ruth Sunderland	Associate City Editor, *Daily Mail*
Tan Chong Meng	Chief Executive Officer, PSA International
Hans Van Geloven	Vice President Projects and Technology Division, Royal Dutch Shell
Nathalie de Wachter	Global Commercial Finance Director, AstraZeneca
Fields Wicker-Miurin	OBE, Co-founder and Partner, Leaders' Quest

Thank you all for your time – this book is also partially yours.

I would like to extend my gratitude to Serge H. Borg CDI EMEA Vice President Markets Development, Oddi Aasheim, Managing Director of Strategy Leadership and Performance (SLP Limited) and Laurent Choain, Chief Human Resources Officer for Mazars, for acting as my advisory board during the creation of this book. Thank you so much for your time, your generosity and helping me stay on course.

Many thanks to Andy Lopata for his great contribution to Chapter 8 – Andy, you are the best! Also to Sue Richardson for turning my writing into 'plain English'.

A very special thank you to Anne-Laure – the indirect cause of all of this – Grégoire and Jean-Marc for so kindly opening their networks to me, and Fabien and Fabrice for sharing coffees, progress and giving me motivational boosts.

Publisher's acknowledgements

We are grateful to the following for permission to reproduce copyright material:

Text

Article on page 1 from Tsusaka, M. (2012) View from Davos, 27 January ©
Boston Consulting Group (this article originally appeared on the Financial
Times website); article on page 41 from Johnson, L. (2012) Beware the
boss with messianic complex, *Financial Times*, 11 September, p.83 © The
Financial Times 2012. All Rights Reserved; article on page 119 from Rigby,
R. (2012) The careerist: Making the workplace fun, *Financial Times*, 30
September © The Financial Times 2012. All Rights Reserved; article on page
223 from Manchester, G. (2012) When times are tough, disrupt, *Financial
Times*, 7 September © Thunderhead.com extract from *The Little Prince* by
Antoine de Saint Exupery © Editions Gallimard 1946. Published by Egmont
UK Ltd and used with permission; extract from 'Fire' by Judy Brown, *A lead-
er's guide to reflective practice*, 2006, Trafford Publishing with permission

Figures

Figure on page 30 courtesy of PwC Projections; on page 263 from HOW
COMPETITIVE FORCES SHAPE STRATEGY, *Harvard Business Review*,
March/April (Porter, M., 1979); Figure on page 266 adapted from The
BCG Portfolio Matrix from the Product Portfolio Matrix © 1970, The
Boston Consulting Group.

Picture credits

Photo on page 28 from www.facebook.com/notes/facebook friend-
ships/469716398919 with permission from Facebook, Inc.

All other images © Pearson Education

In some instances we have been unable to trace the owners of copyright
material, and we would appreciate any information that would enable
us to do so.

Foreword

This is a time when we need leadership, a time for leaders. Our world is crumbling and calling for a new definition of ourselves. I am not only referring to the world of financial services, which is rethinking its codes, purpose and values, but the world at large.

If you take a minute to pause and look around, speed, values, social justice are emerging as new powerful themes to think about. Thanks to the fast development of technology and new powerful tools, such as the so-called social media, we have to face changes with a different attitude. These topics challenge us – as both a corporate community and individuals – to find answers to a very new set of questions.

- How can we remain competitive in the long term when the information base keeps expanding?

- How can we grow and develop our organisations when most financial markets are either in shambles or reinventing themselves?

- How can we balance risk and reward, profitability and compliance, to create a new world that is more sustainable and possibly more equal?

- What is the role of innovation and how do we innovate processes, products and – I will throw this into the mix – people?

Exercising leadership has never been so exciting and so difficult. The pathway to it is more confusing than ever.

When I think about leadership, I think in numbers. Let me explain. When I think about a leader, I do not see a solitary person at the top of a mountain, entrenched in an ivory tower, exercising power and holding the ultimate truth.

Rather, I see someone out there, engaged and doing things. I see someone who tries his or her best to teach and pass on know-how to colleagues. I see someone who behaves like a coach, not just a boss.

A leader should be out there, cutting through complexity and looking forward, towards the future, not holding on to the past.

One of the duties a leader has is to challenge others to think differently – actually, not just to think differently but also to have the courage to put experience into practice and even to fail. A leader should allow (even 'push') for failure in others. Without failure there is no opportunity to learn.

A leader ought to be engaged – not just because he or she is passionate about whatever the work is but because of an inherent desire to learn and constantly develop.

A leader must be 'out there' looking for talented people in order to let them grow and, maybe, make them future top managers. One of the most critical responsibilities of a leader is to feed the talent pipeline of the organisation and build teams. Not just any type, but diverse teams that are able to complement the leader's own skill set, overcome any shortcomings and play on their strengths. Groups of people that can compete, be in conflict and contribute to the common cause. Challenging teams that will debate, push, disagree ... Harmony is not always the sign of a great team. Contributing to a common vision and leading change as one – exchanging, enriching is the name of the game.

A leader should play the role of catalyst for people – helping them build self-confidence so that they reach the best part of themselves. It will translate into profitability for the organisation.

A leader should drive action and be ruthless when it comes to execution. We have to face it, only the concrete realisation of ideas, vision and the ability to lead change counts – they are the ultimate signs of leadership.

I am a strong believer in leadership being more natured than nurtured, however, Marianne here very succinctly summarises a potential recipe for successful leadership.

What is interesting is that she presents a simple yet well thought through model, rooted in three critical and mutually supporting dimensions – the core awareness of the individual, how then this emanates to their immediate environment of influence and, then drives impact on the world at large.

Marianne develops easy-to-follow solutions and methods that have the merit of being tangible and immediately applicable.

If you are experiencing leadership for the first time, this book will help you on your journey and prepare your future path. If, however, you are already a seasoned leader, this book can give you a fresh perspective, a good dose of inspiration to start doing things differently, integrating an understanding of a younger workforce with different needs, dreams and desires. It will also help you kick out complacency or cynicism!

You want to be a leader? Be authentic, open, honest. Do not compromise on who you are ... because one day the music stops and you still need to go on. Happy reading!

Sergio Ermotti
Chief Executive Officer, UBS
Zurich, September 2012

Introduction

In 1996, the new recruits at Arthur Andersen in Luxembourg were sent to the company's training centre in Saint Charles, Illinois. There they got their first real taste of the company culture and started to lay the foundations of the skill sets that they would build on throughout their careers.

When I joined this group of enthusiastic young professionals, fresh from university, one of our instructors – Karen, an American lady in her mid-thirties – made a particularly strong impression on me. She came across as very smart and clearly talented, but there was something else about her. She had an aura, a presence that made everyone listen when she was talking in group settings. She had a particular way of paying attention to the people around her – being very supportive, while at the same time allowing the new recruits to reach the answers by themselves. This made her different, it made her special. I remember thinking, 'This is someone I would like to become one day'. She was my first example of what a leader could be.

In August 2007, I joined Shell as the Global Head of Finance for its aviation business. Shell undertakes a People Survey on an annual basis. The survey consists of a series of questions on the level of satisfaction you feel being a Shell employee and gives feedback from your team on your leadership style. It is compared with your own previous year's score and is benchmarked against different functions of the organisation. In January 2011, after four years in the role, I had helped grow the business by an average of 15 per cent. My scores as a leader were some of the strongest in the group.

My experience begs the question: can anyone become a leader? Can leadership be nurtured or is it an innate part of a person's nature? These are good questions, but have an ambiguous answer: it depends.

A person's nature is indeed fundamentally important to leadership – being a leader requires intellect, empathy, wit and decisiveness. However, what really counts is having the *drive* to become the leader you want to be.

At certain points in my career I hit roadblocks and doubts. Then, the example of Karen came vividly back to my mind. I started thinking a great deal more about my leadership style and 'brand'. I began to spend time observing my environment and consciously adjusting to it. I focused on thinking strategically about my stakeholders and network-building. I also factored time into my schedule for developing my skill set, translating trends and events into business solutions. Above all, I recognised that I needed to develop a much stronger sense of self-awareness and a much higher level of empathy to truly be a successful leader.

Hindsight is a wonderful thing. Looking back at my journey, I can now pinpoint what is essential to becoming a good or even a great leader. It all boils down to three critical pillars of leadership:

- a high level of self-awareness built on a deep understanding of what makes you you – your strengths, fears, hopes, brand or the brand you want to be known for (Finding the leader inside you)

- an ability to read, lead and influence people by developing your credibility and level of empathy, as well as building effective and efficient networks to help and support you (Leading and influencing – bringing others on the journey)

- the skill to craft a compelling vision and, with confidence and inspiration, turn it into a successful strategy, plus most importantly, deliver on it (Building and executing your vision – from ideas to results).

It is this that *The Financial Times Guide to Leadership* is about.

This guide is the result of 15 years of corporate experience – the 11 years it took me to rise from the role of a junior auditor to Global Head of Finance at Shell Aviation and the four years in position as a CFO. These 15 years were spent on three different continents and in six countries. It entailed working with more than 40 different nationalities and managing teams and teams of leaders. I went from analysing financials to working on strategic reformulation and buying and selling equity stakes in different organisations in different countries. Those years took me from being a team member to building teams and, at times, dramatically changing team structures by letting go underperformers and hiring new talent. They saw me learn how to welcome – even embrace – change, then lead and manage it. All of this was done while adjusting to and operating within five different, strong, corporate cultures, mostly in Fortune 100 companies. These five companies had a common feature: they all took fostering and nurturing leaders very seriously. Some of them even had the best in-house leadership development programmes in existence.

What this guide is not is an academic survey of the latest or the greatest theories on leadership. I have no intention of competing with academic literature, nor do I pretend that my work is complete. Leadership is evolving every day and so are individuals. Instead, the goal here is to give you pointers, trigger your thinking and equip you with practical tips and examples to take back to your daily work life. The purpose is to help you either kick-start your leadership journey or further hone some of your leadership skills and/or attributes.

What you are about to read is also the result of meetings with more than 50 fascinating and highly talented individuals, from seasoned corporate leaders to successful entrepreneurs and emerging leaders. Some very kindly agreed to be interviewed, to share their journeys or simply brainstorm their views on leadership with me; some I have worked with and learned from in the past 15 years; some have played the role of mentors in the same period.

What is the quintessential lesson that I learned? Aiming to become a leader is not easy. It is rooted in developing a high level of questioning and self-analysis. It is about constantly challenging yourself, while also being pragmatic and choosing your battles. More importantly, it is a never-ending journey towards excellence.

It is hoped that this will create in you a call for change. The ambition here is to help you assess what is needed for you to become the best you can be, the best possible *leader* that you can be. The aim is to develop you as a global, diverse, collaborative and inclusive leader, ready and able to have an impact on both *your* world and *the* world. As Hillel the Elder (a Jewish religious leader) once said, 'If not now, when? If not you, who?'

How to use this book

The objective of the book is to serve as your 'go-to' resource for tips, exercises, advice. At times, it will also give you a fresh perspective on leadership.

It is an accessible and comprehensive guide for everyone, ranging from young professionals starting their leadership journeys, to mature managers wanting to take their leadership skills to the next level or successful executives looking to stay in tune with their leadership performance. Wherever you are on your path, this guide has been designed to help you become a better leader.

Depending on your position within your organisation, you will need to focus on or acquire different attributes and demonstrate different actions. The table below gives you an indication of how well-rounded leaders or aspiring leaders should allocate their time.

Where are you in your leadership journey?

	The leader inside you	Leading and influencing	From vision to action
	Self-awareness Self-confidence Leadership brand	Credibility Teambuilding Influencing	Vision Strategic thinking Execution
Leader of leaders	0%	0%	100%
Leader of team	33%	33%	34%
Team member	50%	50%	0%

This does not mean that if you are a team member you should not spend any time developing your strategic thinking. Rather, most of your leadership learning efforts should be geared towards increasing your self-awareness and getting a first-hand understanding of your environment. Strategic thinking and vision building are useful skills to develop, but need not be your main focus at this point.

The table represents the map of what needs to be done to build solid leadership foundations and hone your skill set. It will also help you keep an eye on what will be needed at the next level, to proactively work on it and, thus, accelerate your journey. Of course, you may choose a totally different approach, reading from beginning to end, or cherry pick what it is you think you need most right now.

To help you navigate, this guide is structured as follows.

- Each part opens with an article from the *Financial Times* which sets the scene.

- Each chapter starts with a real-life example or a story to highlight some of the issues that the chapter addresses.

- The chapter then provides a general introduction to key concepts that will be covered within it.

- At the end of every subsection are practical examples and exercises (individual and team-based) that you can choose to perform or not, though doing so will help you to consolidate what you have learned. Individual exercises will ask for you to set aside some quiet time to go through either the questioning process about yourself, your team or the organisation, data analysis or the creation of an action plan. Giving yourself a couple of hours to do this, either at the beginning or the end of the week, should be sufficient.

- At the end of each chapter is a summary of tangible key points to remember – these can be actioned immediately and used as refresher notes later.

- If you feel you are overwhelmed by the amount of information, advice and business case studies - consider either pacing yourself by diving into one chapter at a time, on a weekly basis. Alternatively, use this book as a go-to reference if and when needed. Either way, consider selecting what exercises are the most relevant for you or res-onate more with you.

Leadership is not a solitary exercise, nor is learning. To leverage further the impact of this guide, it is highly recommended that you find a spar-ring partner who will go through the journey with you. This person may be a peer or someone from your network with whom you can regularly exchange, compare and contrast, measure and celebrate progress. It is also highly recommended that you put together a feedback group of three to five people you trust and respect to support and help you by observing you in different situations and giving you regular structured and informal feedback.

As mentioned in the Introduction, leadership is a journey towards excellence – your excellence. It can only be triggered by a personal desire to grow and develop and must be rooted in curiosity – about yourself and about the world. The journey of a leader is like Ulysses' quest – at times challenging, always exciting. So, get on board, follow the stars and enjoy the ride!

What is leadership?

'Leaders are made, they are not born. They are made by hard effort, which is the price all of us must pay to achieve any goal that is worthwhile.'

Vince Lombardi, American football coach

View from Davos

By Miki Tsusaka

I arrived at the annual meeting of the World Economic Forum in Davos with a great sense of expectation. This year's summit – under the banner 'The great transformation: shaping new models' – was the first in the wake of some major upheavals in the business and political worlds: the Arab spring, the eurozone crisis and the awakening of Africa. Here, in the beautiful Swiss ski resort, some of the world's most influential people gather to discuss the big issues. So I wondered if I would hear the first answers to the big questions: that the spring would turn to summer; that the major European leaders would find a way through their currency troubles; that Africa, so long dismissed as a basket case, would be recognised as a fast emerging market.

My reaction so far? The discussions – in the formal halls and in the corridors — have been buzzy, thought provoking, and focused. I get the sense that, after so much talk over recent years, senior leaders are feeling that it's time for action – and soon. Key themes come up time and time again: sustainability, corporate social responsibility, job creation, volatility, the talent gap, income disparity, innovation and technology and the connected world are just a few of the buzz words on the lips of delegates.

There is a feeling that we really cannot afford to return to the status quo. Great ideas are all very well, but bold steps to put these ideas into practice are critical. We face a once-in-a-generation test of leadership. In essence, it is 'take control and transform or lose control and be transformed'.

It's happened before. As one high-profile chief executive said, there are not many companies around today that were in the Fortune 50 in the 1950s. Those that are, have changed – and they are changing once more. But this is not easy to do. As several people have made clear, leaders face a web of competing priorities. For instance, in a debate on 'The Global Business Context', we heard how business leaders are frustrated by an apparent contradiction: on the one hand, facing the challenge of creating jobs to overcome the looming threat of a lost generation, and on the other hand, facing a barrage of regulation and anti-entrepreneur comment that arguably prohibits the job creators.

Along similar lines, another panellist reinforced the point that it is no longer sufficient to deliver a good product at the right price – now, corporate social responsibility must be considered a pre-requisite. But the paradox – as John Chambers, the chairman of Cisco, the technology company, rightly pointed out – is that companies do not want to be seen to be 'bragging' about what they are doing in terms of societal contribution. This reminds us that action may not always be self evident but this does not mean it is not happening.

The World Economic Forum's decision to impose a minimum quota for female attendees is certainly setting a good example in terms of challenging the status quo, but let's not put too much emphasis on quantity here. When we look at the women in attendance at this year's event it's an impressive roster. This year's key note speaker, Angela Merkel, the German chancellor, is emblematic of the contribution women are making to this year's meeting. I have been lucky enough to rub shoulders with some very inspirational women this year. For example, I had the opportunity to talk to Nobel Prize winner Leymah Gbowee. She was awarded the prize in 2011 for her non-violent struggle for the safety of women and for women's rights to full participation in peace-building work in Liberia. Listening to her talk about her own experiences of effecting change put the issues that the developing world has to contend with in stark contrast. If anything motivates boldness in tackling the challenges in the context of business and economics hearing about the extremely difficult situations that are all too prevalent in many parts of the world certainly does.

The airline industry has built planes for 1bn consumers but there are 6bn more in the world that it is just beginning to serve. An interesting thought from Tom Enders, the chief executive of Airbus, which neatly summarises the context of this year's meeting. Large parts of the world are awakening – economically and politically – which reminds us we all need to take bold steps to ensure that the opportunity is not lost to turn great expectations into great transformation and for our action to meet our ambition. What's more, engagement of the other half of the world in this process is critical. If women are not part of the solution, there will be no great transformation.

FT *Source:* Tsusaka, M. (2012) View from Davos, *Financial Times*, 27 January.
© The Boston Consulting Group 2012.

Leadership is a concept as old as the world itself. Leaders are a different breed of people. They present different attributes and act differently from most people. Throughout history, leaders have emerged and shaped a future for the next generations. They have challenged the status quo, built empires, enabled breakthroughs and embraced change.

What they have in common with each other, apparently, is a deep level of awareness. This is coupled with a great ability to understand their environment and inspire others to follow them. It is relentlessly expressed in their capacity to execute and reach their objectives.

In this first part, the aim is to analyse the concept of leadership and support the proposed leadership development model, which is rooted in looking inside yourself, influencing around yourself and building and delivering on your vision.

Chapter 1 puts leadership into its historical context to extract what the core traits of successful leaders are. It analyses the stories and attributes of several leaders and looks at what they can still tell us about leadership. This chapter also presents some different pathways to leadership and analyses what it is that leaders really do.

Chapter 2 takes a look at the issues for leadership in the context of the tumultuous conditions of today's world. It aims to answer the fundamental question of what will be required from the leaders of tomorrow and how they should be shaped.

1

A definition of leadership

'If your actions inspire others to dream more, learn more, do more
and become more, you are a leader.'

John Quincy Adams, sixth president of the USA

This chapter covers:

- the different definitions of leadership
- leadership in context – historical examples that have shaped the world
- the pathways to leadership
- a look at what leaders actually do.

The birth of corporate America

In 1868, the 14th Amendment of the US Constitution was voted in. Originally, the amendment was intended to prohibit state and local government from depriving people of life, liberty or property without due process. Savvy corporate lawyers saw the amendment as a way to gain independence from governments and, by demanding the same freedoms afforded individual citizens, managed to free themselves from many government restrictions. They demanded that the amendment also be applied to corporations since they already possessed the right in law to enter into contracts under the same conditions as individuals. This laid the foundations for the emergence of corporate America.

It is clear that the environment shapes the corporate world as much as the corporate world today shapes the world as a whole. By extension, corporate leadership – the topic to be explored in this guide – has also been shaped by numerous influences. Defining leadership, therefore, is a vast and complex task. There are many different schools of thought on leadership – as well as the skills and attributes required for it – to debate, compare and contrast.

The quote at the beginning of the chapter presents a reasonably comprehensive definition of leadership. The quote roots leadership in the attributes of a person. It alludes to a higher purpose and the ability to inspire others. It stresses the need to go above and beyond the call of duty. It expresses the inherent dimensions of the self and our effects on others – elements critical to keep in mind when working on becoming a leader. Finally, it alludes to the constant need for learning and action. The only thing it does not fully embrace is the notion of impact and change that comes with a leader's title. In order to give the most complete overview the chapter will address where leaders come from, how leaders are made and what leaders do.

Leadership in history

History, politics, science, art and religion – these different dimensions that have shaped the world have also shaped our leaders. Galileo, Lorenzo de Medici, Napoleon, Nelson Mandela – all were great leaders at the time. Even though their leadership was expressed in different areas and capacities, they present common traits and attributes that are summed up by the three pillars of leadership listed in the Introduction: self-awareness, influence and execution.

Figure 1.1 shows the main groups of influences on society and leaders that have existed throughout history. Understanding history can help us to understand the future. Understanding historical models of leadership can pave the way to producing better future leaders.

Economics and the sciences

Economics and the sciences are major forces that help to shape the world. From the emergence of mathematics and physics to the Industrial Revolution or the growth of the Internet, from Adam Smith to Keynes or Porter, leaders in the fields of economics and science are models of the ability to challenge the status quo, innovate or merely to think.

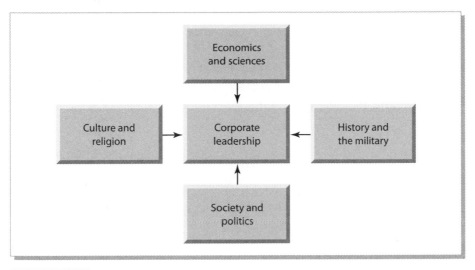

Figure 1.1   Influences on society and leaders

Galileo, the father of modern physics, is a striking example of such leadership. Ruled against in a heresy trial initiated by the Catholic Inquisition, Galileo was forced to deny his theory of heliocentrism, which stated that the sun, not the earth, was at the centre of the universe. He had agreed with Copernicus that the sun was in the centre, with the earth revolving around it. He gave in to his inquisitors and acknowledged, as demanded by them, that a Copernican understanding of the world would be forever seen as heresy.

At the time, Galileo could not understand why they refuted his theory as Pope Urban VIII agreed with him in private. In fact, his theory had previously had both papal support and the blessing of the Inquisition, but, by mentioning the support of the Pope in his manuscript, he had made a potentially fatal political error.

The story of Galileo has it that, on his way out of the Inquisition hearing, he muttered softly 'Eppur si muove' ('And yet it moves'). With these words, his life was irrevocably changed. His manuscript, his life's work – *The Dialogue Concerning the Two Chief World Systems* – was banned from publication. He was placed under house arrest for the rest of his life and never published again.

Later, of course, his theory was accepted and, in time, he was honoured as the father of modern science. Mathematics and physics would become synonymous with progress.

Galileo had a vision. His vision cost him his reputation and his freedom, but he became the proud father of modern science. He was undaunted, courageous and challenged the status quo. He was a man with a vision, authentic and true to himself.

Galileo's leadership can be summed up as having the following attributes:

- **self-awareness** – intelligence, risk-taking, self-confidence, courage
- **understanding others and having influence** – value of self-sacrifice
- **vision and execution** – challenging the status quo, innovating.

It is useful to note that, in hindsight, Galileo perhaps also presented some leadership shortcomings – such as an inability to understand his environment and a propensity to build alliances that ultimately led to his downfall.

History and the military

Military examples are often used to convey the basics of leadership. They are highly representative of the abilities leaders need to engage, empower and motivate others. They also testify to strategic thinking and agility in the decision making process. Napoleon Bonaparte is an emblematic example of this.

Many people would argue that, in the early days of his career, Bonaparte was a true symbol of military genius. His methods were based on the following simple yet effective elements:

- **A compelling vision** Bonaparte wanted to preserve the advantages of the French Revolution. His aim was to protect the country's interests. He had established himself as a fighter for political, civil and religious freedom and a caring leader, protecting his country from all internal and external threats.

- **A team established on the basis of a meritocracy** As a true representative of Revolution principles, Bonaparte chose people based purely on their skills and merit – a truly innovative approach in a period characterised by privilege. He also pushed younger talent, with the average age of those in his team being 35 when, at that time, more commonly those aged 70 would have been employed in the armies of other countries.

- **A decentralised operating model** All those under Bonaparte were given permission to choose how to deliver on the objectives set so long as they delivered. This is what led to the military success of the battle of Marengo, where General Desaix decided of his own accord to come back to the battlefield.

- **The advocacy of feedback** Bonaparte's closest generals were there to pinpoint potential mistakes and keep him honest about his strategy and behaviours.

However, by the time he proclaimed himself Emperor, he seemed to have abandoned his military inheritance and principles of meritocracy, autonomy and feedback. Then, acting as a monarch, he leaned towards ego, complacency and dictatorship.

Bonaparte was an innovative leader who ended by falling tragically. He understood the benefit of empowerment to increase motivation and results, but was not able to sustain this leadership style.

Bonaparte's leadership can be summed up as having the following attributes:

- **self-awareness** – free spirit, driven

- **understanding others and having influence** – empowerment of his team

- **vision and execution** – innovative thinking, a strategist.

He also had shortcomings. He failed to remain true to himself and forgot that leadership is a never-ending journey and requires an openness to feedback.

Society and politics

Political leaders give us striking examples of the ability to influence, great communication skills and vision building.

Nelson Mandela – the first black president of South Africa – is a symbol of courage and resilience. In his book *Mandela's Way: Fifteen lessons on life, love and courage*, Richard Stengel (Virgin, 2010) analyses what made

Nelson Mandela such a model of leadership. He talks about Mandela's incredible physical presence, due to his height and his warm smile. When Walter Sisulu, a famous South African anti-apartheid activist, was looking to establish a youth wing of the ANC, Mandela became the obvious candidate, just by stepping into the room. Stengel also describes how Mandela consciously chose to come to terms with his past and his history. Undoubtedly, his 27 years in prison left profound scars on him and he admitted that, at times, he felt incredibly bitter. However, as a leader, it was important for him to demonstrate that what united South Africans was greater than their divisions. Encouraging reconciliation was the only way to achieve national unity and have a chance of peace and sustainability.

Mandela always made a point of appealing to the heart, but by using knowledge and history. While in prison, he realised that, in order to unite whites and blacks, he had to understand the psyche of the Afrikaners – how they think, how they feel. He even learned how to speak Afrikaans. He also used sport to unite the nation, relying on François Pienaar, the white team captain, to win the 1995 Rugby World Cup.

According to Stengel, Mandela was also ahead of his time when it came to managing his image. He used to say, 'Clothing makes the man: you have to embody the work you are doing'. Being one of the few black lawyers in South Africa when he was young, he would always make a point of wearing a three-piece suit in court. He wanted to convey an image of reliability and belonging to his profession.

He is also incredibly charming, almost seductive, and will make sure he knows who you are before meeting you. When asked a question with an element of choice he would always ask, 'Why can't we have both?', pushing his interlocutor into new ways of thinking. He prioritised the importance of his overarching goal – reconciliation and democracy – but in a pragmatic way, leaving the rest to tactics. He used to say that the ANC's move from non-violent to armed practices was simply a tactic to achieve democracy more quickly; the goal remained unchanged.

Finally, and most importantly, he had a tribal style of leadership, inherited from the Xhosa tradition of cattle herding. He noted that you never herd cattle from the front; you always do so from the back, identifying and gently directing the one cow that will steer the rest of the herd. He applied these techniques in meetings by not speaking much, observing and listening to everyone, then summarising everything that had been said and nudging people in the direction he wanted them to go.

He was known to acknowledge his human failings and, particularly, how scary and terrifying it could feel at times. Nonetheless, he always put on a calm front and reached inside himself to overcome any fear.

Mandela has always been a man with a mission, a symbol of resilience and persistence, an inclusive and reflective leader.

Mandela's leadership can be summed up as having the following attributes:

- **self-awareness** – awareness of traditions, leading by example, humility and empathy

- **understanding others and having influence** – showing empathy and awareness of the importance of trust and image

- **vision and execution** – mission and vision, adapting communication and tactics to any situation.

Culture and religion

Culture and religious trends play an important role in any environment. They put at the forefront the notions of value and integrity, they call for change and symbolise purpose, legacy and intent.

Lorenzo de Medici, head of the Democratic Republic of Florence during the fifteenth century, is the last example of leadership in this chapter and symbolises the part culture and religion play in this role.

Also known as Lorenzo the Magnificent, he was an enigmatic and complex figure. Perceived as the natural heir of Cosimo de Medici, he was groomed for power at an early age. He grew up in the midst of political manoeuvrings, financial concerns and government as practised by his grandfather. A keen poet and artist, Lorenzo was an interesting mix of visionary and savvy statesman. He had a vision for Florence to maintain its artistic and political pre-eminence and reinforce its economic power in fifteenth-century Europe.

To honour his grandfather's legacy, he wanted to strengthen Florence as the intellectual and artistic centre of Italy and Europe. He turned his vision into action, through indirect patronage of the arts, literature and poetry. Under his leadership, artists such as da Vinci, Ghirlandaio, Botticelli and Michelangelo flourished, later courted by Milanese and Venetian families and even France. Lorenzo was at the helm of commissioning masterpieces to both depict the pictorial splendour of Florence and build its reputation.

At the political level, he worked at establishing Florence as the peacekeeper between other nation states, specifically the papal states and the emerging power of the Kingdom of Naples. He spent most of his diplomatic life working on this.

However, he later changed course and strategy to secure additional wealth for the Republic and further develop its power. Florence's economy was based on alum, used to degrease wool and set cotton dyes – both pillars of Florentine industry. A larger reserve of alum was discovered in the boundary between the papal states and Florentine territories and both heads of state were eager to secure this for their own benefit. Despite the mining community rising up against Florence with papal support, Lorenzo decided to suppress the rebellion and made the mine Florentine. This had a disastrous impact on Florence's diplomatic life.

Lorenzo also overlooked the dependence of the Medici bank on papal contracts and the loss of favours that resulted formed the first blow to the Medici empire. Lorenzo then went into a downward spiral. Next, he faced the conspiracy of his most prominent rival, the Pazzi family. The Pazzi plotted to take over the Republic by assassinating the Medici brothers. The conspiracy partially failed, though led to the death of Lorenzo's brother Giuliano. In an emotionally charged reaction, Lorenzo brutally and publicly punished the Pazzi family by tossing the head conspirator from the window of the Palazzo Vecchio.

Unwittingly, he once again triggered a papal outburst. For the first time in the history of Florence, Lorenzo faced the threat of excommunication for the whole city, shortly followed by the risk of a military takeover by Ferdinand de Naples orchestrated by the papal state. However, Lorenzo's strategic genius prevailed. He was proactive and met with Ferdinand to personally surrender and bring peace to the city.

Doubtful accounting practices and rumours of the theft of funds from Florence's treasuries, paired with the constant condemnations of the Italian Dominican friar Savonarola, who was violently opposed to the ideals of the Renaissance, further weakened and ultimately destroyed Lorenzo's reputation as the master of the Republic and the master of Florence.

However, history prevailed and the artists he supported are still considered to be geniuses. For this reason, Lorenzo is highly regarded today for his patronage of the arts and humanities.

Lorenzo de Medici was a man of many talents, aware of his cultural inheritance but driven to build his own legacy. However, he was also a man who failed to fully understand his own impact on people.

The Medici leadership can be summed up as having the following attributes:

- **self-awareness** – awareness of his family history and a willingness to perpetuate it, powerful, emotional

- **understanding others and having influence** – able to create emotional bonds with artists and read political situations, highly credible in his position

- **vision and execution** – paired innovative thinking with in-the-moment strategic thinking, player of long-term games who created things of intrinsic value.

Lorenzo's shortcomings were that he failed to assess or understand the impact of his decisions on the bigger picture and overlooked some important stakeholders.

All of the examples above put leadership in a wide political, social and cultural context. What we can also see is that for these leaders to be successful, they each displayed self-awareness, an understanding of their environment and the ability to deliver on their vision.

The pathways to leadership

Leadership is, above all, driven by context and situation. It may emerge from very different sets of circumstances. It might be a birthright and so the issue of legacy would be at the forefront of such a leader's thinking.

It could be rooted in an act of creation, the leadership journey having started with an idea that turned into an empire and so innovation would lie at the heart of such a leader's thinking. Finally, it might be the result of a lifelong journey of climbing up the ranks, constantly challenging the status quo and pushing for transformation.

From just these three alternative pathways it can be seen how very different types of leaders would result.

Leadership does not appear out of thin air. It is never exercised in a vacuum. The very essence of leadership is contextual, event-driven and people-driven. Therefore, exploring for what purpose and in what circumstances someone can become a leader is critical to defining leadership.

Although there are multiple paths people can take to become leaders, they fall into three main categories:

- creation and innovation
- elevation and transformation
- inheritance and legacy.

These mirror the natural lifecycle of any organisation.

Creation and innovation

This category includes visionary or entrepreneurial leaders. Their rise usually relates to the act of creating an organisation as a result of bringing something new to the world or enhancing something that already exists.

These leaders are usually motivated by a vision or the importance of embedding creativity and innovation in their workforce. They also often allude to leadership being a balancing act between authority and delegation.

After the creation and innovation stage, such leaders stress the importance of letting go of control and reflecting on the timing of their start-ups becoming corporations. Then, the need for better processes and governance becomes important.

Steve Jobs, Mark Zuckerberg, Henry Ford and Charles Merrill are good examples of leaders who have taken this route to leadership.

Elevation and transformation

This pathway involves relatively mature, organised companies producing leaders.

These leaders, having been grown from within, are very interested in sustainability and balancing consistency and change.

The questions that concern them include, 'How do I maintain the established corporate culture while driving change? What is the best path to both protect and enhanced value creation? What is the best strategy to achieve this evolution or revolution?' Also, the search for excellence is usually highly present in these leaders' minds. It is paired with a more fundamental question of, 'How do I balance an increased need for discipline with the imperative to constantly foster innovative skills?'

Individuals such as Jack Welch, the retired former chairman of General Electric, and Peter Voser, Chief Executive Officer of Royal Dutch Shell – both products of their respective organisations – come to mind as examples of this type of leader.

Inheritance and legacy

This is the ultimate 'mapped route' to leadership as, regardless of your entry point or current position in an organisation, you know that you will be given the highest roles or functions.

In such cases, ideas surrounding legacy, risk-taking, legitimacy or choice are the defining concerns of those on this type of leadership journey.

Alexandre de Rothschild and James Murdoch are striking examples of those who have taken this path to leadership.

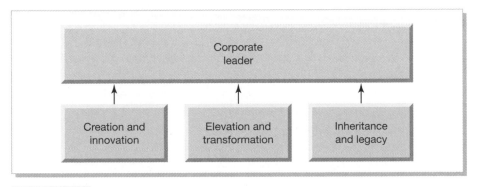

Figure 1.2   **The three main pathways to corporate leadership**

Figure 1.2 summarises visually the three main categories of pathways to corporate leadership discussed above. Next, how these different pathways shape leadership styles is explored via two case studies.

case study   ## Inheritance and legacy: Firmenich and Chemical Industries

The following addresses the inheritance and legacy pathway, viewing it through different cultural lenses. The results are surprisingly similar. Regardless of cultural background, a strong sense of duty, the question of choice and the need to balance individual aspirations with family obligations are at the core of such leaders' thoughts.

Antoine Firmenich is the brother of the current CEO of the largest privately owned company in the perfume and flavouring industry. Founded more than 100 years ago, Swiss-based Firmenich is the leading supplier to the cosmetics and food industries.

Eric Lim is the heir apparent to and the eldest the son of the current Chairman and Executive Director of Chemical Industries (Far East).

Firmenich is European, but educated in the USA, and has had a portfolio life, from working with Paul Berg on the human genome and basic mechanisms of cancer to sitting on the Board of the family company to now creating and running an investment fund in biosciences based on time-proven cash flow and value principles. Lim is Asian and has worked most of his career in the family company, while testing his own business ideas via joint ventures and strategic partnerships.

As noted, regardless of their cultural differences, both have gone on similar journeys. They have both been educated abroad and had exposure at an early stage to diversity and difference. They both admit a certain family pressure to excel in anything they do. They both chose to start their careers outside of the family company as a way to develop their own skills. They both were aware that they needed to prove themselves and build their own credibility first, before feeling at ease within the family business. They both joined their family businesses and both acknowledge a certain desire to break free from family expectations to be able to fully express themselves through their work.

▶

Their leadership can be summed up as having the following attributes:

- **Self-awareness** They are both aware of their family histories and have a strong sense of legacy and the need for sustainability. They both also have a clear sense of duty and respect for the past, even if it is tainted with rebellion or frustration at times. They have a very clear sense of what is best for them and a desire to leave their mark.

- **Understanding others and having influence** This is shown in the way that they influence and manage their relationships with familial stakeholders. They are also able to disagree without hurting the families' feelings or endangering their personal relationships.

- **Vision and execution** They show strategic and innovative thinking, pushing for new directions while protecting values and the past.

case study   Creation and innovation v. elevation and transformation: Steve Jobs and Jack Welch

Steve Jobs is the late co-founder and CEO of Apple Inc. and Jack Welch is the former CEO of General Electric. Both are legendary leaders, the former for creating and running one of the most successful corporations ever and the latter for being a symbol of awe-inspiring corporate success.

Both men embody facets of corporate America – the sheer power and force of innovation for Jobs and what intent can do for Welch. They are both manifestations of what leadership is all about and comparing and contrasting their journeys is particularly telling in terms of the relationship between leadership and:

- purpose and process

- risk and failure

- discipline and independence.

Jobs summed up his thoughts on leadership in his speech to Stanford's 2005 graduates.[1] He presented eight simple and yet powerful principles.

---

[1] See **http://news.stanford.edu/news/2005/june15/jobs-061505.html**

- **Leadership is about doing what you love** and about being in love with what you do. Without passion, nothing can be accomplished. The notion of love is abundantly present in Jobs' speech; he even compares work with a relationship that grows and changes. He also emphasises the need for everyone to nurture and reassess their passion for what they do.

- **Leadership is about having a strong sense of purpose and responsibility** Jobs shared that he dropped out of university as he did not see the immediate value of the teaching and he felt uncomfortable seeing his parents spending money they did not have on his education. He also felt that he had let down a whole community of entrepreneurs after being fired from Apple.

- **Leadership is about resilience and courage** It is critical to know how to make difficult decisions (for Jobs, dropping out from university was such a decision) and be able to put failure into perspective (he was fired from Apple, but admitted that, ultimately, he felt re-energised by the idea of becoming a beginner again).

- **Leadership is about being curious and intuitive** He studied calligraphy because it found it artistic and beautiful, even though he had no practical application for it at the time.

- **Leadership is about trust and self-confidence** Jobs stressed the profound belief that, whatever you do, it will turn out OK in the end. The dots will connect in a way that makes sense, even when the action appears insignificant. Thus, his knowledge of calligraphy pushed him to create all the fonts and formats that, even today, are still the basis of the formatting style palette of any computer.

- **Leadership is about change and decision making** Jobs was very precise on this, specifying *fast* decision making. Live the day as if it was your last, he said. Choose what you do every day and, if you are not satisfied, change it immediately and do not look back.

- **Beware becoming complacent and conformist** Challenge the status quo, challenge yourself. Stay hungry and stay foolish, he urged graduates at the end of his speech.

Jobs' principles are eminently creative and about the importance of change. His message is also about living without any constraints, being a free spirit, a person who is driven but puts creation above everything else. As such, he also recognises failure as being a key learning experience.

Welch is a different kettle of fish. Starting his career as an engineer at General Electric, it took him 20 years to climb the ranks to the CEO role there – a position he then held for another 20 years. In his book *Straight from the Gut* (Headline, 2003) and in the article 'What you can learn from Jack Welch', by *Harvard Business Review*'s editor Walter Kiechel (2001), he defines leadership in four bold statements:

- **Change and action** For Welch, a leader is a change agent, able to identify the pain points of an organisation and courageously act on them. Welch tackled bureaucracy by implementing a flat organisational structure, allowing for a fast decision making process. In General Electric there are only six layers between the CEO and the shop floor. He addressed the perceived passivity of the company by taking action: he made sure the 'army' was always moving forwards, with multiplying deals, and constantly looking for acquisitions that could be made or opportunities to grow. General Electric was one of the first corporations to explore renewable energy. It was also one of the first American companies to invest in the former communist bloc, with its acquisition of the Hungarian lighting company, Tungsram.

- **Discipline and process** In his model, leadership is a synonym for results which come from discipline and through processes. Welch promoted a 'simple' timeline from a January meeting in Boca to define the year's strategic trends, to the quarterly corporate executive council to review progress, a yearly review of the talent pipeline and an annual meeting. General Electric employees therefore know exactly what to do when, depending where they are on the timeline. They learn how to be disciplined and efficient and understand the value of processes. An added outcome or benefit is the strong corporate culture and a sense of belonging.

- **Simplicity and innovation** Welch believes that looking for efficiency and simplicity is part of the leader's role. In the 1980s, he heavily promoted a wide use of Six Sigma, the Motorola-created concept aimed at drastically reducing defects in manufacturing processes. He took it to the next level, using it for all processes to create simplicity and efficiency. He also pushed knowledge of Six Sigma as a criterion for promotion. He championed innovative thinking and transformed the finance function into a worldwide best-in-class community. By deciding to appoint a *business* leader to spearhead the *finance* function, he allowed for the knowledge transfer of business practices to take place and created one of the very first partnerships between business and finance.

■ **Winning and making the numbers** For Welch, leadership is about winning. This filtered through to every part of the company. At the strategic level, he deliberately decided the company had to be number one or number two in any market or quit. It had three simple strategic solutions to achieve that: fix, sell or close. At the workforce level, he promoted the top-20 and bottom-10 concept, letting go all the underperformers. He referred to the professional baseball team coach attitude: look for the potential stars, train them, reward them, have high expectations of them, measure how they deliver and part ways when they don't.

As Welch had climbed up through the ranks, he had developed an intimate knowledge of the nuts and bolts of the company and could understand its pain points and weaknesses. Throughout his tenure as the CEO, he took the company on a relentless change journey to fight bureaucracy, simplify and create a lean organisation. In the process, he managed to create the first finance community that acted as a business partner and one of the most aggressive and energetic corporate cultures to date.

Welch's leadership model is about processes, discipline and excellence; it is about speed and winning. It is very far from Jobs' free-spirited approach. For Welch, failure is just not an option.

Though their leadership styles and models are clearly rooted in their different experience and skill sets, Jobs and Welch also share some attributes:

■ **Self-awareness** For Jobs, understanding his drivers – passion and excellence – plus the ability to articulate what he wanted to stand for and having self-confidence, keeping himself stretched, mastering his fears. For Welch, self-confidence, courage, being a change agent, winning and energy. Self-confidence and drive appear to be the attributes that they have in common.

▶

- **Understanding others and having influence** For Jobs, great communication skills. For Welch, credibility, empowerment and accountability. Jobs' creative nature here contrasts with Welch's execution-driven nature.

- **Vision and execution** For Jobs, innovative thinking, being a strategist, creator, risk-taker, able to make decisions. For Welch, innovative thinking, excellence as a vision and achieving results via financial metrics. So, innovation is important to both leaders, although for one this lies in risk, while for the other it's all about results.

When it comes to their shortcomings, Jobs would have acknowledged that, at times, he failed to trust his own instincts, while perhaps Welch did not take enough time to pause and reflect and was too process-orientated.

These case studies help to shed different lights on leadership, taking into account how it was acquired. However, just as with the examples from history that we looked at, at the beginning of this chapter, these leaders' successes can be seen to lie in them having demonstrated significant levels of self-awareness, understanding of their environments and the ability to deliver their clear visions.

What leaders do

Most leadership literature makes a clear distinction between *leaders* and *managers*. Leaders should solely invest their time in setting the vision or direction for the organisation. They should put their efforts into aligning resources to facilitate delivery of that vision and try to be active role models to inspire and motivate their workforces. Finally, they should have the ability to handle a crisis and have at heart legacy and passing on to those who will follow.

Leadership experts have highlighted that leaders think in terms of actions, are not passive, want to shape goals and not react to them, and have the ability to alter people's moods, expectations and perceptions about a particular situation.

Harvard Business School scholar John Kotter extended and deepened these insights, stating that leaders push for change and are there to help organisations embrace or at least cope with change. Leaders, he says, do three main things:

- **Set direction** This includes the development of strategies that will support the direction chosen and, ultimately, enable delivery of the vision. This requires a lot of observation, the leader needing to stay attuned to the environment, looking for trends, patterns and pain points. Leaders, therefore, decide *what* should happen, partially explain *why* it should happen and clearly articulate *how* to get there. They are not interested in the mundane details, only the broad, high-level picture. The direction might be rooted in innovation, but it doesn't have to be. It must, though, be grounded and serve the interests of the stakeholders and, above all, it has to be realistic in order to effectively harness resources and energy.

- **Align people** This means getting people's buy-in. Leaders must first establish their legitimacy, then invest time in communicating a clear and powerful vision. This comes about by first building credibility and demonstrating that they can be trusted. It comes through diverse experiences, giving assignments that stretch them, mentoring and emulating role models. Only then can they communicate at all levels, inside and outside the organisation as well as across functional boundaries. Ultimately, leaders are looking to create an impact and a tipping point for their vision to come to life. To achieve success, leaders develop a deep understanding of stakeholders and spend time assessing not only how to leverage anyone who can help convey their message or embrace their vision but also, more importantly, seek to manage or influence those who can block change and progress. Finally, leaders align people by empowering them. Once the vision has become clear and compelling, they draw on the power of collective vision while mitigating the risk of divergence and stalling.

- **Motivate and inspire people** This is a critical part of any leader's role. To have people deliver, leaders need to be in tune with their motivations and their needs. They also need to spend time not only connecting with people but also influencing them to move forward, praising and recognising behaviours, results and progress made.

Thus, leaders need to energise people, be able to call on their emotions and their need for recognition, to have an impact and achieve. They spend time involving others and asking for feedback and ideas. In modern organisations, where multiple leaders can have multiple visions, leaders also need to spend time developing and maintaining networks. This allows the coordination of visions to create even greater value.

The above actions need to be complemented by the following:

- **Be good in a crisis** It is usually in times of crisis that leadership strength is most clearly revealed. Consider the actions of John F. Kennedy during the Cuban Missile crisis in 1962 or those of George Bush at the time of 9/11 in the USA. Everything depends on how well and how fast leaders react, reach out to necessary stakeholders and assess risks and consequences. Leaders need to be confident in their own ability to handle anything that may be thrown at them. To adapt the words of Kipling, if you can keep your head when all about you are losing theirs and blaming it on you, you'll be a leader.

- **Leave a legacy** The greatest leader will always keep in mind how important it is to create a *culture* of leadership – not only as a guarantee of sustainability in an ever-changing environment – but also to serve as a mentor and potential role model. Some of a leader's time must be dedicated to identifying young talented people, nurturing and stretching them. Leaders must accept that they will be challenged by them and engage with these challenges because it is the only way to stay current. Legacy is the last duty of leaders. As the former CEO and Chairman of Solvay once said, 'In the tenure of one's career, one's motivation changes. First you work mostly for the money and recognition, then you work to achieve power and finally you want to leave a trace in history.' Jack Welch is a resounding example of the desire to leave a legacy.

Summary

People become leaders in many different ways and their leadership styles can be shaped by a variety of different influences. What leaders do has been analysed in depth over time. Looking at examples of great leaders from the past can also provide useful insights into what you should be focusing on when developing your leadership skills.

Contrary to the myth of people being natural born leaders, the skill set required can be developed by working on the following three key attributes:

- build your self-awareness to get a sense of who you are

- understand the environment and influence others to get a sense of what they need and want

- develop a vision and relentlessly work to execute it.

Here's a reminder of some of the key points from this chapter:

- leadership is deeply influenced by the environment, so proactively taking the measure of your environment is vital in any leadership journey

- the different pathways to leadership shape different types of leaders

- leaders have well-defined roles and responsibilities, the best definition for leadership being that it is a mix of attributes (embedded in the very core of an individual) and actions (which are tangible and identifiable)

- you can develop your leadership skills or explore your leadership potential by looking inside yourself, around you and making a point of setting things in motion

- leadership is an exciting and challenging journey that requires you to invest time in analysing and questioning yourself and the world around you, dedication – as it is never ending – and resilience – as it requires you to be able to evolve and step out of your comfort zone.

2

Leadership today

'Heretics are the new leaders. The ones who challenge the status quo, who get out in front of their tribes, who create movements.'

Seth Godin, American entrepreneur and author

This chapter covers:

- how the characteristics and emerging trends of today's world are affecting the issue of leadership

- in these times of change, what new attributes and skills will be required by leaders of tomorrow

- how the leader's development journey may be built on the foundations of self-awareness, influence and execution.

A cause without a leader: the case of the Arab Spring

In December 2010, a wave of protests started in North Africa and slowly spread to the Middle East, leading to regime change in Tunisia, Egypt, Libya and the Yemen.

The wave started with the self-immolation of one young Tunisian in protest at police violence and ill-treatment. Social media gave everyone the opportunity to keep updated and watch the protest, playing the role of catalyst in spreading the rebellion and hope from one country to another. It might even be said that the perception of the power of social media has changed forever as a result. What is even more interesting to note is that, for the first time in the history of revolution, no leader emerged – there was no Malcolm X, Che Guevara or Lenin. There will be no celebrity revolutionary leader recorded in history to symbolise the events of the Arab Spring for future generations. The world appears connected, fluid and following a dynamic of its own.

One of the key leadership attributes is the ability to grasp the environment you are in and stay in tune with it. Leadership is also about looking around you. In order to be able to develop into the leader of tomorrow, it is important to analyse the contemporary world and assess how it impacts the roles and attributes of future leaders.

A fast-changing world

New trends are emerging that put back into the equation values such as integrity and accountability. The world is calling for the reconciliation within organisations of profit and social justice. Technology is empowering and giving unprecedented speed and impact to knowledge. A major demographic shift is pushing diversity and complexity in the workforce. Leaders of tomorrow need to be acutely aware of the environment to be able to adequately perform.

In the first decade of the twenty-first century, Lehman Brothers, a symbol of corporate America, was left to collapse. This opened the debate on the real value of financial services and introduced the notion of moral hazard in a capitalist society.

Not long after, the BP issue in the Gulf of Mexico opened the debate on leadership and accountability – when to discard it and when to retain it.

These were manifestations of a shockwave that hit the status quo, a sign of a deep transformation from an old to a new system.

A crisis of values

One of the emerging trends is for individuals and organisations alike to seek a change to current models. Summarised below are just a few that are relevant from a leadership perspective as they impact human behaviour and thinking.

The Occupy movement

Inspired by the Arab Spring and the financial crisis, this movement stresses the need to rethink and realign economic power and social needs. For its members, it is critical to rebuild a sustainable way of living and embrace democracy.

The Occupy movement also draws on statistics from the Congressional Budget Office report, which notes the concentration of wealth among the top 1 per cent of income earners. These top earners have seen their income triple in the past 30 years, with minimal progress being made by the other 99 per cent.

This controversial international movement has been gaining political importance. The rebalancing of wealth is top of its agenda.

Social, or, impact investing

According to a JP Morgan study, the field of social, or, impact investing – funding projects that will have positive results or outcomes for local communities or society as a whole – is valued at $3 trillion. As with investing on the stock exchange or buying stakes in unlisted companies, the field of impact investing is becoming an asset class of it own. Scott Lawson – the Founder of SOW Asia, a non-profit organisation looking at expanding the spectrum of philanthropy and funding Asian projects with highly social impacts – has said, 'The impact investing space is new and big and is trying to resolve the current tension between profit and justice. It can be defined as visionary leadership because it is looking for alternative ways to solve critical and strategic problems.' This was echoed by Wolfgang Hafenmayer, Managing Partner of the Venture Philanthropy arm of private bank LGT: 'Every industry has "impact" potential. Social entrepreneurship and corporation can cross-fertilise and there is an important leadership role in there.'

This field is growing fast in Europe, Asia and Latin America. International organisations such the World Entrepreneurship Forum and the European and Asian Venture Philanthropy Associations are gaining momentum. Each in their different ways is assessing how to impact the poorest people on the planet by promoting social entrepreneurship. Together, they aim to define new models of investment to support growth, harmonise the definition of impact investing across the board and create adequate metrics for it. This trend is also spreading to wealth-management activities

Responsible leadership

Companies such as Leaders' Quest are emerging. They aim to create a global community of leaders aware of their impact on the world.

There is an urgent need to bridge sectors, nations, cultures and different outlooks. To do this, there is a requirement to foster and nurture leaders able to stand in the shoes of others so as to ensure that a wiser decision making process becomes the norm. Leaders' Quest pushes leaders to get in touch with their humanity and ask themselves, 'How can I contribute, how can I make a difference to myself, to my organisation, my community and the wider world?'

There is an emerging call for corporations to rediscover themselves, a re-affirmation that their primary role is to create value while serving a community. To discharge this responsibility, they need to be fully aware of their impact on the world at a macro *and* micro levels.

Future successful leaders cannot afford to overlook this and the above dimensions or fail to integrate them into their practice.

Boundaryless technology

The picture of Facebook traffic on the African continent[1] (shown in Figure 2.1) highlights just how well-connected our world now is.

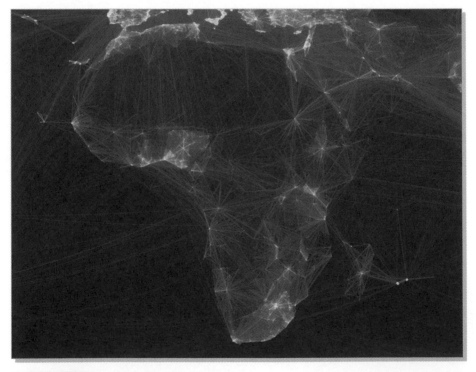

Figure 2.1 Facebook traffic in Africa

[1] Ictworks.org, 'Facebook usage in Africa is doubling every 7 months', Facebook, Inc.

Everyone is part of a community and expresses opinions about every-thing and everyone. There are fewer and fewer boundaries between our work and private lives – new types of applications enable us to keep in touch with office contacts and personal ones while at work or play. This creates a new set of issues when it comes to people management and style of leadership. What is appropriate, in terms of time spent and use of these tools? Should we allow and encourage their use or control and suppress them? How does all this connectivity impact company policies? How can you use these tools in your leadership? These are important questions for future leaders.

New ways of working are also emerging that are highly mobile and flexible. They frame an increasing need to balance flexibility and pro-ductivity and call for a transformation of the notion of office space. Trust and accountability now lie at the heart of the working rela-tionship, as does the work–life balance. In today's world everyone is expected to be accessible at all times to everyone else and this is chal-lenging the notion of the possibility of real time off. New leaders need to adjust their perspectives and examine their sense of what is impor-tant and urgent as well as balance purpose with process.

Knowledge has also become readily available, spreading virally. The notion of competitive advantage is experiencing a fast-decreasing life-span. Leaders need to constantly look for and harness mega trends in order to build a sustainable future.

These are real changes that are impacting every organisation and cannot be ignored if organisations expect to survive. Leaders of the future ought to be aware of and address such issues as they will be called on to decide and strategise, harness or react to what the world throws at them.

Leaders now need to have an understanding of the risks and rewards of a well thought out social media strategy and use these media as market-ing or even strategic tools. There is also an imperative to think about ways to use flexible working options to retain an increasingly vola-tile workforce in a world where talent is diminishing. Finally, there is a need to shift from thinking in terms of competition to thinking in terms of collaboration.

Diverse and increasingly complex mega trends

Complexity and diversity are touching every dimension that goes to create our modern world – economics, culture, gender and demographics.

At an economic level, different forces are competing. The emergence of the BRIC countries as the engines of global growth (as shown in Figure 2.2) is accelerating the need for cultural awareness.

Business growth and sustainability require an understanding of the driving forces of diverse economies, with every organisation and every leader needing to be looking East and West. Rather than being focused on one geographical or regional entity, leaders need to be looking at very specific issues and opportunities. How can doing business in a country like Singapore – a services and trading pole and wealthy and politically stable state – compare with setting up business in agricultural and tourism-dependent Vietnam or unstable and corruption-ridden Indonesia? How could, for example, the South African economic model be applied to the reality of Uganda or an oil-rich Nigeria?

At a cultural level, it is more and more important to have a deep understanding of a country's psyche. So, it is necessary to fully comprehend the colonial and tribal heritage of all the main countries in Africa to have any chance of tapping into opportunities of this next big emerging market. Equally, understanding the subtle hierarchy and sense

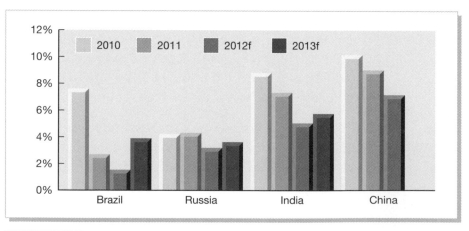

Figure 2.2   **Real GDP forecasts for BRIC economies**

Source: Figures as at November, 2012 – PwC Projections

of duty in Chinese or Japanese cultures leads to better negotiations. The Western European and/or North American models are becoming increasingly challenged, both as economic and as leadership models.

At a gender level, there is increasing recognition that women are a growing economic force. According to the article 'The female economy',[2] globally, women control about $20 trillion in annual consumer spending, which could reach $30 trillion in the next five years. Women represent, in aggregate, a growth market twice as big as China and India combined.

It is also recognised that women are adding tremendous value to the business environment and via their roles on the Board of corporations. They tend to provide a focus on risk and controls and present highly developed emotional intelligence. 'Companies with the highest number of executive women had a 35% higher return on equity and 34% higher return to shareholders compared to those with few women at the top', states the diversity thinktank Catalyst.[3]

Understanding women as a market is increasingly a must for companies if they are to retain or build competitive advantage. At a deeper level, nurturing, fostering and developing women's talent is a critical mission for new leaders. Also leaders must set the tone for organisations to drive and embrace more diversity generally, as well as comply with regulatory pressure to ensure the equal representation of women on the Boards of companies.

At a demographic level, by 2015, about 50 per cent of the global workforce will be composed of people born between 1977 and 1997. Four different demographic trends will soon coexist in the workforce. They will present totally new and radically different drivers – a result of the technology revolution experienced in the past 20 years that is still ongoing. This is demonstrated in the list of the main demographic trends of the past 80 years[4] below.

---

[2] Michael J. Siverstein and Kate Sayre (2009), *Harvard Business Review*, 1 September.

[3] Rachel Soares, Christopher Marquis and Matthew Lee (2011) 'Gender and corporate social responsibility: It's a matter of sustainability', Catalyst and Harvard Business School, November.

[4] H. Schuman and J. Scott (1989) 'Generations and collective memories', *American Sociological Review*, 54: 359–81.

Baby Boomer I – born between 1946 and 1953

Memorable events

Assassinations of JFK and Martin Luther King, political unrest, independence in Africa, a man on the moon, Vietnam War, anti-war protests, student protests, social experimentation, sexual freedom, civil rights movement in the USA, environmental movement, women's movement, protests and riots, experimentation with various intoxicating recreational substances.

Key characteristics

Experimental, individualistic, free-spirited, social causes orientated.

Baby Boomer II, 'Generation Jones' – born between 1954 and 1965

Memorable events

Watergate, Nixon's resignation, the Cold War, the oil embargo, raging inflation, disco, oil shortages.

Key characteristics

Less optimistic than Baby Boomer I, pragmatic, cynical.

Generation X – born between 1965 and 1980

Memorable events

Challenger explosion, Iran–Contra, Reaganomics, AIDS, Star Wars, MTV, the home computer, safe sex, divorce, single-parent families, end of Cold War, fall of Berlin Wall, Desert Storm.

Key characteristics

Searching for emotional security, independent, informal, entrepreneurial.

Generation Y – born between 1981 and 1999

Memorable events

Rise of the Internet, September 11 attacks, cultural diversity, two wars in the Middle East.

Key characteristics

Accepting of change, technically savvy, environmentally aware.

One additional force at play is the Baby Boomers' tendency to exit the market in droves while still at the top of their intellectual abilities. This represents a wild card in the current tough dynamics of the talent market. As they opt for second careers as entrepreneurs, they may begin to present attractive employment propositions for volatile and purpose-driven Generation Ys.

As a leader, how could you build a human resource strategy to attract, retain and foster young talent? As a leader how could you reconcile and motivate such a disparate workforce?

'I dream of having a company with people who think like me, where we would all collaborate to innovate and create value, using technology. Leadership in the future is not only about someone who inspires, it's about someone who enables you with technology, who is accessible, open to difference and who will tell you the truth about the company. As Gen Y, we have a hard time making decisions, we are option people and like to challenge. I think we have a hard time accepting leadership, but at the same time we do not know how to be leaders. The leader of the future is just like an app – one that gives you the truth, makes decisions and cherishes speed over process.'

Interview with Ruth Marshall-Johnson, WGS

As a future leader you need to be able to make everyone come together around a vision and goals in a way that is equally appealing to all of them. You also need to address the looming knowledge gap that the existing mature and long-lasting workforce will soon leave in its wake.

Codes are changing fast and there is considerable volatility – uncertainty, complexity and ambiguity are the new attributes of the current world. Only someone well aware of this can dream of becoming a future model of leadership.

New conundrums … new leaders

To cope with a world filled with new paradigms, any aspiring leader needs to integrate a very specific set of attributes, while demonstrating new types of values. To cope with dilemmas and solve problems, new leaders must look to develop a new sense of collaboration. To match the increasingly global and complex environment, future leaders need to feel at ease with innovation and apprehend the world in a diverse and ever-evolving way. They also need to accept and trigger positive conflicts.

The underpinning value required is that of accepting, embracing and promoting diversity, with inclusiveness becoming the differentiating factor with new leaders.

As renowned business psychologist Douglas LaBier said in an interview for the *Washington Post* in November 2008, 'If Google were a person, it displays, in many respects, the model of a psychologically healthy adult in today's world. Its corporate culture and management practices depend upon qualities like transparency, flexibility and collaboration with diverse people; non-defensiveness, informality, a creative mindset and nimbleness, all aimed at aggressively competing for clear goals within a constantly evolving environment.'

This elegantly summarises what leaders of tomorrow should aim to be and strive to do.

The new meaning of collaboration

The increasingly complex environment today is challenging the traditional problem solving and analytical skill sets of today's leaders.

As Bob Johansen states in his book *Leaders Make the Future* (Berrett-Koehler, 2012), 'In years ahead there will be fewer problems that can be solved. Instead we will have dilemmas that are basically insoluble problems.' Such dilemmas require a radically different approach, collaboration becoming critical to finding the best possible solution.

According to Ernst and Young's Economist Intelligence Unit,[5] the collaborative leadership of the future will embrace all of the following means of achieving solutions:

- **Purposefully bring together people from different backgrounds** Diversity appears to be the ultimate driver of value creation, as indicated by 53 per cent of the 1050 leaders working in global companies. For about 560 of these leaders, there was a strong correlation between reputation, financial performance and diversity. Championing diversity is part of the leadership package of the future and this includes spotting conscious and unconscious bias

---

[5] 'Winning in a polycentric world', Ernst and Young, 21st Century Workforce series, Economist Intelligence Unit, January 2011.

and breaking conformity patterns. 'However, as diversity is messy, hence difficult to embrace, let alone to manage and requires a supreme level of self-awareness and ability to sense your environment', cautioned Clara Gaymard, Vice President of General Electric International and France country chair in an interview, empathy and emotional intelligence will be key.

- **Become idea catalysts** Leaders of tomorrow will need to be idea catalysts. Discussion and debate are necessary for the emergence of new ideas. There will be requirements to subtly stir the debate in a non-threatening way while consciously pushing for divergence. This will only enhance the chance for innovation to occur or make it stronger.

- **Being at ease with conflict** Future leadership roles will require the ability to spark healthy tension. Leaders will constantly have to move teams and organisations out of their comfort zones and fight complacency, which could give rise to conflict. The ability to survive in an increasingly agile environment depends on it. As iconic leader Jack Welch might say, the forces will have to be constantly kept alert and moving.

This new collaborative leadership style will have to come from a deep appreciation of the value of individuals, combined with a willingness to put them constantly to the test. It will need to be able to match up to the increasingly uncertain nature of the business world and of the world at large.

Balancing innovative thinking with global realities

Above and beyond collaboration, future leaders will have to be able to grasp the global picture and/or create their own solutions.

So, how will innovative leaders be defined in the new paradigm?:

- **They will have confidence in their own abilities** Such leaders will have confronted and conquered their fears of failure and be willing to challenge the status quo, ready to do things differently, not abide by any one model.

Google

Google's culture is a great example of such confidence. Google's leaders promote transparency, flexibility and collaboration. They foster a working environment that is quite opposite to that expected in most big corporations – it could even be perceived as counterproductive, yet they embrace it and challenge all other models. They also make a point of granting a day a week to some of their employees to work on their own projects or ideas. It is a way to keep their creativity afloat, yet allow them to stay grounded in reality. It is also a strategic way to keep an eye on up-and-coming technology and potentially create additional value for the company.

- **They will factor in time to pause and think** In today's hyper-fast, hyper-connected, hyper-here-and-now environment, leaders need to be able to go into standby mode and observe the team, the organisation and the world. The new leaders will be disciplined enough to be able to block out the outside world and be in the moment. This, in fact, is the critical competitive advantage of the innovative leaders. Of course, leadership is all about action and delivery, but the upstream time spent in allowing ideas to incubate is critical to innovation.

- **They will be the ultimate change agents, able to embrace it and create positive change every day and at every level** This ability allows the organisation not only to stay current but also get ahead. So 'innovative' takes on a broader meaning – of innovation in every way, from product strategy, to marketing, to business model creation or process re-engineering – anything that allows something new to come to light – to ultimately have an impact within or outside of the organisation – is a sign of an innovative leader.

- **They will not only trigger change but also be able to manage it** Simply finding the world's or the organisation's pain points and creating a vision is not enough for innovative leaders. They also have a supreme ability to unite around change and communicate. Can you reassure others when they are faced with the unknown, the different, the new? Can you influence and convince others to commit to embracing change? This is the acid test of a true leader.

- **Above all they will have the ability to think globally** Muhtar Kent, Chairman and CEO of the Coca-Cola Company, put it well in an interview for Ernst and Young's 2010 'Globalization Report'. 'Leading is a global mindset. It is about putting all actions and decisions through a global filter. For instance, how does a decision made for a business in the US impact our business in India? How will this innovation in Poland translate in North America's market? What can we learn from our experiences in Mexico that can apply to China?' How can we explain what global thinking really means when applied to business problems? The aptitude to develop a locally fit-for-purpose ecosystem that also allows for the delivery of a global objective is perhaps best described using the following equation:

$$\text{Unique global selling points} + \text{Local business and/or Local delivery models} = \text{Global thinking}$$

Another way to describe global thinking is as the ability to integrate all cultural dimensions when developing new business solutions – that is politics, consumer behaviours, infrastructure availability, history and people's psyches. It is strongly related to spotting tension points and creating solutions that are locally fit for purpose and being able to deliver the global vision, which is also known as integrated strategic thinking. For example, if you were to realise that the infrastructure for consumer food was weak in African countries and local behaviours were to buy from small, local, independent shops, you would not provide cans but small glass bottles of fizzy drinks, as is the case in Tunisia.

Without doubt, there are other attributes that define innovative and globally aware leaders (those relating to technologically savvy social media experts, for instance). However, being fearless, willing to put time aside to think and being a change agent appear to be the key foundations on which tomorrow's leadership will be built.

The power of 'inclusiveness'

As mentioned above, integrating diverse and global market dimensions, above and beyond our own limited cultural context, is critical to the successful business.

Human beings make decisions based on heuristics. Their judgement is founded on simple and efficient rules, hardwired during the evolutionary process. These rules provide a shorthand for categorising people and behaviour. Moreover, whatever is familiar to an individual, whatever is aligned with their own patterns, their own culture, or those that seem similar to them, will always appear more appealing and acceptable. Consequently, the last must-have skill for the leaders of tomorrow is *inclusiveness*.

Inclusiveness is the willingness to break out of your own patterns, a desire to get out of an emotional or personal comfort zone and not only embrace difference but also learn how to value it. It is the talent not only to understand but also to manage different ecosystems.

Inclusive leaders multiply professional experience outside their comfort zones, working in places or areas of a business they have never experienced before, with people they do not know and in markets they have never visited before. They also care for the people around them and show genuine interest and true respect.

In fact, inclusiveness can be associated with the concept of servant leadership, as developed by Robert Greenleaf, since inclusive leaders have at heart a commitment to the well-being of their people and their community. They place their main focus on people and how to promote their personal development. Inclusive leaders have the aptitude to create highly diverse teams while creating a safe space for co-creation. All viewpoints can be expressed, truly heard and debated.

Finally, inclusiveness can also be seen as the power to manage both conflicts and consensus.

Summary

New conundrums call for new leaders – more self-aware and more emotionally intelligent than ever before, innovative and inclusive. The following, then, may be added to the list of desirable leadership attributes and actions to take to become a leader of tomorrow:

- **self-awareness** courage, integrity, fearlessness, being culturally savvy, a thinker

- **understanding others and having influence** inclusive, collaborative

- **vision and execution** think globally, act locally, be truly innovative, a change agent, reconcile profit and fairness, have an impact.

Here's a reminder of some of the key points from this chapter:

- the world is undergoing a massive transformation, changing codes, values and purpose and embracing technology, to become an increasingly connected and complicated world

- The best leadership models are deeply rooted in the reality of the world around them, so aspiring leaders too need to always be in tune with the needs of their environment. It requires them to be in tune with current values, retain flexibility and enhance their strategic thinking.

- aspiring leaders need to demonstrate that they are collaborative and innovative in their thinking and actions

- they must embrace diversity, champion inclusiveness and multiply experiences, sharing these with others

- these attributes need to be integrated into the three cornerstones model which involves looking inside yourself (self-awareness), looking around you (understanding) and setting things in motion (vision and execution).

2

Finding the leader inside you

'Knowing others is intelligence; knowing yourself is true wisdom.
Mastering others is strength; mastering yourself is true power.'

Lao Tzu, ancient Chinese philosopher

Beware the boss with messianic complex

Luke Johnson

'I do whatever the f–k I want.' This is a remark by the world's richest restaurateur, a billionaire called Tilman Fertitta, as quoted in *Forbes* magazine recently. Does it reflect a widespread belief among successful entrepreneurs?

Unquestionably, self-determination matters a lot to them. At a recent gathering of business high-flyers, I conducted a survey of their chief motivations. Rather than wealth, power or fame, the most important driver among these self-made men and women was almost uniformly the desire for autonomy.

Certainly if you are your own boss, no one can fire you. For plenty of entrepreneurs, from Michael Bloomberg down, getting the sack was the spark to start their own show: they all vow that being given the boot will never happen to them again.

Wealthy entrepreneurs can also wear what they want, be late and get away with it, buy their way out of trouble, take a year's holiday, retire early or carry on until they drop, shut their business, sell it, give it away, put their name over the door or stick their picture up in every branch – as the founder of PizzaExpress once wanted to do (my partner and I convinced him it wasn't such a good idea).

If you possess a major business, such ownership gives you the power to make all the corporate decisions you ever fancy. By contrast, public company chief executives have to convince a board to back them, and sometimes take matters to a shareholder vote. They are in essence hired hands. Indeed, being the chief executive of a large corporation is a precarious job – the average incumbent lasts only six years in the post.

There are exceptions – Steve Jobs was one. All the profiles of him since his death describe what an autocrat he was, and how he could bully subordinates and even dictate to customers. But his remarkable achievements at Apple allowed him to get away with such seemingly unreasonable behaviour. Of course, private companies still have other stakeholders, even if all the shares are controlled by one individual. There are staff, suppliers, customers and probably lenders.

Some entrepreneurs give the impression they don't care a fig about any of them. I know one near-billionaire who appears to treat everyone like dirt – and not suffer for it. He brushes off the lawsuits and rows, and seems to grow richer and more arrogant with each deal. Yet because he has the magic touch, everyone he comes into contact with tolerates his coarseness.

Politicians give the impression of holding power, but they are very temporary custodians, and once they step down or are voted out of public office, all their influence disappears. Moreover, their every move is supervised by civil servants, and watched like a hawk by the media. Generally speaking, those in public life have very restricted freedom.

Sometimes dictators spring up, and a few cling to power for extended periods. But almost all, like Muammer Gaddafi, come to a sticky end because their hegemony is illegal and gained through force. Eventually the citizens revolt and overthrow tyrants.

By contrast, tycoons create empires through commercial flair (or perhaps inheritance), and in any event their possessions and dominance – once amassed – are protected by civil law.

Many seemingly invincible entrepreneurs are lord of all they survey in the office, but second-in-command at home. They think they can do whatever they want, but actually their spouse calls the shots about domestic matters, family – and often more.

My view has always been that we all answer to someone – be it the bank, a partner, regulators – indeed, the list can be a long one. Anyone who imagines they have total independence from the rest of society is delusional.

Perhaps while in uniform, all of those at the top have moments when they imagine they are god – be they generals, surgeons or corporate chieftains. But unless they are sociopaths – which some entrepreneurs probably are – then any momentary lapse into a messianic complex will soon be corrected.

In my experience, leaders who lack conscience and suffer from excessive self-confidence end up in trouble. Business is a collaborative art that requires persuasion and negotiation. As the Greeks knew, nemesis awaits those who are afflicted by hubris.

'Mastering yourself is true power' – and this is even truer for anyone determined to unlock their leadership potential. Leaders set things in motion because of who they are. Leadership is, first and foremost, rooted in a deep sense of self-awareness that is expressed in day-to-day attitudes and behaviours in the workplace. It is also essential to assess the fit with the intrinsic culture of the organisation.

Part 1 provided a high-level overview of the rich historical context of leadership and complemented that with an exploration of the desirable attributes of tomorrow's leaders.

This second part focuses solely on the personal dimensions of aspiring leaders. It provides a comprehensive view of what is needed in order to find the leader inside you by successively analysing the following key aspects:

- **Self-awareness** This is the most important element if you are to develop the level of empathy required to become both an effective and authentic leader. A deep understanding of who you are, rooted in the deep layers of your life story, will give you insights into your strengths, weaknesses and biases. The greater your understanding, the better you will be able to relate to and influence others. Different methods and techniques to reach an adequate level of self-awareness are presented (see Chapter 3).

- **Self-confidence** Self-confidence plays a critical role in establishing yourself as someone who is not only respected and listened to but also inspiring. Gaining self-confidence is not an easy exercise. It requires the development of a strong feeling of self-worth, by means of reprogramming yourself, shifting perspectives and how you filter information. You will also need to understand your fears and find ways to overcome them (see Chapter 4).

- **Your leadership 'brand'** This means how you convey your identity and is a way to communicate what is powerful, inspiring and effective about your leadership, at every level of the organisation and externally. Developing your leadership brand requires you to clearly define what you want to be known for, always bearing in mind your authenticity. It asks for you to 'walk the talk' and consistently demonstrate in your behaviours what you stand for. Finally, it asks you to build your charisma and gravitas by being aware of how you carry yourself and how you communicate (see Chapter 5).

3

Building your self-awareness

'Retire into yourself as much as possible. Associate with people who are likely to improve you. Welcome those whom you are capable of improving. The process is a mutual one. People learn as they teach.'

Seneca, Roman Stoic philosopher

This chapter covers:

- the importance of self-awareness when building a leadership skill set

- the three basic processes you can follow to achieve adequate levels of self-awareness – self-questioning, experiencing and proactively seeking feedback

- how to discover when you perform at your best and, subsequently, build and/or maintain an environment that is conducive to bringing this about

- the commonest leadership styles and how to identify what yours is and when and how to adjust it to circumstances.

The Oracle of Delphi and Bill George

In ancient Greece, the Oracle of Delphi was a major influence on people's lives. Proud rulers, anxious to know what the future would hold for their empires, would take a trip to consult Apollo's Oracle. Meeting an oracle was perceived as a life-changing experience, where the requestor would be given, most of the time, an ambiguous and somewhat cryptic answer.

The principle of an oracle was that it would guide enquirers so that they would become aligned with their destinies. Every answer could be found from within.

Over time, the oracle's purpose evolved into one of learning how to be who you are. The more consciously you understand what is contained within you as an individual – your goodness and your badness – the better equipped you will be to go through life.

At the beginning of 2012, Bill George, former CEO of Medtronic and Professor of Management Practice at Harvard Business School, challenged the 'great man' theory, declaring that trying to emulate other great leaders is the surest way to failure. The key to leadership, he asserts, is not emulation, nor having the perfect competences or leadership styles, nor even having the power or the title to lead, but merely being authentic and true to yourself in what you do.

Building your self-awareness, finding the essence of what makes you you and keeping your authenticity are keys to successful leadership. You can develop your self-awareness by examining the following questions:

- What do I stand for as an individual?
- What are the necessary conditions for me to perform best as a person and a leader?
- What is my most natural leadership style, one that allows me to stay authentic while being able to flex when circumstances dictate?

Note that it might be helpful to keep the answers you give for the exercises included later in this chapter as they may be useful when you come to undertake the exercises in Chapter 4.

Finding the keys to your self

Self-awareness is your ability to understand how you feel and think. This knowledge is essential as it enables you to stay in tune with your emotions, understand and help your decision making process and develop authentic relationships with your team. After all, if you don't know yourself, how can you lead yourself? If you can't lead yourself, how can you lead others?

To acquire an adequate level of self-awareness, it is necessary to commit to yourself and work on understanding exactly who you are. It demands the development of sound self-questioning abilities, coupled with a pro-active approach to the experience of leadership. Finally, it requires you to avidly request feedback and act on it. Taking time to reflect on your values, goals, your personal definition of success and how your actions relate to these is a necessary starting point for anyone who wants to lead.

Inquisitive self-questioning

To develop your self-awareness you must begin by looking inside yourself. The following questions are good starting points:

- Who am I?
- What are my most important beliefs and values?
- What are my strengths and weaknesses?

These should be looked at through the filter of, 'What does this tell me about my ability to lead, to become a leader or differentiate?' Let us look at each question in turn.

Who am I?

This is the most fundamental question. Identify the different elements that have influenced you and assess how they appear or translate in your behaviours and might be shaping who you are as a leader.

You can break this down by looking at different aspects, such as the following:

- Your cultural background, in terms of where you were born, your religion and so on. This might give you insights into your tolerance of difference (if, for example, you are from a minority group) or your flexibility (if your parents are from two different cultures, say). It might be indicative of how at ease you are with diversity, compromise, adaptability.

- The environment you grew up in. Your environment defines you. Early exposure to either leaders or the problems of leadership – at any level and in any field of activity – will give you a head start on the behaviours you will need to exhibit or actual role models you do or do not want to emulate. If you come from a medical or academic background, for example, you might have more empathy, an already rich frame of reference or a greater ability to think strategically.

- What is your family history and your position in the family. Are your parents divorced? Do you have siblings? Are you the eldest, youngest, the one in the middle? These things will have an influence not only on how you relate to others but also how you establish trust and what role you tend to take in groups. It will also shed some light on the origins of your drivers – a need to be noticed, successful or loved, for instance.

What are my most important beliefs and values?

Your beliefs and value system are constructed out of a complex series of factors, including your upbringing, education and religion. These define you at moral and ethical levels. They represent the framework of what it is acceptable for you to do or be. They also frame your relationships with others and how you build respect and trust. (More on beliefs and values can be found in Chapter 6.)

What are my strengths and weaknesses?

Understanding your strengths and weaknesses is helpful in defining your current potential and forces you to think in terms of leveraging your strengths and compensating for your weaknesses.

The questions to focus on could be, but are not restricted to, these:

- What am I good at or not so good at and why?
- What do I enjoy and not enjoy doing and why?

Assessing strengths and weaknesses also presents additional benefits. It acts as a training ground for you to assess others, ultimately developing your teambuilding and leading abilities while honing your delegation skills – in other words, what and to whom to delegate. It helps you to very quickly gauge your fit with or appetite for a particular position and highlights how you can differentiate to be more successful. Ultimately, it will buff up your career management skills (for more on this, see Chapter 6).

Working on your self-awareness can be a difficult exercise, so consider hiring a personal development coach. Some organisations will even offer coaching sessions to their top performers, identified talents or executives. A professional coach will help facilitate the change required and answer any questions or doubts you may have. Coaching can crystallise your responsibilities and commitment to your own change. It has a ripple effect, as it can also train you to more effectively coach and help others develop.

Exercises and action points

Starting your self-questioning process

A self-questioning process is best started by putting yourself into a particular state of mind. You need to allow space and time to reminisce about your past, and look for behavioural clues or patterns. It is important to keep in mind that you are, first and foremost, a person, not only a professional. Whether you are a team member, a manager or a leader, examining your personal life is an important part of becoming more self-aware.

▶

The following might help you get started on your thinking process:

- Make sure you are relaxed and emotionally ready for the exercise. Rather than think in terms of 'I have to', say to yourself, 'I am investing time in myself because I want to'.

- Set aside an adequate amount of time to go through the questioning process.

- Create the right surroundings. Find a quiet room, put some music on if it helps to isolate you from the rest of the world – whatever you need to create your own bubble.

- Find the most comfortable way for you to record your thoughts and experiences. This might be by writing, drawing or using audio. Some people have a leadership folder where they record their thoughts, experiences and ideas, but you might like to use notebooks or sticky notes. What is important is to capture everything in one place and provide yourself with a resource you can revisit.

- If you are feeling like nothing is coming to you, break down every question into smaller questions.

- This process can be repeated – you might need a couple of sessions to capture all the important influences.

In terms of frequency, most organisations will have a well-defined performance assessment cycle that will generally consist of a mid-year review of objectives and a year-end review of performance. It can be beneficial to mirror this frequency and factor some self-awareness-building time either just before or right after your performance meetings.

Personal SWOT analysis

SWOT analysis is a recognised strategic thinking tool that can also be useful for your personal development. 'SWOT' stands for strengths, weaknesses, opportunities and threats. It is particularly effective or recommended when you take on a new role or hit a roadblock in your current organisation and are debating if you should consider a change of direction.

Specifically, SWOT will enable you to recognise and take advantage of your abilities. It provides you with a deep analysis of your strengths, uncovers the opportunities to leverage your talents, reveals your blindspots when looking at your weaknesses and helps you to see the potential threats to your own success.

Performing a comprehensive personal SWOT will take a couple of hours. Make sure you are as precise as possible in your answers to the questions about each area below, illustrating them with examples whenever possible:

- **Strengths**
  What do you consider to be your leadership strengths?
  How do you leverage those strengths?
  What do others see as your strengths?
  What technical knowledge/skills do you possess/leverage?
  What functional expertise/experience do you possess/leverage?

- **Weaknesses**
  What skills, behaviours or knowledge would you like to develop?
  What would you like to stop doing?
  What would you like to do better?

- **Opportunities**
  (Positive external conditions/factors that you do not necessarily control but can leverage.)
  What opportunities do you have to elicit feedback on your leadership competences?
  What opportunities do you have to leverage other people's strengths?
  What opportunities are there to create value from the ideas and opinions of others?

- **Threats**
  (Negative external conditions/factors that you do not necessarily control, but may be able to overcome.)
  What obstacles or challenges could you experience when eliciting feedback?
  What might prevent you from leveraging other people's strengths?
  What might prevent you from leveraging your leadership strengths?

It might be useful to share your personal SWOT with your feedback group to get an independent and unbiased opinion.

The ultimate outcome of performing a personal SWOT analysis is to craft an action plan to take advantage of your new knowledge and develop as a leader. For more on action plans and how to keep up momentum to deliver on them, see later in this chapter.

▶

Myers-Briggs type indicator (MBTI)

While self-awareness may be enhanced by self-questioning exercises, it can also be useful to invest time in some well-recognised tools and questionnaires. One tool particularly popular in FTSE 500 companies is the Myers-Briggs type indicator (MBTI).

The MBTI personality assessment tool is based on Jungian psychological types. The basic premise is that an individual's apparently random behaviour gives us insight into the way that individual prefers to apply his or her perception and judgement.

It takes into account four pairs of elements, which are four different types of preferences in certain given situations:

- focus on the outer (**Extrovert or E**) or inner world (**Introvert or I**)

- handling information by either focusing on basic information you take in (**Sensing or S**) or having a preference for interpreting and adding meaning (**Intuition or N**)

- making decisions, with a preference for looking at logic and consistency (**Thinking or T**) or looking at the people side and special circumstances (**Feeling or F**)

- handling the outside world – either having a preference for reaching a decision (**Judging or J**) or staying open to new information and options (**Perceiving or P**).

Completing a MBTI questionnaire may take two to four hours, depending on the version you use (there are two that can be found online at: **http://myersbriggs.org**).

The real value of an MBTI is in getting an expert analysis of the results and preparing a summary of key points for you to keep. You may also decide to share this with your team to give them some insight into your preferences and how they can best handle you.

Practice makes perfect

Leadership is far from being a scholarly concept. The essence of leadership is rooted in delivering a product or service and having an impact on others. It is important to multiply your leadership experiences or, in the words of Alain Bloch, Affiliate Professor Director of HEC

Entrepreneurs, 'Leadership is like learning how to ride a bicycle – you do not learn by looking at the diagrams in a book. You go out there, and you try.'

Where do you find opportunities to test your skills and learn how to lead? Virtually anywhere. Leadership is absolutely not constrained to an organisational or corporate framework. Anytime, anywhere there is a problem to solve, people to influence, people to engage on an issue, work with to deliver a project or merely create, do something or find ideas and decisions to be made, there are leadership opportunities.

Proactively looking for 'qualifying' leadership experiences early in your career will definitely help you to build a clear competitive advantage. It is crucial, however, to take adequate time to reflect on what you have learned, and how you might shape the next leadership experience. Testing, experiencing and becoming better at it is the name of the game.

Have a think about the following questions after you feel you have closed one leadership experience but before you embark on a new one.

- What insight have I gained about myself?
- How do these influences affect my role as leader?

Also consider sharing your learning with your feedback group, so they too can help you recalibrate your behaviours.

Exercises and action points

Ten quick ways to increase your experience of leadership

The following list shows ways to kick-start your acquisition of leadership experience:

- while at school or university:
  - get elected on to the committee of a student association and, subsequently, run it
  - create a new association that addresses some pain points for students or academic staff

▶

▶
- Leverage your hobbies:
  - become the captain of your local sports team or club
  - become a member of the leadership team of any other interest or hobby-focused group you belong to
- via work:
  - organise a work assignment or ask to be put in charge of a particular project within – or preferably outside – your area of influence
  - explore opportunities to head up or take charge of one of your company's networks or associations or become a non-executive director on the Board of a start-up company.
- via family activities:
  - take charge of the parents' association at your children's school
  - run your local church or other group's annual fundraising event
  - fundraise for a charity when you take part in your sporting activities.

Learning from feedback

The question of *giving* feedback is addressed in full in Chapter 7, but it is useful to look here at the best ways to learn from feedback you *receive*.

To achieve self-awareness, you need to look at yourself as a constant work-in-progress, approaching this endeavour with humility and a pro-active approach to changing your behaviours. Feedback is the best tool for helping you to become the self-aware leader of tomorrow.

Feedback should come from a variety of sources within your organisation (such as peers, bosses and team members) and outside it (friends or family) to give you the most accurate picture of who you are. Requesting feedback is not an easy task. It can feel somewhat counterintuitive when trying to establish yourself as a leader. However, having the courage and openness to ask others to help you on your journey is already a sign of leadership potential. The trick is to start thinking about feedback as being part of your learning and personal commitment to the goal of becoming the best professional you can possibly be. Any discomfort – or even shame – you might feel will not last.

There are multiple ways to gather feedback, which can be either structured or ad hoc. Both types are important: the former, giving a certain formality to the exercise, allows you appropriate time to reflect, absorb and build on it in the long term; the latter can be very effective for addressing immediate issues and behaviours that are easy to fix.

Structured feedback is usually given face to face in a formal evaluation of performance with your boss, usually twice a year. However, you may request feedback as often as you think you need it – once a quarter or once every couple of months or at different milestones, such as at the end of big projects. Structured feedback may also be obtained by using 360-degree or similar multi-rated assessment tools, with a view to helping you increase your level of self-awareness. However, generally, the feedback received from these tools addresses the 'what' and 'how' of your performance and not necessarily the 'who you are'.

Asking the following questions during your feedback sessions can help you build a more complete picture of who you are.

- What do you want me to continue doing?
- What do you want me to do more of?
- What do you want me to start doing?
- What do you want me to stop doing?

Another way to use these questions is as a means of gaining feedback from your team. This will keep you honest and committed and enable you to start building trust with them.

The other type of feedback – *ad hoc feedback* – can be obtained via a pool of trusted people you enrol in your leadership journey. Give them the task of observing you in situ and systematically debriefing you on your behaviours, how you came across and what you did well or not. This is a very powerful technique as it allows you to focus your dos and don'ts on recent and tangible experiences.

Gathering feedback is relatively easy – once you get past any initial dis-comfort. What is important to your development as a leader, though, is that you also commit to proactively work on the feedback received. This will happen if you follow the thorough process described next.

Keep track of all feedback received in notes or drawings in your leader-ship folder, if you are keeping one. Make a point, on a monthly basis, of systematically going through these notes to identify trends and recur-ring points – good or bad – that you can then integrate into an action plan. This is the real value-adding part – creating a comprehensive action plan to deliver on and allow you to track the desired changes.

Your action plan should include or address the following:

- the top two or three recurrent patterns or the most immediate derail-ers – these may be a mix of soft or technical skills – that you can then address sequentially or all at the same time

- tangible actions to be taken in a determined period of time

- people who could help you to achieve your goals

- a feedback mechanism to keep the momentum going.

Table 3.1 shows an example of a comprehensive action or improvement plan.

Table 3.1 Example of an action or improvement plan

Skills	Actions	Deadline	Resources	Feedback
Listening	• Do not interrupt people in meetings • Count to three before taking a turn in the conversation • Take notes	End of March	None	Ask direct reports
Public speaking	• Volunteer to present at the March leadership team meeting • Join a public speaking association	Ongoing	Public speaking association	Business vp
Industry knowledge	• Read energy news every day • Read 'The prize'	End of June	End of June	Company economist

What really matters about the plan is that you commit to it and deliver on it.

Finding the keys to your self – and, ultimately, your leadership – is an ongoing process that requires the development of your self-questioning, experiencing what leadership entails, getting constant feedback and committing to act systematically on it.

It requires the investment of a lot of time and discipline if you are to lay solid foundations on which to build your leadership.

Exercises and action points

Undertake a 360-degree assessment

Undertaking a 360-degree assessment every couple of years will definitely keep you on track in your self-awareness journey and enable you to clearly identify bias and patterns and measure your progress.

It is one of the most popular tools used in organisations to elicit feedback, so most HR teams could help facilitate one for you.

What is it?

This Web-based tool is designed to aggregate feedback on your leadership competences from a range of diverse populations, internally and externally.

How does it work?

First, you complete a questionnaire about yourself, your preferences and your behaviours.

You are then invited to select a sample of people to request feedback from.

The recommended number is 10 to 20 people, in different capacities, who interact with you on a regular basis.

The selected people then answer the same set of questions about you.

The questionnaire consists of a mix of multiple-choice closed questions and open questions, so concrete situations and examples can be mentioned. The information given is kept completely anonymous, to prevent any discomfort for both you and the other people. The output is a report.

▶

How can it be used?

A 360-degree assessment gives you the chance to view your assessment of yourself and compare this with the assessments given by others. It helps to quickly identify any gaps between others' perceptions of you and your own. It also stresses what you are good at and what can be perceived as your limiting behaviours.

It is a very powerful tool to help you start your self-awareness journey. To make the most of it, consider the following before you start:

- when choosing people for your sample, take into consideration culture, gender and the status of your relationship with each of them

- aim for a good balance between people you have difficult relationships with and your strong advocates or supporters

- consider including external stakeholders as well, to get the most accurate picture possible

- when you have picked your people, give them each a courtesy call to reaffirm how you are committed to your leadership journey and that they are an important part of it

- if you are comfortable with the idea, enquire if they would be open to having a face-to-face debrief session to enhance the benefit of the assessment.

Set up a feedback group

One important part of starting a leadership development programme is to have an efficient support system around you. Having a feedback group can be a huge help.

Identify a group of people – no fewer than three and no more than five – you trust, and with whom you feel you can be completely honest and open in sharing your shortcomings, doubts and fears. It is best to put together a mix of peers, direct reports and people you consider to be mentors.

When you approach them, it's a good idea to share your development project, stressing the following:

- why you are doing this – you have a genuine desire to grow and learn, for example

- why you would like them to be involved – for instance, because you respect and trust them, you can learn from them, you see their potential or you admire them

▶

> ▣ that this will require them to invest some time (regular meetings or phone calls) and they need to be OK with this
>
> ▣ that you might engage them in different parts of your development (self-awareness, fears, vision building and so on) and their role may range from holding the mirror up to you and keeping you honest to challenging and pushing you, listening to your fears, helping you reframe or change perspective – the idea is that they will essentially become a 'go to' person for you
>
> ▣ the importance of confidentiality and trust – be open about your emotional state.
>
> One way to get buy in is to offer to reciprocate if you find that someone you have asked to join your group wants to start their own journey.

Defining your personal leadership style

Are you challenging or supportive? Collaborative or autocratic? Responsible and valuing accountability? Laissez-faire? These attributes define different leadership styles. Different individuals will demonstrate different natural leadership styles. What is critical for future leaders – on top of perfectly understanding their natural leadership style – is to be fully knowledgeable about what other styles of leadership are available to them and develop the ability to flex their own style, while remaining authentic and creating the right sort of leadership in any given situation.

Building your knowledge: the three main styles of leadership

Leadership is often defined as the activity of providing direction, implementing plans and monitoring people. In the 1940s, psychologist Kurt Lewin defined the three main leadership styles as autocratic, democratic and laissez-faire.

Autocratic leadership

This style is characterised by the leader providing clear expectations regarding:

- what needs to be done

- when it should be done

- how it should be done.

Autocratic leaders prefer to make decisions by themselves, based on their own ideas or judgements, with little or no input from the rest of the group. One great example of an autocratic leader is Howell Raines, Executive Editor of the *New York Times*, 2001–3. Widely cited as a 'hard-charging' executive editor, Raines was known for his policy of 'flooding the zone' – that is, using all of the *New York Times*' resources to cover what he deemed to be important stories. He was known to push people. Autocratic leadership involves having total control over the group.

The key attributes of this style of leadership are that:

- there is little or no input from members of the group

- the leader makes the decisions

- the group leader dictates all the work methods and processes

- the members of the group are rarely trusted with decisions or important tasks.

Democratic leadership

Also known as participative leadership, democratic leaders prefer to offer guidance to their group. They feel that they are part of the group and look for members' input. When it comes to decision making, democratic leaders encourage participation from the group's members, but retain the final say and make the decisions. Usually, democratic leaders will ensure that members of the group are engaged in the process, encourage creativity and make them feel valued.

A prominent example of a democratic leader would be General Dwight Eisenhower. While it may seem counter-intuitive to cite a military leader as an example of democratic leadership, what Eisenhower achieved in the Second World War was truly exceptional. It was imperative that a common strategy be adopted if the Nazis were to be defeated. Eisenhower grasped this very early on and strived to make sure that everyone worked together, having a common understanding ... and the rest is history.

The key attributes of this style of leadership are that:

- members of the group are encouraged to share ideas and opinions, even though the leader retains the final say
- members of the group feel engaged in the decision process
- creativity is encouraged and rewarded.

Laissez-faire leadership

Also known as delegative leadership, laissez-faire leaders offer little or no guidance and leave decision making to members of the group. Lewin's study showed that this leadership style is generally to be avoided, unless you are leading a team of highly qualified or expert individuals who can be left to act ably of their own accord.

The key attributes of this style of leadership are that:

- there is very little guidance from the leader
- group members have complete freedom to make decisions
- the leader provides the tools and resources needed
- members of the group are expected to solve problems on their own.

Assessing your baseline leadership style

Having established the basics of your leadership style, it is important to assess where you naturally sit in relation to Lewin's classification. This can be done by answering the questions in the following exercise.

Exercises and action points

What is your baseline leadership style?

1   In a group setting, do you find yourself breaking the ice:

(a) always □?   (b) occasionally □?   (c) never □?

2   In a group setting, do you generally find yourself organising the activities:

(a) always □?   (b) occasionally □?   (c) never?

▶

3 In a group setting, do you generally find yourself telling other people what to do:

(a) always ☐?   (b) occasionally ☐?   (c) never ☐?

4 In a group setting, how would you describe how much time on average you spend speaking and how does this compare with others:

(a) above average ☐?   (b) average ☐?   (c) below average ☐?

(Above average = you dominate most conversations. Below average = you are more often than not a quiet participant.)

5 In a group setting, would you ask for help or guidance when performing a task:

(a) most of the time ☐?   (b) occasionally when challenged ☐?
(c) never ☐?

6 In a group setting, would you normally be paying attention to how everyone else is doing:

(a) yes ☐?   (b) no ☐?   (c) often be solely focused on yourself ☐?

7 Have you ever caught yourself offering help or advice without being prompted:

(a) yes ☐?   (b) no ☐?

8 In a group setting, would you pay attention to how others are performing:

(a) yes ☐?   (b) no ☐?   (c) compare them with yourself ☐?

9 In a group setting, would you generally be happier:

(a) being left on your own to do your own thing in your own time ☐? (b) engaging in social interaction, even competition ☐?

10 How do you react to being challenged:

(a) well ☐?   (b) neutrally ☐?   (c) rather badly ☐?

11 Would you define yourself as a people person:

(a) yes ☐?   (b) never thought about it ☐?   (c) not really ☐?

12 How do you make decisions:

(a) by consulting others ☐?   (b) by yourself ☐?   (c) do not generally like to be the decision maker ☐?

▶

13 How do you feel about authority?

(a) it's useful ☐? (b) it's difficult ☐? (c) do not generally think in terms of hierarchy ☐?

Select the answers or statements that resonate most with you. To make the exercise more valuable, take time to reflect on different instances in both your personal and your professional lives.

They are both relevant to establishing your baseline leadership style.

Another very effective tactic is to have these questions in mind as you go into your next team meeting and answer them after the meeting. That way you will have tangible examples to help you with your answers.

Finally, you might decide to ask a member of your feedback group to attend one of your meetings then answer the questions. Then you could have a face-to-face debrief session to assess what is your most natural leadership style.

How to score:
Autocratic (A) Democratic/Participative (P) Delegative (D)

Check your responses for each question against the list below:

1 (a) P (b) D (c) A

2 (a) A (b) P/D (c) P/D

3 (a) A (b) P (c) D

4 (a) A (b) P (c) D

5 (a) P (b) P (c) A/D

6 (a) P (b) A/D (c) A

7 (a) P (b) A

8 (a) A (b) P/D (c) A

9 (a) D (b) A

10 (a) P (b) P/D (c) A

11 (a) P (b) D (c) A

12 (a) P (b) A (c) D

13 (a) D (b) A (c) P

When you believe you have answered all the questions, take some time to compare and contrast your answers with the characteristics and attributes

▶

of each of the profiles of Lewin's styles. This will help you to determine your baseline leadership style. For example, if you generally:

- break the ice

- organise activities

- tell others what to do

- try to solve problems on your own

- do a lot of the talking

- focus on yourself

- do not particularly offer help or advice

- are very competitive

- do not like to be challenged

- make decisions alone

you are naturally an autocratic leader.

Do not be concerned if you do not seem to have a clear-cut leadership style. Simply pick the one that *most* resonates with you and represents you. Bear in mind that no leadership style is better or worse than any other. The point of the exercise is to be aware of your natural inclination, as an important element of your self-awareness. In times of extreme pressure or intense stress, human beings return to their comfort zone. In this case, it would be the leadership style that is most natural for you.

If you are to be an authentic leader, you will need to understand your natural leadership styles and use them to best effect.

Becoming an 'authentic chameleon'

Next, you need to build on the knowledge you acquired from completing the above exercise. That is because, while everyone has a natural leadership style, the most effective leaders are those who can switch from one style to another as required. To do this well, it is vital that leaders can read the environment and the situation and quickly assess what leadership style will result in the most favourable outcome.

Table 3.2 illustrates the pros and cons of each leadership style. It also indicates which style is best suited to a given set of circumstances.

Table 3.2 Leadership styles and how to use them effectively

Style	Benefits	Disadvantages	Best to use when?
Autocratic	• Quick decision making process • Strong delivery • Group members focus on tasks at hand • Develops expertise in group members	• Hinders team spirit • Potential demotivation/ resentment • Impairs creativity	• Crisis situations • Leader is most knowledgeable • Leader has privileged information
Democratic	• Creativity and idea generation • Greater team spirit • Greater team commitment • Higher levels of productivity	• If role unclear, can lead to communication failure, lack of delivery • Slows down decision making process • Impairs quality of decision making	• Team members are skilled • Team members are eager to share their knowledge • When time is not of the essence
Laissez-faire	• Allows thinking time for leaders • High levels of autonomy of group members	• Risk of non-delivery • Lack of problem solving • High levels of autonomy of group members	• Team is skilled or experienced • Team is self-motivated • Leaders are still available for consultation and feedback

This kind of situational leadership is also rooted in assessing everything through social, circumstantial and cultural lenses. It is important to factor other considerations into your natural leadership and decision making preferences, too.

Knowledge of team members

Knowing what their skills are and where they are on their learning curves is vital. Selecting an authoritarian style for a new employee who is just learning the job may help him or her feel at ease by alleviating fear of the unknown. Equally, using a democratic style with workers who know their jobs well – especially when it is likely that you do not know all the information – will make the team feel valued. A laissez-faire approach is likely to be best when you are faced with a team member or a co-worker who knows more about the job than you.

For the best possible performance, it may be highly effective to use all three styles. For example, you might tell your employees that a procedure is not working correctly and a new one must be established (autocratic). You could then ask for their ideas and input to create a new procedure (democratic). Finally, you could delegate tasks in order to implement the new procedure (laissez-faire).

Corporate culture

Leadership learning comes also from observing others and finding role models. Your environment shapes what it needs from you if you are to become a leader, which will mean that, at times, you will need to adjust your natural leadership style.

case study   General Electric

General Electric is known as a company with an especially effective corporate culture that fosters good leaders. Its corporate culture is geared towards excellence and execution. This can only be achieved by having flawless processes and extreme discipline.

The constant pace of change should naturally foster an autocratic leadership style, but, surprisingly, most of General Electric's leaders appear to be democratic, as success is first and foremost a team effort. Everyone is regularly stretched and trust and delegation are critical success factors. The decision making process, however, remains an autocratic leadership act.

Ability to assess the cultural environment

Culture and diversity also play an important part in deciding which leadership style to use. The power difference index (PDI)[1] records the extent to which the less powerful members of a society expect and accept that power is distributed unequally. The higher the number for a country, the more autocratic and/or paternalistic is its leadership. This means that employees in countries with high scores tend to be more afraid or unwilling to disagree with their bosses than those in countries with low scores. In such countries, a more democratic style of leadership is found and there employees tend not to be as afraid of their bosses.

Example: Cultural differences in the acceptance of inequalities in the distribution of power

The last revolution in Sweden disposed of King Gustav IV, whom the Swedes considered incompetent, and, surprisingly, led to Jean-Baptiste Bernadotte, a French general who served under Napoleon, being invited to become the new King of Sweden. He accepted and became King Charles XIV.

Soon afterwards, the new king needed to address the Swedish Parliament. Wanting to be accepted, he tried to make the speech in Swedish. His imperfect use of the language amused the Swedes so much that they roared with laughter. The Frenchman was so upset that he never tried to speak Swedish again.

Bernadotte was a victim of culture shock — never in his French upbringing and military career had he experienced subordinates laughing at the mistakes of their superiors. That is because Sweden differs from France in the way that its society handles power inequalities. This is illustrated by Sweden having a relatively low PDI score of 31, while France has a PDI of 68.

This story has a happy ending as Bernadotte was considered a very good king and ruled the country as a highly respected constitutional monarch until 1844 and his descendants still occupy the Swedish throne.

For example, Malaysia has the highest PDI score (104), while Austria has the lowest (11). The USA's is 40 and the UK's is 35. Being aware of such differences will help you to choose the most appropriate leadership style.

Thus, bringing all these factors together, it can be seen that understanding your natural leadership style and being able to adjust it to circumstances and cultural differences are critical knowledge and skills to master. Only then will you be able to blossom into the inclusive and adaptable leader that the world is looking for.

---

[1] Geert Hofstede (2003) *Culture's Consequences*, Sage, and co-authored with Gert Jan Hofstede and Michael Minkov (2010) *Cultures and Organizations: Software of the Mind*, McGraw-Hill.

Creating your own performance card

Reflecting on how to adequately manage your performance is part of developing self-awareness. It is first critical to define what performance means for you and the organisation, then ensure you are always performing to the best of your ability – that is, you are delivering consistently and in a sustainable fashion. This type of self-awareness is built on understanding what external and internal conditions are required in order for you to perform. This allows you to create the most favourable environment for you and, ultimately, quickly adjust and recalibrate when you feel your performance is sliding.

Let's use the example of a marathon runner to explore this further. A marathon runner will need enough physical strength to endure a 40-km run. He will need to be able to maintain a certain speed without too much difficulty to avoid putting pressure on his body. This should be complemented by a huge dose of mental strength to overcome pain and keep going when he hits 'the wall'. In order to develop these three key elements of high performance, the aspiring marathon runner needs to follow some basic rules, such as never settle into a routine, constantly challenge himself and use a mix of physical and mental training techniques.

After a certain period of trial and error, all marathon runners learn what it is that they need to do to ensure they are at the peak of their ability on the day. They know with absolute precision how strict or relaxed their training programme needs to be, which sequence of cardio and strength training is best for them. They know what they need to eat, when and how often. They know what their most restful sleep patterns are and when to exercise for best results. By keeping track of all internal or external triggers, once they have defined what performance means for them, they can always assess whether or not they will be in good shape to finish their race.

Becoming a leader is a bit like marathon training that lasts a lifetime. It demands the integration and practice of four essential elements:

■ defining what performing well means for you and for the organisation

■ assessing what the necessary conditions are for you to perform well

- defining monitoring mechanisms to quickly assess when you are at risk of going off the rails – for instance, when facing an increased workload or heightened stress levels

- keeping the momentum going to minimise the risks of derailing.

The best possible way to reflect on what performing well means and address the four questions above would be to set aside a couple of hours at the end of a weekend – or, preferably, a holiday, when you are relaxed and refreshed.

It is also recommended that you set aside another couple of hours to revisit your answers after two weeks to assess potential deviations. This should give you a proper baseline to start working from.

Defining what performing well means

Before delving into how to create the most favourable environment for you to perform, it is important to first assess what performing well means for you and your organisation by looking at the following questions:

- What are the critical success factors in my current role?

- Why are they critical to my success?

- Why are they critical to the company's success?

- What types of behaviours/state of mind do they require?

The critical success factors can be a mix of technical and soft skills. They represent the yardsticks by which your performance is measured. These are the attitudes or behaviours that you need to keep under control at all times and excel at. Discussions with your line manager or your most important stakeholders can be good sources of data to help you answer these questions.

Looking at these factors from the point of view of the organisation and its culture is key if you are to ensure that you are focusing on the vital sustaining behaviours and attributes for your organisation. In other words, it will help you apply your energy to the right things and assess how good a fit or match you are for the organisation. It is also a good idea to get input from your manager.

Only once you have clearly articulated what performing well means for you can you then work on assessing the conditions required for you to do so.

Assessing what the necessary conditions are for you to perform well

Some of the areas you might focus on are:

- sleep patterns
- eating patterns
- social and/or cultural activities
- status of relationships with your loved ones
- exercise schedule
- status of relationship with direct reports, boss, other colleagues
- schedule of important events
- travel schedule
- overall emotional state while at your work.

It is important to look at anything that you feel has a positive or negative impact on your being able to demonstrate your best behaviours and perform at your best. To do this, keep a diary for one to two months, jotting down instances when you performed well and others when you didn't, articulating the outcome in each case. At the end of the two-month period, it is a good idea to summarise your findings in a list of the top five behaviours or activities you need to constantly watch to stay in your optimum performance zone. This list is what goes on your performance card.

Defining monitoring mechanisms

Type or write your outcome list on a card to create your personal performance card. Refer back to it on a regular basis or when you foresee a change in pace in your working life. This will allow you to immediately spot when your discipline is starting to slide and take corrective action.

Keeping the momentum going

To help maintain your discipline, keep several copies of your card positioned in strategic places both at home and in the office.

At home, the most popular and useful place would be on the fridge or on the bathroom mirror, so you can see it daily or even several times a day.

In the office, again, if possible, keep it where you can see it – so, on your desk or by your computer screen would be good places. However, if this feels too public, keep it in a top drawer or in a folder by your computer.

Supplement these with an electronic version on your phone or in your diary, so you can be reminded of what it is you have to keep doing when you are travelling.

With the pressures of your daily work, it can be easy to slip off course. Integrating your performance band factors into your work environment will not only make them easier for you to implement but also encourage you to share this knowledge with your peers and your team, which can help create a mutually supportive environment.

Exercises and action points

Defining the conditions for you to perform at your best

Imagine you are the commercial director of the business unit of a Fortune 500 company, in charge of global accounts that represent about 80 per cent of the company's turnover and about 40 per cent of its profitability. Now answer the following questions:

- What are the critical success factors in my current role?
- Why are they critical to my success?
- Why are they critical to the company's success?
- What types of behaviours/state of mind do they require?

Your answers to the first three questions could be along the following lines:

- 'The ability to adequately read body language and demonstrate empathy are critical to my performing as a commercial director.'

- 'They are critical to my success because they help me to bond with customers and influence them without them noticing – for example, when I am negotiating contracts.'

- 'My ability to secure long-term, profitable contracts is essential as it contributes to the company's value while satisfying the shareholder requirements.'

- 'To demonstrate empathy, I need to always be 100 per cent focused on what is happening in the client meeting and not let my mind wander. I need to be alert and pay particular attention to body language so as to be able to match or mirror my customers. It would also be helpful for me to act as an observer more and hone my listening skills, so I will avoid being the first to speak whenever possible. I will ask questions but also be sure to leave some silence for others to volunteer more.'

Let us now translate these points into tangible actions that might improve how well you perform.

- 'Bearing in mind that I am not a morning person, it will be best to organise meetings with customers for late morning.'

- 'I will keep 30 to 45 minutes before the meeting free to clear my mind of current issues and get myself into observing mode. I might spend time re-reading some high-level explanations of the principles of body language.'

Summary

Leadership is a lifestyle and being able to analyse what you need to do, design an holistic strategy to achieve it – ranging from intellectual self-awareness, to an ability to understand yourself and down to creating and managing the most favourable environment to enable you to consistently perform well – and integrate it into your life is the ultimate step you can take towards self-awareness.

Here's a reminder of some of the key points from this chapter:

- self-awareness is based on inquisitive self-questioning

- create time and space for yourself to analyse who you are and make sure you investigate as many angles as possible – from your cultural background and childhood to your aspirations and adult experiences

- self-awareness also requires you to be comfortable with feedback and consider yourself as a work-in-progress. Proactively seek all types of feedback – formal, structured, ad hoc

- creating a feedback group to observe and support your leadership development can be helpful, acting as an honest yet caring mirror for your behaviours

- dedicate sufficient time to analysing feedback and crafting an improvement plan, focusing on three key behaviours or skills at a time via tangible, measurable and time-bound actions

- develop an understanding of your natural leadership style by questioning and reflecting on your behaviours in your personal and professional lives

- be aware that another type of leadership style might be more effective, depending on the situation, cultural environment or corporate culture, so adjust your style to suit the situation and increase efficiency

- think of yourself as a marathon runner and define the conditions that will result in your optimal performance, including work and lifestyle elements

- make monitoring your performance a regular activity, as by being disciplined you will minimise your chances of going off the rails

- shift your perspective on leadership from it being purely a work thing to it being part of your lifestyle – all experiences and interactions matter and can become opportunities to develop and grow as a leader.

4

Gaining self-confidence

'They can because they think they can.'

Virgil, Roman poet

This chapter covers:

- the concept of self-confidence and why it is a critical attribute for leadership
- self-belief and positive reinforcement – the first building blocks of self-confidence
- why fear holds you back and how to overcome this stumbling block to progress.

Playing the piano and the British Army

Estelle Clark is Group Business Assurance Director for Lloyd's Register. She was born without index fingers and significant deformity to most of her other fingers. At the age of four, she undertook extensive plastic surgery, the doctors constructing some of her fingers from scratch. On the last day of her stay at the hospital, the chief surgeon brought some of his students by to discuss the great results achieved – only to end with a tasteless joke: 'Well, of course, she will never be a pianist!' The whole audience laughed politely.

That was a defining moment for Estelle when it came to assessing her self-confidence. That very day she decided no one would ever say for her what she could or could not do. She would be fully accountable for who she could be and would be whatever she wanted to be. Estelle is now, by the way, a very good pianist!

The founder of a very successful consultancy business started his professional career serving in the British Army, where he stayed for several years before joining the business world. During his time in the Army, he served in a war zone and experienced being physically threatened. It irrevocably altered his perspective on life and his understanding of fear. Regardless of how complex or critical the business situation is, he is now convinced that he can handle it as it is never life-threatening. His experiences have given him ultimate confidence in his abilities.

What do these examples tell us? Making your own decisions as to what you can or cannot do, believing in your self-worth and letting go of your fears are important attitudes of mind for leaders.

They are also great confidence boosters. Self-confidence is the driver to achieving great things, taking risks and challenging the status quo. It is one of the key elements allowing innovation to happen and also generates a high level of influence on others. The aura or energy of a self-confident person usually draws others towards them, as they become a source of inspiration and a role model. Having self-confidence is very helpful for getting people's buy in and motivating them.

Most successful CEOs ooze self-confidence and it is the foundation of solid leadership. Marshall Goldsmith, the author of *What Got You Here Won't Get You There* (Profile Books, 2008), argues that self-confidence is usually grossly overlooked in leadership programmes and literature.

The three cornerstones of self-esteem

Self-worth or self-esteem are fundamental building blocks when it comes to gaining self-confidence. Who in today's volatile, complex and uncertain world would follow you if you didn't believe in yourself? Building self-esteem is a long-term process. It often requires you to deconstruct patterns formed during childhood. It can be achieved by mastering control of your own perceptions, developing the healthy habit of filtering and reframing events and your ideas about failure. Finally, it requires you to embrace and advocate positive reinforcement.

It is well known from psychological studies that self-confidence and self-esteem are built mostly during the early stages of your childhood. Often education and parenting emphasise what attitudes should be avoided to stay safe and, consequently, impose constraints on young children, the effects of which often last into adulthood. Moving towards a strong belief in yourself involves overcoming or deconstructing those years of natural programming and changing your perspective.

Your perception is your reality

Believing you are great at what you do, being convinced that you can achieve anything that your heart or your mind desires are important attitudes to develop quickly in your leadership journey.

Human beings build their own mental prisons and have a hard time understanding that they have the power to break free from them any time they please. Being able to recalibrate your own perception of yourself and imprint a better one requires you to focus on your strengths and systematically take stock of the positive aspects of any experience. This is what self-esteem or self-worth is about.

Build on your strengths

This helps you to create a positive feeling about yourself. The aim is to change your internal 'parental' voice from, 'I cannot' and 'I should not' to the liberating 'I can' and to do this because you feel you have the capacity or intellectual ability to do so. It is also useful to change your perception of failure. Because you are purposefully focusing on what you are good or gifted at, failure becomes a less and less likely event.

Systematically take stock of positive aspects of any experiences

This is the next step. It helps you to project or create a future where everything is possible for you. By building your inventory of positive experience and success, you are freeing yourself from your own limitations.

Imagine you are going out on to a ski slope for the first time. It is a black run slope and you are a bit scared about it. If you start thinking, 'I am going to fall, I am going to fall', it is highly likely you will end up falling. If, instead, you consciously recall that this slope looks very similar to the slope you went on the day before, and you managed just fine because you took long turns and avoided the bumpy part, it is quite likely you will not fall at all.

Focus on the positive

Negative experiences are to be expected in any career. How you choose to react to failure – consider it a learning opportunity or not – is entirely your choice, but it can make a huge difference to your level of self-worth. Two words need to be at the top of your mind when dealing with failure or negative events: perspective and filtering.

Perspective

This is the state of your mind and it can easily be changed by shedding a
different light on failure or negative feedback. Do this by asking yourself
these two questions:

- What have I done right?
- What have I learned?

Replacing asking 'What have I done wrong?' with the above questions
will help you to analyse failure by focusing on the positive aspects of it.
This will help you to rebalance the experience and recover quickly. That
is because the eye sees what the mind sees. So, reframing your reactions
to negative experiences will help your self-confidence.

View any situation as an experiment, a way for you to grow. Believing
in yourself comes from trusting your abilities. Only when your abilities
have been tested can you start to trust them. So, all experiences, good or
bad, help you to build your inventory of abilities, which in turn develops your self-confidence. Learning to ask 'What have I learned?' will
also allow you to invite feedback more readily and naturally.

Filtering

This is the next important building block. Shaky self-confidence comes
from listening to harsh assessments or words from individuals who
are either relatively close – such as a friend or family member – and/or
highly respected – such as a manager, mentor or role model.

It is natural to swallow their feedback whole, but exercising your
filters will help you to stay immune to negative feedback and
assess which to classify as relevant and valid and which to ignore.
Inherently, it is a matter of applying the following thoughts as filters
to any negative comments:

- 'Everyone is entitled to their opinion'
- 'Some of their opinions may be wrong because no one can be
  always right'
- 'These particular opinions represent a data point rather than an
  absolute truth'.

You can develop your filtering ability by asking yourself the following question when faced with negative feedback, unfair comments or any situation that has had an impact on you:

- 'Is this the first time I am receiving this type of feedback?'

Apply this questioning process to your professional and personal lives to come up with different instances. If the answer is 'yes', just let it go – reframe it as a one-off and move on. If the answer is 'no', then try to recall the specifics and timings of the previous similar situations. If you then start to realise that you have received recurring feedback on this area, make a note to yourself to address the issue in your action plan.

Applying filters does not mean that you have to discard all the negative feedback you are given. It merely helps you cultivate your ability to choose what feedback is relevant and what is not and stay in control of your self-confidence, even when receiving criticism.

Become a strong advocate of positive reinforcement

Example: The positive effects of positive reinforcement

The Health, Safety, Security and Environment Director at BHP Billiton Iron Ore Business Development fully embraced the importance of positive reinforcement. He had extensive experience, having led projects where safety was a key metric in environments as hostile as northern Canada, the Indonesian rainforest and even the Amazon. It was critical there to develop safe behaviours in the local workforce.

He chose to introduce a new programme, based on the positive reinforcement of good behaviours developed by an Australian company. The principle was very simple. On a weekly basis, every team would gather and collectively share their week from a health, safety, security and environment perspective. They would discuss any incidents and the progress necessary to make the preferred behaviour the natural thing to do, but added praise and celebrated any positive change. In the meetings, they were also asked to congratulate themselves for being aware of these issues. The director's actions led him to create one of the most safely run operations in the world.

From a psychological perspective, positive reinforcement helps crystallise a feeling of empowerment and recognition. Individuals thrive when they regularly experience this feeling, then when repeating the behaviour that led to it. It is also a strong enabler of self-confidence.

Consider reflecting on the following question on a weekly basis as this will greatly help reinforce your self-esteem by means of positive reinforcement:

■ What can I be proud of this week?

Your answers might range from having handled a difficult discussion with a subordinate to having convinced a difficult customer or simply be that you managed to complete everything you had set yourself to do this week.

As a parting comment, a high level of self-esteem is essential if you are to appear to be a self-confident leader. However, self-esteem should not be mistaken for arrogance. A self-confident leader is not a 'know it all', but someone who is at ease with him- or herself, fully aware of his or her own abilities as well as limitations. Leaders with self-confidence are fully capable of adjusting their perspectives to cope with varied and significant events. They focus on what they can control and let go of the rest. They have enough inner strength to calibrate feedback.

Exercises and action points

Anchoring your strengths

Anchoring is about going deeply into what it is that you are good at. Doing this helps to create a positive mental picture of your abilities.

It is useful to crystallise the strengths you identify in a specific and very tangible moment as then you can draw on or go back to them any time you want. Establishing an emotional connection with the event can also be very useful for replicating positive feelings.

The best way to start the anchoring process is to use the strengths you identified in the exercises in Chapter 3, especially the SWOT analysis. Select a couple and ask the following questions:

■ Why is this strength important? What does it give me and for what purpose? How does it help me to achieve any other objective?

■ What are the past situations in which I have demonstrated this strength? (Make the situations as accurate and real as possible.)

■ How did this make me feel?

There is no particular timeframe for performing an anchoring exercise. It can easily be added to your self-questioning rhythm or the performance assessment cycle of your organisation.

▶

The outcome of your anchoring session might look like Table 4.1.

Table 4.1 Expanding your strengths

Strength	Why is this so important?	How can it be useful?	Recent examples	How did I feel?
Ability to connect	• Enables me to quickly build networks • Enables me to communicate effectively through emotion • Allows me to get information on what people want/need	• I can quickly find the right resource to help with the current problem • I can come up with business opportunities based on others' needs • I can negotiate better with customers/partners	• Meeting with VP/Sales • Discussion with Russian contacts	• Knowledgeable • Confident • Helpful
Current industry knowledge	• Enables me to quickly detect trends • Enables me to propose innovative strategic solutions before anyone else	• I can become the reference point and influence decisions • I can think at a macro level and spot strategic positions	• Tom asking for my input for his project – before Board meeting • Being asked to lead the next strategic review	• Expert • Respected • Having an impact
...	...	...	...	...

Building a 'positivity' inventory

Systematically keeping track of all the positive experiences or successes you have achieved is a huge self-esteem booster. Keeping this data helps you track the progress you have made on your personal journey. Having a record is also helpful when you are experiencing self-doubt, when you have a heavy workload or find yourself under intense pressure. It is also a useful tool for ensuring that you receive positive reinforcement.

Reflect on the following questions:

- What new things have I done this week? These could include anything from doing a presentation for the first time to organising the next teambuilding event or attending a leadership meeting.

- How did I feel before and after? Your answers will help you gauge your normal learning process.

- How successful was I? The process of answering this question will help demonstrate that, most of the time, you will overcome your discomfort or stress in order to learn what you need to learn.

Analyse your answers, keeping in mind the following angles:

- What do they say about your tolerance of risk or fear? Are you proactively looking for new experiences and stepping out of your comfort zone or not?

- What do they say about your natural learning process? Do you tend to feel anxiety at the start of the project or excitement? Being aware of your usual progression will help rationalise your emotions and, as a result, deconstruct any fear.

The purpose of this exercise is to make you realise, by giving you unbiased supporting evidence, that when you put your head and your heart into doing something, even if it feels frightening at first, most of the time you *will* succeed.

This is part of your reprogramming, so it will require some investment of time before you notice changes. Consider setting aside 45 minutes to an hour on a weekly basis for a minimum period of a month to start noticing a change in your attitude. It is preferable to perform this exercise at the end of the week, so you can better absorb and process what you have learned from it over the weekend.

Practising positive visualisation

One methodology commonly used on coaching courses that is known to help develop self-belief is visualisation. If you are interested in this, look at *Creative Visualization: Use the power of your imagination to create what you want in life*, by Shakti Gawain (New World Library, 2002). The chapter entitled 'Accepting yourself' is particularly relevant:

'Imagine yourself in an everyday situation and picture someone (someone you know, or even a stranger) looking at you with great love and admiration and telling you something they really like about you. Now picture a few more people coming up and agreeing that you are a very wonderful person. If this embarrasses you, stick with it. Imagine more and more people arriving and gazing at you with tremendous love and respect in their eyes. Picture yourself in a parade or on a stage, with throngs of cheering, applauding people. People, all loving and appreciating you. Hear their applause ringing in your ears. Stand up and take a bow, and thank them for their support and appreciation.'

Here are some affirmations that may help to develop your self-belief:

- I love and accept myself completely as I am.
- I do not have to try to please anyone else. I like myself and that's what counts.
- I am highly pleasing to myself in the presence of other people.
- I express myself freely, fully and easily.
- I am a powerful, loving and creative being.

Letting go of your fears

Fear is a primal instinct that gives our body a way of signalling danger. It helps us stay alive and safe. In today's world, fear is the only thing that can hold a person back. Fear may prevent someone from reaching what it is they really want or, at times, unlocking their real potential.

Freeing yourself from your fears starts with understanding the different categories of fears any individual can face. You then need to reflect on and identify what it is you are most fearful of and, more importantly, why. Spending time assessing what you can reasonably envisage overcoming and what you will have to accept and deal with is the next step.

Finally, once you have established what your biggest fears are, you can proactively design an action plan to either keep them in check or build your comfort level to free yourself from fear.

Fear is simply the anticipation that something is going to happen soon that needs to be prepared for. Anthony Robbins in his book, *Awaken the Giant Within* (Pocket Books, 2001) states 'Nothing makes anyone more uncomfortable than fear'. Joseph Murphy states in *The Power of our Subconscious Mind* (Wilder, 2008) 'Fear is man's greatest enemy.'

Leadership is about inspiring others, being a role model and, at times, demonstrating decisiveness and courage. Mastering one's own fears is a part of a leader's learning. Even if it is an uncomfortable moment, even if it feels counter-intuitive, acknowledging that you, as a leader, can be afraid is ultimately liberating. Addressing and confronting your fears is not only a huge confidence booster but also part of learning to get in touch with your vulnerability. Accepting and at times showing your vulnerability can help you to connect more deeply with your team.

Understanding the whole picture: the seven fears

A course on behavioural management held at the Erasmus University in Rotterdam described the seven specific fears standing between any individual and true freedom. These are also addressed in Napoleon Hill's best-selling book on personal success, *Think and Grow Rich* (Wilder, 2008).

Fear of failure

This is the irrational fear that we will not succeed. It is often the cause of procrastination – an important derailer of delivery and execution for leaders.

Fear of failure is based on a number of factors, including uncertainty about the future, upsetting others and devaluing one's own or, as explored below, others' fundamental fears. It is also acknowledged that fear of failure is largely triggered by social pressures and the cultural environment.

Guillaume Gauthereau, enthusiastic French émigré to New York City and founder of Totsy.com – a private sales website aimed at mothers with young children and one of the top five fast-growing ventures on the east coast in the USA – puts it this way:

'Having been educated in a French culture, but having lived for most of my professional life in the US, I have experienced first hand how failure is stigmatised on one side of the pond and merely considered a normal route to success on the other. At times, failure is even praised as the true success of your trial and error period'.

Fear of solitude

This fear can be rooted in a variety of experiences, from fear of death to sad or lonely experiences in childhood. It is characterised by the urge to be constantly among others. It encourages you to remain distracted and creates a state of self-avoidance in the person's mindset.

Fear of public speaking

In their book ... *And Death Came Third*, Lopata and Roper (Ecademy Press, 2011) explain that this comes from a fear of sharing your thoughts. The idea of sending a message to the world is utterly threatening, as it makes individuals truly exposed. It draws on a complex mix of fear of being listened to and deemed to be not smart enough, fear of not having something innovative or worth saying and the fear of not being heard at all. Public speaking represents the ultimate risk of being heard and, therefore, judged.

Fear of criticism

This is destructive of self-reliance and individuality. It is another form of the fear mentioned above of being judged or deemed not good enough. Fear of criticism is often described as a learned behaviour rooted in socialisation. People ache for a sense of belonging, the need to be part of a group. The fear of criticism is the fear of being ostracised or excluded from the group. It also relates to the pressing need to conform.

Fear of success

This is commonly found with sportspeople. A tennis player, for example, performs superbly for most of the match. At the critical moment, she suddenly makes mistake after mistake, losing point after point. Sports commentators refer to this situation as 'fear of winning'. When, in our example, the tennis player is so close to reaching her objectives, doubts creep in, paralysing her abilities, impairing thought and the ability to act on winning strategies. This happens because people often shy away from success as it comes with expectations, responsibilities and pressure.

Fear of being hurt

This is usually considered one of the deepest fears, affecting both professional and personal lives. It is usually referred to as a fear of being loved or simply a fear of living. Like the fear of criticism, it stems from the need to belong and be accepted for what you are. Like fear of uncertainty, too, it is triggered by a need to control or an inability to let go.

Fear of the unknown or uncertainty

This fear is often defined as an aversion to risk and the anxiety of not knowing the potential outcome of every decision. It is often demonstrated by a need to control every part of the environment or every part of your life. Fear of the unknown can lead to a fake sense of danger and trigger dictatorial, almost obsessive, types of behaviour.

It is interesting that there is a high level of interdependency with these different fears. For instance, the fear of public speaking is linked to the fear of failure. One fear can act as a trigger for another – for instance, your fear of being hurt may trigger a fear of criticism. How to combat or let go of these fears will be addressed later in this chapter.

Assessing your 'fear factor'

As professionals and human beings, individuals are the sum of their experiences, good or bad. Specific behaviours or beliefs are unknowingly hardwired within individuals. Spending time consciously and purposefully reflecting on fear is instrumental in deconstructing behaviours that can be detrimental to self-confidence and leadership. In other words, confronting fear is a way to address parts of our psyche that we do not know or do not want to know.

The best way to summarise and then address your fear factor is by means of a sequence of questioning and analysing, followed by the creation of a comprehensive action plan.

Questioning and analysing

Your questioning should be articulated around the following three fundamental questions:

■ What am I afraid of or what do I fear most?

■ Why am I afraid or where does this come from?

■ What am I prepared to do to free myself from fears?

These questions address the need to clearly articulate and express your fears, which is the first step to being able to overcome them. They help you to analyse the rationale of your fears whenever possible, which will prove useful in assessing what is actionable and what is not (or, indeed, when you might require professional help). While reflecting on the above questions, keep in mind the seven fears described above. This will help to trigger your thinking and guide you as you categorise your findings.

Finally, these questions call for you to take an action-orientated approach – in other words, commit to doing something about your fears and, ultimately, enable you to craft a fit-for-purpose action plan.

An action plan

Working on your fears is not easy. The best approach is to focus on either the most limiting fear or the one you think will be easiest to overcome. Figure 4.1 may help you to choose what you want to focus on first.

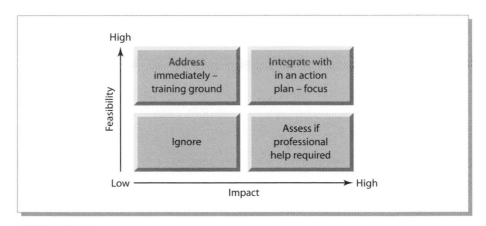

Figure 4.1   Assessing your fears so that you can plan to overcome them

Clearly focus on the top right-hand corner of Figure 4.1 and reflect on what would be the best actions you could take to address your fears. These could be to expose yourself to your fears more in order to increase your comfort level with them, factor in additional training or simply reframe and systematically change your perspective on them. Whatever you decide, make your plan tangible by considering the frequency with which you will take action and think of people who might be able to help you with this process – your feedback group is a good place to start.

Since most fears are interrelated, if you proactively work on overcoming your top fear you will naturally address some of your minor fears as well.

When you start to work on your fears, it might be difficult to assess and measure results, which might not come to you either easily or straight away. One option is to reach out regularly to your feedback group and, specifically, ask for their help in assessing whether or not you appear more self-confident or if they see other changes in you.

Overcoming the seven fears

Here are some simple ways to overcome some of the commonest fears. This list of practical actions essentially builds on the reframing and filtering techniques explored above.

Failure

Simply accept the idea of failure and reframe it as continuous learning. This will lead to risk-taking and innovation – critical parts of a leader's role.

Solitude

Think rationally. Mobile phones, e-mails, chat clients and voice over enable individuals to be reachable, communicate, share and be engaged at all times. In our modern society, there is no such a thing as solitude, unless we proactively seek it out. So, being alone expresses your choice as an individual to withdraw.

To overcome the fear of solitude, consider counting your blessings – think about your family, your friends and the last time someone called you just to say, 'Hi.'

Consider reaching out and communicating to reverse the cycle. Send a message into the world and something will come back.

Public speaking

Believing in yourself is the first step.

Any time you experience a fear of public speaking or a more general fear of expressing yourself, reframe the situation as being the opportunity to share your thoughts, have an impact or change the world. These activities are an intrinsic part of being a leader.

Find role models and collect examples that inspire you to remember the importance of expressing your opinions.

> ### Role models to help reframe the idea of pubic speaking
>
> The mission of TED (Technology Entertainment and Design) is to spread ideas, as ideas are powerful tools for changing attitudes, lives and, ultimately, the world.
>
> At TED, they believe that humanity is an ever-evolving work in progress and everyone is an important part of it. They are constantly wanting new ideas and count on their listeners to reach out. Their USP is people's courage to express new ideas to change the world.
>
> An inspirational example is the Arab Spring. Starting in 2010, it spread out from Egypt, then Tunisia to Libya and on. It began on Facebook and Twitter, where certain parts of the population – especially the young – expressed their opinions and found a community of like-minded people. This triggered revolutions that are still ongoing.

Criticism

Accept this fear as you become aware of it. It is at best a data point, at worst a trend you are either already aware of and working on or you need to reflect on and address.

Above all, try to avoid obsessing about it. Do not give others power over you – consider criticism a test of your ability to rebound.

Success

Assessing what it is you really want is an important part of overcoming the fear of success. Understanding what you can handle happening is also an important step in overcoming this fear.

Change your perspective – success is earned. Success is the result of your hard work, not the outcome of luck or other uncontrollable factors. Remember that you are the author of your own success.

Keep any sense of guilt about your achievements at bay and commit to working on your personal development every day. Commit also to growing and celebrating your success.

Being hurt

Being hurt and feeling pain are an inherent part of life and cannot be avoided.

Change your perspective on it – what matters is turning the pain into something positive. With every difficult or painful experience comes an opportunity to learn about yourself and others.

Consider all experiences of pain as opportunities to learn.

The unknown or uncertainty

Rationalise the situation. It is truly impossible to control everything at all times, so you cannot predict every possibility in every situation. Accept this and let go of your fear.

Make an effort to focus on the present. The present is the only tangible thing and the only time when you can truly have an impact. The past is already gone and can only give you regrets. The future is in the making and can only give you worries. Only the here and the now matter.

If this is not enough to banish your fear, listen to ancient wisdom – Horace's *Carpe Diem* (Ode, 1.11) – to the Jewish teaching, 'If not now, then when?' (Pirkey Avoth, 1.14) and embrace every moment. Do what you can to live today, to be the best you can be today and try again every day.

Exercises and action points

Beating your fears

This practical exercise demonstrates how to put together a comprehensive action plan for addressing your fear factors:

- To carry out a full and comprehensive review of your fear factor, it is recommended that you invest a couple of hours in questioning and categorising your fears.

- Refer frequently to the descriptions of the seven fears earlier in this chapter.

- Consider undertaking this exercise in the comfort of your own home or somewhere you can find some peace and quiet and be undisturbed.

Questioning and analysing

Table 4.2 Mastering your fears

What am I most afraid of?	Why?	The seven fears
• Being excluded	• Because I am an extrovert and I need the energy of the group • Because others' perceptions of me are important	• Fear of being alone • Fear of criticism
• Not being recognised	• Because I was the last of a brood of eight and never got attention from my parents • Because I am afraid of speaking as I am never sure what I am saying is interesting or relevant	• Fear of being alone • Fear of criticism • Fear of public speaking
• Not being able to get to the next level	• My last promotion turned out to be a disaster and I did not succeed • Because I have been lucky so far and one day my luck will disappear	• Fear of success • Fear of failure

▶

Creating your action plan

Table 4.3 An action plan

My top three fears	Action plan
• Fear of criticism	• After every difficult meeting I will reframe the outcome and understand what I could have done differently • I will volunteer to be exposed to others' opinions, etc. (meetings, presentation, public speaking) • I will set aside the time necessary to fully prepare my presentation/intervention, including running question and answer sessions • I will read all the positive evaluations I have ever had or the congratulatory e-mails I can find
• Fear of success	• I will make a list of role models and examples of successful people I admire • I will have handy a list of all my achievements that I can go to every time I am in doubt • I will look at my résumé to measure progress made and how successful I have been in my career so far • I will write every morning why I deserve to be successful
• Fear of public speaking	• I will make a point of asking questions when in a group meeting or attending a presentation • I will proactively look for opportunities to speak in public in my community or work starting with small audiences, then getting bigger • I will practise both the content and form with my friends or family beforehand • I will identify one of my peers who I find particularly good at public speaking and analyse the techniques and language used • I will read books on public speaking • I will enrol on an acting class if need be

Since fears tend to evolve over long periods of time, consider recalibrating your fear factor on a yearly basis.

Summary

Gaining self-confidence asks of you that you go to the core of who you are and not only work on reprogramming some of your more fundamental patterns but also confront your fears. Even more so than when building self-awareness, gaining self-confidence requires discipline, patience and constant observation.

Being aware is what matters – a heightened awareness is the sign of a leader.

When uncertain or in doubt, the following two quotes may be helpful:

'The less you bet, the more you lose when you lose.'
Estelle Clark, piano-playing Group Business Assurance Director
for Lloyd's Register

'Our deepest fear is not that we are inadequate. Our deepest fear is that we are powerful beyond measure. It is our light, not our darkness, that most frightens us. We ask ourselves, "Who am I to be brilliant, gorgeous, talented, fabulous?" ... There is nothing enlightened about shrinking so that other people won't feel insecure around you. We are all meant to shine, as children do ... And as we let our own light shine, we unconsciously give other people permission to do the same. As we are liberated from our own fear, our presence automatically liberates others.'
Marianne Williamson, A Return To Love: Reflections on the Principles of a Course in Miracles *(Thorsons, 1996)*

Here's a reminder of some of the key points from this chapter:

- know your strengths and build on them – you are the sum of your strengths, they are the core of your self-confidence, assess them and keep them in mind at all times

- everything is a question of perspective and you are in control of how you let negative feedback or experiences impact you – reframe any negative feedback in terms of how frequently it occurs and its relevance

■ failure is only an opportunity to learn – there is nothing wrong with failing, as without doing so, you cannot assess the limits of what you can or cannot do

■ do not take isolated negative feedback as reality – nothing is ever as dark as you think and grounding feedback in real-life examples is key to distancing yourself from it and changing your perceptions

■ reframe, reframe and reframe – develop and start exercising your filters

■ acknowledge your fears – it is the best way to start conquering them – but this will require you to be honest and realistic, building on the inquisitive self-questioning techniques set out earlier

■ be proactive in confronting your fears, crafting a realistic action plan – the key is to multiply experiences to expand your comfort zones

■ do not hesitate to ask for help anywhere you can, including friends, family and colleagues – read books and make sure you keep up the momentum with any development work.

5

Developing your leadership brand

'Your brand is what people say about you when you're not in the room.'

Jeff Bezos, founder of Amazon

This chapter covers:

- ▓ the definition of personal branding and why it is important to consider yourself as a product
- ▓ the process of building your brand by walking your talk
- ▓ the importance of keeping your leadership brand current
- ▓ the notion of charisma and gravitas and how to build them using clothing, body language, vocabulary.

The rise of Nazism and how your brain stores information

In 1933, a man benefiting from the total disarray of the political situation in a country crippled by one of the deepest ever economic crises was elected as the new German chancellor. He was passionate about his country and used simple, yet powerful rhetoric that resonated deeply with the frustrations, desires and fears of an increasingly unsettled and anxious German population.

He was viewed as a saviour with the ability to wash away the humiliation of the First World War defeat. His public presence was impeccable. He used controlled gestures, an engaging vocabulary and ways of speaking and flawless rhythm in his speeches. His rhetoric was never left to chance. He would systematically start in a lower tone of voice and finish shouting. The effect he always aimed for was to hammer thoughts into people's minds. He had charisma and gravitas.

This man was Adolf Hitler and he led the world into one of the deadliest wars of all time. He changed for ever the notion of cruelty and crime towards other human beings.   ★ ★ ★ ★ ★   ▶

▶

> The brain contains about 180 billion neurons, processing information via 15,000 synapses per second. It is bombarded with millions of pieces of information a day, all needing to be assessed, filtered and stored – and this never stops.
>
> The brain needs to be supremely efficient in order to cope with this. It also has a way of creating shortcuts for processing everything by using what is called a prediction filter, against which any information that comes its way is assessed. If it fits, then it is stored. A new storage process is only created when the brain receives error messages – in other words, when the stereotyping does not work any more. This happens when an individual disrupts pre-set patterns, forcing the brain to adjust. The more an individual demonstrates consistent behaviours, the harder it will become for the other person to remember any old behaviours. This concept is known as heuristics.

Why are these examples relevant to the concept of a leadership brand? Well, establishing your leadership brand requires you to package what makes you unique and make this resonate with your environment, as Hitler managed to do. You also need to be disciplined and consistent in your behaviours so others register or 'store' you in the way that you want, as the concept of heuristics demonstrates.

To develop your leadership brand, you will need to mix self-questioning and feedback, with tangible actions and integrate the notions of charisma and gravitas.

Building a powerful leadership brand

The concept of a 'leadership brand' is ultimately about making others see your value and allowing you to focus your actions on what will help you deliver on it.

Developing your leadership brand requires you to analyse what it is you want to be known for and want to stand for, while taking into consideration what you know about yourself. It also invites you to understand what leadership means in your organisation.

To adequately build your leadership brand, you need to follow the same approach of self-questioning, calibrating this with feedback and focusing on a tangible action plan that has been outlined in previous chapters.

'I am honest in everything I do, I have a can-do attitude and I am known to be a good coach and push people to develop into the best they can do. I want my peers and my bosses to associate who I am with efficiency and execution. So I invest time in not only creating networks but also making sure everything that is thrown at me is treated with the highest quality level possible.'

Camilla Hartvig, Country President for AstraZeneca, Spain

This executive knows exactly what perception of herself she wants people to take away after meeting her. She also knows what perception she needs to create in order to continue her career journey onwards and upwards.

To aim towards achieving this level of self-awareness, it is important to look both inside yourself and around yourself. Being aware of how people perceive you and to act on their feedback will help you to develop. Investing time in developing a consistent and actionable approach is the ultimate step towards building a powerful leadership brand for yourself.

Looking inside yourself

This is about leveraging your self-awareness and translating it into dimensions, actions or attributes that will allow you to be perceived as a leader. While it may involve focusing on your ability to deliver or execute, it might also be more geared towards softer attributes, such as demonstrating empathy or the ability to influence your internal and external stakeholders.

To look inside yourself, try answering the following questions:

- What do I want to achieve?
- What do I wish to be known for?
- What do I want people to say about me?

The first question will enable you to ground your brand in delivery and address the needs of different groups. To answer it, think about how you can add value to what your customers, stakeholders, employees or investors need or want. Consider what you can do to meet their expectations, but also what they need from you.

The second question will allow you to work on how people perceive you. To answer it, look at the list of possible attributes below and pick three to six that you can or want to make yours.

- Analytical
- Approachable
- Assertive
- Attentive
- Benevolent
- Bold
- Bright
- Calm
- Caring
- Charismatic
- Clever
- Collaborative
- Committed
- Compassionate
- Competent
- Concerned
- Confident
- Confrontative
- Conscientious
- Considerate
- Consistent
- Creative
- Curious
- Decisive
- Dedicated
- Deliberate

- Dependable
- Determined
- Diplomatic
- Disciplined
- Driven
- Easy-going
- Efficient
- Emotional
- Energetic
- Enthusiastic
- Even-tempered
- Fast
- Flexible
- Focused
- Forgiving
- Friendly
- Fun-loving
- Good listener
- Happy
- Helpful
- Honest
- Hopeful
- Humble
- Independent
- Innovative
- Insightful

- Inspired
- Interactive
- Intelligent
- Intimate
- Inventive
- Kind
- Lively
- Logical
- Loving
- Loyal
- Nurturing
- Optimistic
- Organised
- Outgoing
- Passionate
- Patient
- Peaceful
- Pensive
- Persistent
- Personal
- Playful
- Pleasant
- Polite
- Positive
- Pragmatic
- Prepared

- Proactive
- Productive
- Quality-orientated
- Reality-based
- Religious
- Respectful
- Responsible
- Responsive
- Results-orientated
- Satisfied
- Savvy
- Self-confident
- Selfless
- Sensitive
- Service-orientated
- Sincere
- Sociable
- Straightforward
- Thorough
- Thoughtful
- Tireless
- Tolerant
- Trusting
- Trustworthy
- Unyielding
- Values-driven.

The third question will help you to construct a tangible action plan at a later stage. It will translate your thoughts into actions and ensure you demonstrate what it is you want to be known for.

Exercises and action points

The elevator pitch

The name of this exercise comes from the idea that it should be possible to deliver a summary of a business idea in the time it takes an elevator or lift to get to the floor you want – approximately 30 seconds to 2 minutes.

To adequately capture what it is you want to be known for, consider creating a statement of a couple of sentences or so that will act as your catchphrase or motto, your elevator pitch. The statement should represent a summary of who you are and what your values are and be concise and tangible. Remember, this is about you, not your business, and is for you to sell yourself. Here is an example.

If you were in a lift with the CEO of the company of your dreams and you knew she was looking for people, what would you say to her?

'I am a driven individual, passionate about innovation in our industry and committed to delivering results.'

Equally, your personal elevator pitch could be given by someone else talking about you and then it could look like this.

'... is a charismatic individual, thorough and with unyielding integrity, who has always delivered superior financial outcomes for the business.'

If a person who knows you was in an elevator with the CEO of the company of your dreams, what would you like them to say about you?

Looking around yourself

This is the second critical step towards adequately defining your leadership brand. It involves looking around you so that, ultimately, you can be in a position where you can harmoniously mesh who you are with the organisational culture in which you are operating.

To do this, you need to observe and absorb the culture around you. In other words, establish what it is you need to demonstrate to become a respected leader within that culture.

So, reflect on the following question.

■ What are the perceived attributes of a leader in my organisation?

This is helpful for gauging what you should aim to become and assessing the potential stretch necessary, given your natural aptitudes and abilities. To do this, you can look for leadership models in your organisation. Who are these people, what behaviours do they demonstrate, what have they achieved and how can you emulate them?

The corporate culture part of this step is very important to bear in mind, but especially when you are changing company or even moving from one part of the organisation another.

The importance of corporate culture: General Electric versus Royal Dutch Shell

General Electric defines leaders as those who can imagine, solve, build and lead with uncompromising integrity. It praises the values of curiosity, passion, resourcefulness, accountability, a teamwork orientation, commitment, openness and being energising. The company is very pro functional technical expertise (marketing, finance, technology, for instance) and the use of teamwork to produce innovation and deliver results.

Royal Dutch Shell promotes a health, safety and environmental culture. It looks for leaders who are highly intellectual, can develop networks and promote consensus in the decision making process. It also generally wants to develop well-rounded individuals without putting so much emphasis on natural strengths.

So, if you want to be perceived as a respected leader, you will need to demonstrate different skill sets and attributes that align with the corporate culture in which you are operating.

Testing and recalibrating your brand

There is a saying that 'people's perceptions are their reality'. Testing how your leadership brand works in your environment is critical. This is because how you see it and how others see it can differ, so it is important to expose your brand to others to check whether or not your perceptions are correct and recalibrate if necessary. Gathering feedback to make your brand more effective is the objective. It is recommended that you look for feedback within your organisation and reach out to external sources as well.

Internally

For truly comprehensive feedback, a good sample size is required. Consider making a list of seven to ten people you trust and respect in the following professional groups:

- peers
- team members
- major stakeholders
- managers
- mentors.

It is a good idea to add a couple of people from your personal network to this list for a balanced perspective and see how your corporate persona fits with who you really are.

With each member of your feedback group, present and discuss:

- the attributes you have chosen for yourself
- ask them if these are qualities that you demonstrate and/or whether or not they are traits that someone in your particular leadership position should demonstrate
- your leadership catchphrase
- ask if this is truly representative of you, if they would feel comfortable saying this about you and/or if there is something missing that should be added.

Based on the feedback received, rework some or all of your leadership statement. Authenticity is an important trait in a leader, so if you feel that some of the feedback does not ring true for you, try to slip into the shoes of the person who gave you that feedback and replay some of your behaviours. If you conclude that your behaviour was more circumstances driven than rooted in the core of who you are – qualify the feedback.

Externally

You may also consider speaking with external stakeholders, such as customers or investors. As this can appear awkward and put you in a vulnerable position, consider shifting the focus of the exercise. Do not ask for direct feedback, but give it a data-gathering format instead. Ask them what their expectations are, what attributes they expect to see in a person in your position and if they see you demonstrating them.

The questioning and feedback phases can be sequenced in any way that you feel comfortable with, as long as you consider both the personal and external dimensions and recalibrate your brand as required in an iterative process.

Exercises and action points

The baseline approach

The 'baseline' is the natural or unaltered state of your leadership brand, your default position.

Starting from your natural state is another way to go about building your leadership brand. This will allow you to assess if there is any perceptual gap between you and, say, your feedback group. You will be able to compare what you *think* you are projecting with what they *see*.

It is helpful to remove any chance of bias, so make sure you do not present your feedback group with answers, but, instead, ask open questions to develop your brand. Here are some examples of open questions you could use.

- How would you describe me as a leader, using three adjectives, three sentences or three bullet points?
- What do you like most about me and why?
- What do you dislike most about me and why?

This exercise is particularly beneficial if you are hitting a roadblock regarding your leadership brand and need to adjust it quickly.

Developing a consistent and actionable approach

In his book *The Tipping Point*, Malcolm Gladwell presents a new way of understanding why, at times, change happens as quickly and unexpectedly as it does. He describes what we could call a 'recipe' codifying how change happens. One element presented in the book is the 'stickiness' factor – that is, the attributes that give a particular message impact and prevent it from going in one ear and out the other. Gladwell likens such messages to catchy songs that you cannot get out of your head.

How can you make your leadership brand stick? By developing concrete actions and being disciplined about it.

Concrete actions

Bringing your leadership brand to life really comes down to taking action and committing to exhibiting certain behaviours. It should be evident in the way you make decisions, choices and communicate. For every attribute you have decided to include in your leadership catch-phrase, write down the tangible behaviours required and the action you need to take to make them happen.

Also reflect on the specific language you should start to use to get your message across and create the right perceptions of you. Only a mix of actions and ways of communicating will get you the results you need and allow your environment to experience the leadership brand you have or want to develop.

Here are some examples of things you can do to master this process.

- **You want to be known as a reliable leader** 'Reliable' means that there are no surprises in terms of either your behaviour or expected outcomes. Consider doing the following:
  - always be on time for meetings
  - do not cancel at the last minute – if you are forced to, reschedule promptly
  - make a point of not missing deadlines
  - if you absolutely cannot avoid missing a deadline, give plenty of notice and agree in advance when you *will* deliver.
- **You want to be known as a nurturing leader** 'Nurturing' means paying attention to people's development and encouraging their personal growth. Consider doing the following:
  - multiplying mentoring opportunities
  - regularly scheduling coaching sessions with your top talent

- systematically sharing knowledge (sharing your notes on leadership team meetings or preparing digests of your reading on economic trends or technological advances in one of your fields, for example)
- making a point of inviting renowned speakers on relevant topics to your team meetings (for example, industry experts or innovation experts).

■ **You want to be known as results-orientated leader** 'Results-orientated' means you meet your objectives and push performance. Consider doing the following:
- do not miss deadlines and ensure your team does the same
- in meetings, make a point of asking tangible questions, such as 'When can this be delivered?' or 'What is a realistic deadline for this?'
- in meetings, also make a point of bringing the conversation back to tangibility, focusing on questions such as, 'What are we really trying to achieve?' and 'What will the impact be on the bottom line?'

Being disciplined

Be consistent in your behaviours and sustain this for the long term. Heuristics is the term used for the human need to identify predictable patterns of behaviour in the world around us (facts), which then allow us to react to instances of these without having to analyse them each time. By establishing and maintaining a consistent brand, you can take advantage of this evolutionary mechanism that is hardwired into all of us.

Consistency is critical when you either want to create a particular perception of you or change people's perceptions of your leadership brand. Once you have defined the actions and vocabulary that will convey your newly identified leadership brand, ensure you demonstrate them. Consistently use your chosen words in your interactions.

As a leader or aspiring leader, your impact will be measured as much by your behaviour in the most mundane situations – the fact that you say, 'Good morning' to everyone or walk into the office with a smile – as in the more obvious ones – such as in team meetings or in one-on-ones with your boss.

> **Example: The importance of consistency**
>
> The Executive Vice President of Strategy of one of the big oil companies was always very aware of the impact he could have on others, and how this, in turn, could impact his leadership brand. He consistently made a point of calling catering staff by their names and asking how they were doing while ordering his coffee. This might have seemed rather unnecessary, or even irrelevant, as it did not have any direct impact on his business success, but, it helped create an overall perception of him as being a respectful and inclusive person and, hence, a respectful and inclusive leader.

Habits will make this perfect, but living and breathing your leadership brand will require discipline from you and constant awareness.

Exercises and action points

'The five steps to building your personal brand'

This is the title of an article in the *Harvard Business Review* by Dave Ulrich and Norm Smallwood who list the following steps:

1 determine what results you want to achieve in the next year

2 decide what you wish to be known for

3 define your identity

4 construct your leadership brand statement and test it:
   '*I want to be known for being _____ so that I can deliver_____*'

5 make your brand identity real.

Keeping your brand current

Once you have invested time and effort in building your leadership brand, you also need to keep it alive, as you are evolving and so is your environment.

> **Example: Evolving the leadership brand at General Electric**
>
> The change in the General Electric company's view of which attributes of leaders should be valued is a good example of how to keep your brand current.
>
> Jack Welch, the legendary former CEO of General Electric, argues that the best leaders display the 'Four Es': very high *energy* levels, the ability to *energise others* around common goals, the *edge* to make tough 'Yes' and 'No' decisions and the ability to constantly *execute* and deliver on their promises.[1]
>
> Jeffrey Immelt, Welch's successor and current CEO of General Electric, adjusted the above definition, adding concepts such as imagination and innovation, and, thus, bringing the desired values into line with what is needed to remain competitive in today's increasingly cut-throat world of business.

Environments change ever so rapidly – people even more so. All experiences and challenges will shape you as a leader or future leader. Success and failure alike will have an impact on you. Never take your leadership brand for granted, never forget the essence of the leader you want to be or the leader you want other people to see. If you do, you will probably let it slide and will have to start from scratch again. Maintaining your leadership brand is an ongoing process, by consciously thinking about it, it will help it become part and parcel of your leadership DNA.

Keeping the adjectives 'disciplined' and 'iterative' in mind will help greatly.

Disciplined

When it comes to your leadership brand, be deliberate in what you do and ensure you maintain momentum and focus on your actions.

This can be achieved by factoring in some kind of review mechanism with either your feedback group or on your own to keep your eye on the ball. Timing a review of your leadership brand with the performance evaluation process of the organisation can be a good way to go about it.

Iterative

You will never stop evolving, changing and adjusting – never expect to be finished! It has been demonstrated that leaders with the self-awareness and drive to evolve their leadership brand continuously are more likely to succeed in the long term than those who don't.

---

[1] Walter Kiechel (2005) in 'What you can learn from Jack Welch', *The Results-driven Manager: Becoming an effective leader*. Boston, MA: Harvard Business School Press.

To keep you plugged in and evolving, you need to be able to quickly assess the following:

- how effective you are at delivering on your leadership brand strategy

- what it is you need to do – if anything – to readjust your course of action and deliver on your own promises

- whether your leadership brand is still current *vis-à-vis* who you have developed into, the role you are in or growing into and what the environment requires of you.

It is important not only to measure progress made but also assess what you want to keep focusing on to further enhance your brand or any new elements you want to start integrating to remain competitive or match up to a potential new job or career change.

This toolkit may be useful in times of crisis, when your leadership brand is no longer yielding the results you expect. Equally, if a negative chain of events has tainted your leadership brand, start with the questioning (see page 46), gather feedback, craft and deliver an action-orientated plan and get back on track.

It can also have great impact when you embark on your brand transition – in other words, when you are using a career change to reinvent yourself.

In the Harvard Business Review article (March 2011) 'Spotlight on landing the next big job: Reinventing your personal brand', Dorie Clark presents five key steps for any personal rebranding:

1 define your destination and acquire the necessary skills

2 craft a unique selling proposition and distinguish yourself by leveraging your points of difference

3 develop a narrative that describes your transition in terms of the value it offers to others

4 re-introduce yourself using digital media and seize opportunities to showcase your capabilities

5 prove your worth by establishing and promoting your track record.

It would be interesting to integrate these into any new brand building exercise. Be aware that traces of your old brand may linger, but a carefully considered strategy and the ability to create unique value in your changed role will help your new brand stick.

The best example of the power of rebuilding a brand remains Michael Milken, who was once best known as a 1980s high-flyer, jailed for securities violations. However, his long-term efforts have dramatically redeemed his reputation. In the course of more than three decades of committed philanthropy, he has raised hundreds of millions of dollars to combat prostate cancer, melanoma, epilepsy and more, earning him a 2004 *Fortune* cover story – and huge rebrand – as 'The man who changed medicine'.

What, then, is it important to keep in mind?

The essence of the influences on your leadership brand are expressed in Figure 5.1.

Your leadership brand needs to be rooted in what comes naturally to you, based on your natural strengths. It also needs to serve a purpose and deliver something to the different groups you want to lead.

This leads on to the fact that your leadership brand has to be authentic. There is no point in claiming traits that you do not believe you can truly exhibit, even if you stretch yourself. That is why gathering and analysing feedback can be incredibly insightful.

Building a leadership brand requires investments of time and patience. Consider setting aside one to two hours to comprehensively reflect on your personal brand in order to kick-start the process. It is preferable to do this outside the office, when you have the opportunity to pause and

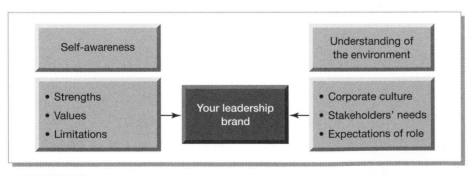

Figure 5.1 Defining your leadership brand

think. It is also important to find the most appropriate environment and timing (refer back to the advice given in Chapter 4).

You will not always see results straight away and, at times, you will have to fight the temptation to go back to your old habits. You might feel as if you are behaving artificially and be discouraged by this, but it is entirely natural and to be expected. Just keep things in perspective and recommit to your personal development.

It can take three to six months for you to see the results of your newly established leadership brand. After this time you should experience a 'tipping' point in people's interactions with you based on your new attributes – then you will know that you have made an impact. When in doubt, remember that a strong leadership brand is a key element of corporate success.

Exercises and action points

Three practical ways to maintain your leadership brand

Using your feedback group

It is recommended that you do the following two to three times a year, to both allow your progress to be measured and keep pace with changes in the organisation or the environment.

Set aside some time with your feedback group and specifically ask them if they feel you are living and breathing your leadership brand.

If they say 'No', ask for concrete examples of situations where you did not live up to your leadership statement. Ask what you should do or could have done differently.

Also invite them to provide you with any observations regarding your behaviours, traits or emerging habits in your leadership. These could be positive or negative, but extremely valuable.

On your own

The most efficient way would be to do the following once a year, preferably at the year-end to allow you to factor in what you learn and set proper objectives for the following year:

▶

▶

■ Take some time to revisit your leadership statement and the attributes you have chosen to focus on.

■ Ask yourself if they are still current. Do they still match what it is you need to achieve or the expectations you are facing?

■ Ask yourself if the attributes still resonate with you. Do they still convey your authentic self?

On an ongoing basis

You may decide to specifically pick one member of your feedback group as your leadership brand 'custodian'. This person can be in charge of observing and giving you feedback on your leadership brand and style. You could organise this as follows:

■ Schedule regular catch-ups to debrief regarding your custodian's observations of times when you've had the opportunity to convey your leadership brand. To establish a working relationship, consider having a bi-weekly meeting.

■ Consider more ad hoc interaction, using the custodian as a sounding board when preparing for potentially important milestones when you will push your leadership brand (a team meeting, an internal conference or an industry event, for example).

At all times and with any plan you pursue, ensure that you take immediate note of the feedback given and develop a subsequent action plan.

Brand accelerators: charisma and gravitas

Charisma and gravitas are powerful accelerators when you are building your leadership brand. They are part of what gives you presence and impact. Many people might argue that you cannot teach anyone how to have charisma or demonstrate gravitas, as they are an intrinsic part of an individual, but, by paying attention to the way you carry and present yourself, and communicate, you will be able to prove otherwise.

'Charisma' is usually defined as a mix of charm and grace. It is the ability to draw people towards you without demonstrating any type of authority. Typically, political and religious leaders demonstrate significant charisma. Think of Barack Obama, Steve Jobs or Mother Teresa. Charisma is usually perceived as inherent, rather than cultivated or taught.

'Gravitas' is associated with an impression of weight, influence or authority. It relates to sobriety, seriousness and maturity. Someone with gravitas is someone whose words you want to listen to, someone who inspires trust and respect. Consider Warren Buffett, Jack Welch or George Soros. Gravitas could be considered to stem from nurture rather than nature.

In order to grasp the diverse forms charisma and gravitas can take, the following examples might help:

- **Jeffrey Immelt** The current CEO of General Electric is over 6 feet tall. He played American football in college and is still very athletic. When he enters the room or is about to speak, everything stops for a split second. When he is listening to a pitch, you can almost see how fast his brain is processing the information.

- **Tan Chong Men** Former Executive Vice President, Global Business-to-Business & Lubricants, Shell Downstream, a part of the Royal Dutch Shell Group, now Group Chief Executive Officer of the Port of Singapore Authority, is a Chinese Malaysian of average height. He radiates calmness and serenity and is very softly spoken, but, make no mistake, his brain is swift and he has the uncanny ability to cut through complexity and pinpoint the right angle and the question you simply had not thought of. He motivates and inspires people with his visionary mind and sensible, down-to-earth problem solving pragmatism.

- **Gerard Lopez** Founder of Mangrove Capital Partners, owner of the Lotus Formula One team is extremely tall. He will make a point of waiting for you to come to him when you meet him for the first time to carefully manage the power balance. In meetings, he does not say much, but listens intensely – he is processing every possible angle to find any potential flaw in the reasoning. When it is his turn to speak, he makes decisions very quickly and is known for his strategic thinking.

■ **Clara Gaymard** The current Vice President of General Electric International, she is a petite, slender, beautiful woman. Her smile is always engaging and she is extremely approachable. She is the type of leader who will come in person to greet you and escort you to the meeting room when you are meeting with her.

There are two main points that are universally true when it comes to charisma and gravitas:

■ they require an understanding of the power of your physical presence and demeanour – how you carry yourself, how you present yourself and the way you dress – and how to use it

■ they require that you pay attention to the ways in which you are communicating – this is, mainly, how you speak and when you choose to speak.

How to make the most of your physical presence

Studies have shown that physical attributes such as height and attractiveness play a part in whether or not you are perceived to have leadership potential.

A study carried out by Erik Lindqvist of the Stockholm School of Economics for the Research Institute of Industrial Economics in May 2010 underscored the relationship between height and leadership. Using data from a representative sample of Swedish men, the study found that tall men are significantly more likely to attain managerial positions than short men. An increase in height of 10 centimetres (3.94 inches) is associated with a 2.2 percentage point increase in the probability of holding a managerial position. Selection for managerial positions explains about 15 per cent of the unconditional height–pay premium. However, at least half of the height–leadership correlation is due to people perceiving there to be a positive correlation between height and cognitive ability.

What does this mean? The taller you are, the more intelligent people will perceive you to be or the more commanding people will believe you to be.

Why? Because in our primal brain, height is still synonymous with strength, hence increasing the chance of survival of the group. Height, therefore, even now, is considered synonymous with intrinsic leadership ability.

If you are not naturally tall, you can always wear shoes that make you look taller. However, you may find that there are other ways to compensate – by, say, carrying yourself with a lot of authority or demonstrating a great deal of energy.

Using body language well or even the way you dress can help you to create your leadership presence or establish your leadership potential. This is particularly important when you are meeting people for the first time. Princeton University research confirms the old saying that, 'You'll never have a second chance to make a first impression.'[2] People evaluate others in the first tenth of a second of their initial meeting. This means establishing your leadership potential from the start is critical.

The following six principles are easy to remember and can create an immediate positive impact:

1 Always walk into a room confidently, commanding as much space as possible. This will create a perception of self-confidence and assurance.

2 Always introduce yourself with a firm handshake. It will put you in a position of calm assertiveness and power.

3 Always maintain good eye contact when you introduce yourself. Consider maintaining good eye contact at all times. This creates an impression of openness, commands trust and establishes your self-confidence.

4 Don't 'over-smile'. Although it sounds counter-intuitive, charisma and gravitas require a certain element of aloofness at first. Being perceived as too helpful or approachable can hinder your credibility as a potential leader.

5 While in a meeting, make sure you sit comfortably on your chair. Stay calm and poised. This will convey a feeling of you being comfortable in your own skin and self-assurance about your ability to

---

[2] J. Willis and A. Todorov (2006) 'First impressions: Making up your mind after 100-ms exposure to a face', *Psychological Science*, July, 17(7): 592–8.

cope with anything. Control your body at all times. Do not fidget or play with a pen or with your hair. Stillness and natural tranquillity create an impression of authority.

6   If someone says something that particularly resonates with you, make a point to nod. Showing that you are listening intensely and subtly expressing your opinion will help build your credibility.

If you are a woman, consider the following additional things.

7   Sweep back your hair from your face to ensure that people can see your features clearly. This will lead to you being perceived as self-confident and self-assured.

8   Keep make-up subtle or to a minimum. This will be perceived as a sign of self-confidence in your intellectual abilities.

Effective power dressing

The way you dress is also a key factor in establishing your leadership presence. Humans are visual beings and image counts. In the absence of other relevant information, people will look for visual clues as to how a person regards him- or herself and how professional he or she seems. The way you dress helps establish your credibility and your brand. This is all part of creating your corporate persona and establishing your potential.

Most personal coaches recommend dressing for the job you *want*, not for the job you *have*. How, then, do you identify the dress code for leadership material? How do you reconcile embodying the leadership traits of your corporate culture with dressing for leadership (power dressing, if you will)?

For instance, would you be perceived as a credible leader wearing a dark pinstripe suit to see a company such as Google or Facebook? At the opposite end of the spectrum, would you be considered leadership material at a private bank or wealth management company in chinos and a polo shirt?

This is a difficult balance to strike. However, adhering to the following two rules may help.

- Dressing for a leadership position means dressing to command power and in a sophisticated way. It does not necessarily mean dressing conservatively. Even if most dark colours (grey, black, navy blue) do fit the profile, they are not the only ones. Consider wearing red accents if you want to make a statement of power or more neutral colours if you are in the role of observer.

- Dress in accordance with your sector and appropriately for the occasion. If you have team meetings or customer meetings, consider dressing in a way that fits in with their culture as well. If you were visiting Google, you would not wear a suit. If you are giving a presentation or going to be sitting for most of the day, wear comfortable shoes and clothes in a material that does not wrinkle. Overall, remember that it is always better to be slightly overdressed than underdressed.

Example: Dress to impress

To convey the image of your choice, keep the following in mind:

For both genders

- Avoid any scruffiness whatsoever.
- Always make sure your shoes are clean and polished.
- Always ensure you have a neat haircut.
- Invest in quality clothes.
- Wear clothes you feel confident in.

For men

- Consider matching the colour of your belt and shoes.
- Do not wear a short-sleeved shirt with a suit.
- Your accessories should not be distracting.

For women

- Keep your nails clean and tidy.
- Neutral-toned make-up reads as subtle and sophisticated.
- Ensure you have statement and professional accessories.
- Adopt the mantra, 'Dress shabbily, they notice the dress. Dress impeccably, they notice the woman.'[3]

---

[3] Coco Chanel, French fashion designer, Founder of the Chanel brand.

Charismatic communication

It's not only what you say, but how you say it that will establish you as someone with gravitas and charisma.

It is important to start by being perceived as knowledgeable and insightful. This is about inspiring respect, trust and demonstrating a certain calm.

Additionally, visuals and words go hand in hand, so what people say verbally about themselves will then either support or contradict the initial visual impression, not the other way around.

Investing time in becoming the best communicator you can be is the final key element to consider when honing your charisma and gravitas. This can be achieved when thinking about the following seven attributes for all occasions:

1   **Preparation** Always be prepared and knowledgeable about your area. Invest time in researching facts to sustain your vision and ensure that you are crystallising one theme at a time. Allocate enough time for rehearsal and practise question and answer sessions.

2   **The library analogy** Always use a deep tone of voice when expressing yourself, as if you were talking in the middle of a library. The brain associates deep voices with the notion of authority.

3   **Slow your pace down** This will give the impression of you being in control and create a greater sense of gravitas.

4   **Master your language** Even today, Winston Churchill remains the leading example of the true master of communication. His lessons can be boiled down to the following four elements:

   –   **use the right words**: when addressing an audience, invest time in thinking about what you really mean and what words would most concisely, practically and elegantly express your vision

   –   **use rhythm**: think in terms of musicality, repeat your statements out loud, talk to yourself, using pauses and silence to create impact

   –   **use analogies**: they help clarify, simplify and make the point – proverbs can also be useful engage emotionally: 'For an audience to cry, the speaker must feel pain.' Engaging emotionally also entails identifying with your audience. Find themes and stories that will resonate with them; these might refer to common history or historical figures, heroes, and so on.

5 **Establish a credible verbal presence** Avoid starting your sentences with expressions of doubt, such as, 'I guess it might' or 'I could be wrong, but …'. Speak confidently and use hard data to prove your points.

6 **Less is more** Use the time you have to speak wisely. It is not about how much you say, but the impact you have when you say something. When in meetings, consciously allocate yourself a certain numbers of interventions and interact when the topic matters the most.

7 **Walk the room** Learn how to 'walk a room', moving fluidly from one person to another. Being interested in everyone is part of building your leader's persona. At all times, give your undivided attention to the person you are talking to. In that moment, you need to make him or her feel like the most important person in the world. This will allow you to connect with that person, creating the level of trust needed.

Exercises and action points

How to further enhance your communication style

Some of the following are additional techniques that you can practise to help you strengthen your charisma and gravitas:

- Identify one or two people in your immediate environment you consider to be leadership models. Observe the way they move, speak, carry meetings and the way they dress. Be inspired by others and emulate them.

- Many politicians develop a charismatic communication style as they need to gather a large number of followers. Consider studying videos of their speeches and the ways in which they interact with others as a way of learning.[4]

---

[4] Chris Abbott (2010) *21 Speeches that Shaped our World*, Rider, is – a good source of powerful and inspiring speeches. So is the website **www.voicegig.com**

▶

> ▪ Consider hiring a style consultant to find a way of dressing that will yield the necessary results.
>
> ▪ Consider investing in communications training to analyse both your spoken presentation and your body language.

Charisma and gravitas will come more naturally to some than others, but they can be built on and will help you strengthen your leadership brand.

Summary

Building an effective leadership brand can actually be summed up in one word: energy. It has been proven that the most successful people are usually the most energetic. Think about how to create energy around you in the way you talk, listen, interact with and connect with people.

Branding demands commitment – to continual reinvention, striking chords with people to stir their emotions and to imagination.

Here's a reminder of some of the key points from this chapter:

▪ human beings need to categorise the world around them and put people into boxes – proactively building your leadership brand will allow you to build your *own* box and be in control

▪ even if it is important to take your environment into consideration, authenticity should prevail – remaining true to yourself is key (keep in mind the self-awareness developed in Chapter 3)

▪ build a brand that you can deliver on, being realistic about what you can deliver, even if this does include some stretching of your current abilities, and pay particular attention to your strengths, what you want to be known for and how this meshes with the expectations of your environment

▪ take proactive steps to develop and then live your brand, such as using your feedback group and your leadership statement

- your leadership brand should not be static – it will evolve with you and your experiences – make sure you regularly reflect on progress and changes you need to make

- charisma and gravitas are elements of leadership that can be worked on by attending to the way you carry yourself, and how you dress and communicate

- dress for success and the occasion, always adjusting to the environment and keeping the purpose of the meeting in mind, dress impeccably – overdressing is better than underdressing – and do not shy away from colours – they can make a very positive statement

- think about how you say what you say – lower your tone of voice, pause and use your time wisely – invest time in preparing any communication and make a point of looking for the right word – your use of language should be pristine

- do not be afraid to ask professional consultants and advisers to maximise or leverage your body language, dress code and oratorical skills.

Leading and influencing – bringing others on the journey

'As we look ahead into the next century, leaders will be those who empower others.'

Bill Gates, founder of Microsoft

The careerist: Making the workplace fun

by Rhymer Rigby

The idea that work should be fun is much talked about but rarely well implemented. Is it possible to have career-enhancing fun?

Isn't work meant to be serious?

'You should take your work seriously' says Jessica Pryce-Jones of workplace consultancy iOpener – but not take yourself too seriously. 'Fun is good for business. It tends to lead to unexpected things being juxtaposed and good connections being made – it can make you more innovative and creative.'

John Williams, author of *Screw Work Let's Play* adds: 'In corporations people will naturally want to work with those who are fun to be with.'

What can I do on a day-to-day basis?

'Be willing to spend time talking to people and having a laugh with them,' says Octavius Black, founder of The Mind Gym. 'Take a bit of time out for the pleasures of conversation.' Just helping other people can also make work more fun. 'If you ask leaders to look back on their careers, they'll often say the most enjoyable part of it was helping others.'

Ms Pryce-Jones advises cutting back on email: 'It wastes time and prevents face-to-face contact, which builds bonds and makes people happier.'

If you do communicate electronically, using social media may be more fun and encourages brevity.

Mr Williams says that just not moaning helps. 'Put yourself on a complaining diet for 30 days, where you don't complain about anything. It's actually quite hard, but if you use the energy and time you would have spent moaning to encourage optimism, the results can be impressive.' What projects can I take? 'If there's a fun project up for grabs, jump at it,' says Mr Williams. 'Put in the extra work and deliver, so you get asked first next time.' You might do something such as organise a social event: 'Everyone will enjoy themselves and you will get known for that.'

Look too at 30-day projects, says Mr Williams. 'Ask if you can spend a small amount of time working on a business-related project that you enjoy for a month. The idea is to deliver something at the end, even if it's small.'

Ms Pryce-Jones suggests mixing up work and life outside the workplace. '[Activities] like volunteering [through a workplace scheme] can bring another dimension to work. There's also being able to work where and when you want – such as in the park on a sunny day – and initiatives such as having pets in the office.'

How do I plan for long-term enjoyment?

'Try to shape what you do around the things you enjoy,' says Mr Black. 'Also, take the time to understand what you really enjoy rather than what you think you should enjoy. Thinking about what makes life fun outside work can help. If, for instance, you enjoy marathons, you might also like long projects.'

If work still seems like a grind, look at it holistically: 'Rather than give up your job, ask yourself if it's your mood or state of mind,' he adds. 'Think about life generally. Are you engaged with it?'

Leadership is like a journey that starts at an individual level, within oneself, then expands to the team, the organisation and, ultimately, to the world at large.

Leadership success requires people to come together, stay together, then be able to work together and achieve success. Part 3 looks at these 'people' dimensions of leadership under the headings shown in the figure below.

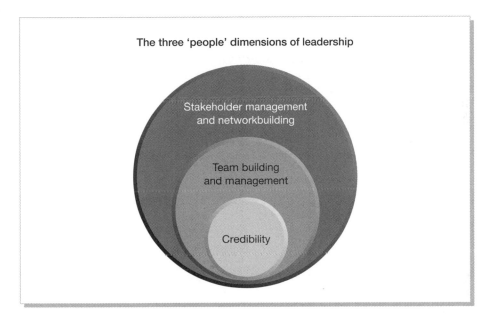

The three 'people' dimensions of leadership

Stakeholder management and networkbuilding

Team building and management

Credibility

- **Credibility** This involves you exploring the question, 'Why would someone be led by you?'[*] and looks at how you can go about building credibility. Everyone around you is a participant in leadership. In a world of highly empowered employees, it is critical to establish a certain level of authority over the people around you. How can you do this so that you become the natural or providential leader? (This will be explored in Chapter 6.)

- **Teambuilding and management** Once credibility has been gained, leaders' successes are not achieved on their own. How

---

[*] Robert Goffee and Gareth Jones (2006) *Why Should Anyone Be Led by You?*, Harvard Business School Press.

does the team dimension come into play and how can you build on it? Chapter 7 will delve specifically into knowing others and building rapport. It will then explore techniques and tools that can be used to create positive team dynamics and, finally, looks at how to motivate people – in other words, how to develop immediate areas of influence.

■ **Stakeholder management and networkbuilding** It is essential to look at the topic of influence and how you can expand it outside your team boundaries. Chapter 8 looks beyond the natural area of influence, and explains the basics of stakeholder management, the strategies for building efficient networks and how to master the subtleties of body language.

6

Building your credibility as a leader

'Coming together is a beginning. Keeping together is progress.
Working together is success.'

Henry Ford, American industrialist

This chapter covers:

- how credibility results from experiences and value set. It can take on different meanings for different stakeholder groups
- what types of experiences – technical and situational – will provide or accelerate credibility building
- why values are essential to being a leader and how to demonstrate and promote your value set
- how to balance credibility and authenticity.

Beauty is in the eyes of the beholder

When asked how you would define beauty, you might feel as able to do so as you would if you had been asked to dissect a soap bubble. The commonest answer is usually along the lines, of 'I know it when I see it.'

The concept of beauty has had different meanings in different eras. Ancient philosophers give it a moral slant – 'What is beautiful is good,' says Plato. Poets are similarly lofty – 'Beauty is truth, truth beauty,' wrote Keats, although Anatole France thought of beauty as 'more profound than truth itself'. The definition of feminine physical beauty has also evolved over time, from the curvaceous and lavish pale beauties of the nineteenth century to the painfully thin models of the noughties.

The concept of credibility is, to some extent, similar to the concept of beauty – you know it when you see it. Credibility is what makes a person a long-lasting leader. It is rooted in what others expect from a leader – 'others' here being a diverse group of stakeholders (teams, peers, bosses), each with specific filters and each with ever-changing expectations.

Establishing credibility and maintaining it is essential. How is it possible, though, to please so many and meet such different demands? How can anyone truly build unquestionable credibility?

The secret is to work at simultaneously developing the following three elements:

- **experience**: efficient career management will help you demonstrate what you can do – credibility is based on experience

- **values**: these are pivotal in helping to establish who you are – credibility can't be maintained without values

- **authenticity**: this cardinal point is that you always embrace who you are – credibility only stands up if a leader is true to him- or herself.

Mastering career management

Ensuring that you get the right experience boils down to one thing: adequate career management. This is usually done by defining what is the right experience for what you want to achieve. You will generally need to be exposed to the top three or four well-recognised skills and character-building events, as appropriate for your organisation. It requires you to be crystal clear on your intent, proactive in looking for opportunities to be stretched and willing to confidently grasp any unusual or difficult assignments thrown your way. Finally, to accelerate your career path, differentiating and adjusting to ever-changing market trends is key.

Identifying what is the right experience

Some 80 per cent of leaders would tell you that you mostly develop by means of 'on-the job' activities and this is the best way for you to gain experience. The 'right' experience for you is that which caters for and meshes harmoniously your needs as a professional with the needs of your organisation. This might be defined as a range of skills acquired via diverse experiences where you have been successful. It allows you to move beyond your comfort zone and learn and develop both your technical and interpersonal skills. It is experience that takes you one step closer to your objectives (what you want to achieve) and is aligned with what your organisation needs you to know in order to fulfil a role. It is experience that would add to your credibility within your area's or corporation's culture.

The right experience includes diversity and stretches you

Jack Welch has always been a huge advocate of experience and learning on the job, pushing this to another level with the concept of stretch.

One of his fundamental leadership concepts is to build leaders up by putting them through different and diverse experiences – 'Push them up the rank, never let them rest' is one of Welch's maxims. In General Electric, the average tenure in one position for someone recognised as having high potential (a possible future leader) is about 18 months: 3 to 6 months to learn the business and assess critical problems, 6 months to work on solutions and strategy and the remaining time to implement and test results.

By undergoing such intense and relatively short assignments, these individuals are constantly increasing their ability to learn, act quickly and decisively and, of course, make mistakes, as they never stay in their comfort zone for very long. Through the process, they create a wider frame of reference to build on, develop a certain self-confidence in their own ability and, without doubt, gain a huge amount of credibility.

The right experience involves proactive learning

Building credibility is not about multiplying experiences for the sake of it but getting the right experience for what it is you want to achieve.

As Loren Gary states in her chapter 'Pulling yourself up through the ranks',[1] there are about 16 critical events that are relevant or fast experience builders and drive huge credibility and leadership success.

---

[1] In (2005) *The Results-driven Manager: Becoming an effective leader*. Harvard Business School Press.

They include:

- turning around a business or a group
- starting a business from scratch
- dealing with employee/workforce issues
- handling your own mistakes and failures.

Most leaders in Fortune 500 organisations would add the following to the list:

- being accountable for financial results
- handling difficult people
- negotiating an important contract
- finding and closing an investment.

These last are particularly relevant to building credibility as they draw on a complete skill set, including technical skills, finding resources, strategic thinking, challenging leadership skills, people skills and a flawless ability to deliver.

The right experience gives you the right mix of technical and soft skills

The right experience builds skills in two main dimensions – technical and interpersonal (communication, having influence and leadership).

The right experience relates to what you want to achieve

If, for example, you want to become a chief financial officer, having solid experience in financial planning and analysis will give you a head start and develop your numeracy and business thinking. If you are more drawn to a chief executive officer role, then having spent some time leading different business units, in different cultural contexts or in a mergers and acquisitions department will be critical to you being credible in such a position.

All the above qualities also need to be complemented by a solid understanding of the industry you are in. Having knowledge is the overarching requirement for top-notch credibility. The current Executive

Director and member of the Board of the French shipping company CMA-CGM has over 30 years' experience in shipping. There is not a cycle, situation or issue that he has not either seen or experienced in his career. When he talks about shipping, he is able to give you the history of the industry with the strategic implications and potential competitive responses. That is what credibility is all about.

Exercises and action points

Examples of the right kinds of experience

Negotiating an important contract is a perfect way to gain the right experience and build your credibility. It employs both technical and soft skills.

At the technical level, negotiating an important contract helps develop the following:

- **Business acumen** As you need to be able to assess the opportunity, understand who brings what to the table and analyse what risk–reward equation will be acceptable for both parties.

- **Strategic skills** As you need to possess the ability to develop a negotiation strategy that will include but not be restricted to the following questions.

  - What are the must haves for you – in other words, the elements that you ought to gain from the deal?

  - What are the bargaining chips you are ready to give up? Are they quantitative (for instance, an additional discount if you are in a customer negotiation) or qualitative (for instance, a ramping up of performance if you are in a supplier negotiation)?

  - Are you in a position of power? If you are, how can you use it or tone it down, balancing short- and long-term outcomes? If not, what would be needed for you change this? Looking at other parties' strengths and weaknesses, opportunities to partner or collaborate can help.

  - What is your 'walk away' position – in other words, what would not be acceptable for you?

- As a corollary, what is your best alternative to the negotiated agreement (BATNA) – inherently, what next possible way would the current negotiation fail and would it be acceptable (for instance, could you to use a completely new supplier or open a tender process)?

- What is the most desirable outcome for you? This should take into consideration who is in the position of power and the short-, medium- or long-term vision for the relationship.

- What is the best possible outcome of the negotiation – for you *and* the other party?

Your negotiation strategy would also need to take into account who plays what role – good cop/bad cop, decision maker or influencer – and the potential triggering points for playing bargaining chips or utilising the balance of power:

■ **Contract management skills** As you need to be able to understand the local regulatory framework in order to assess what is possible and what is not. Even if your organisation has an extensive legal department, being able to ask the right questions and translate contract clauses in tangible ways is incredibly useful.

At the interpersonal level, negotiating an important contract helps develop the following:

■ **Empathy** As you need to be able to slip into the other party's shoes in order to assess what will be acceptable to them, work out their BATNA and what their desirable outcomes are. During the negotiation itself, you will need to be able to sense the atmosphere and read body language. This will give you the edge in terms of being able to sense the impact different elements of the proposal will have, who is the decision maker or how the alliances are naturally formed (body language is explored in Chapter 8).

■ **Communication** As you need to be able to control and influence the meeting, knowing what to say and when to say it. The skills of assessing or sensing when to make a proposal using your bargaining chips, to ask for time out to discuss a point with your team or 'fake' leaving the meeting can make all the difference.

▶

Create a credibility document

Robert Rozek, Chief Financial Officer of Korn Ferry International, used what he called a 'Roadmap to CFO' to gain the right experience and, thereby, increase his credibility. It is an eight-page document that:

- maps out what is required to become a credible CFO

- takes into consideration how the role has changed over time, CFOs having evolved from simply being concerned with the figures to strategic business partners with a keen focus on governance and compliance

- includes the seven key competences required to become a great CFO – technical ones: financial expertise to operational expertise, to business process improvements and governance/Board experience; interpersonal ones: teamwork and facilitation, knowledge sharing and change management/leadership

- includes a separate page for each of these seven competences, exploring what each means, what it entails and, more importantly, the experience in each he had acquired over the years.

Rozek would review this document on a yearly basis to update himself based on the latest developments in his experience. It was his credibility document.

This very powerful tool allows you to articulate a clear pathway to achieving your goals. It helps you keep track of what has been achieved and changes in the environment. It is a great credibility tool for anyone serious about managing their careers.

Gaining your experience

Gaining the right experience or, as previously mentioned, adequately managing your career, building on both your technical and soft skills, is based on three distinct elements.

Asking yourself the right questions

In Part 2, you spent some time finding the leader inside you. This included understanding your natural leadership make-up and the things that motivate you to succeed. You identified your strengths and your areas for development, as well as your fears and how to overcome them. You also reflected on your leadership/personal brand.

Your reasoning or questioning around gaining the right experience should relate to all of the above dimensions, with a specific focus on the following two questions:

- What do I want to achieve?
- What makes someone credible in such a role?

The first question allows you to ask yourself not only what function or position you want to attain but also, more generally, how you can express 'who you are' in career terms and so, ultimately, gain credibility. For example, if you are not particularly numerate, it might be unwise to choose to aim for a high-ranking finance position. Look at what you like doing, what you are naturally good at, then look for positions that require these qualities and skills. What do they really entail? What kinds of people are currently holding these positions? Why are they credible in these roles?

The second question focuses on the meaning of your desired role and what its attributes are, so will help you visualise how to get there. To answer it think about someone you feel is credible in that role and the attributes they demonstrate. You will then be able to hold a mirror up to your own attributes and assess the gaps between your experience and where you want to end up. Then you can decide what you want to address immediately or sooner rather than later.

Translating your goals into tangible skills or attributes

This process should be based on what you have defined as the must have skills or attributes of people who are credible in the role you ultimately want to achieve. Complement this by assessing the gaps in your current experiences or attributes. Ultimately, you will need to proactively develop a comprehensive plan to fill these gaps.

Staying flexible and grasping opportunities

Even when you have a well laid-out action plan, as defined above, stay tuned in to any potential opportunities that will either:

■ stretch you and take you out of your comfort zone

■ present a high strategic stake

■ allow you to focus on your long-term strategy

■ allow you to build your network and demonstrate influence.

Also, stay open to opportunities outside of your current organisation.

Exercises and action points

From goals to actions

This exercise helps you develop a comprehensive understanding of potential gaps in your experience and craft an action plan to resolve this. To do this you will need to meet and discuss with others, gather data and then spend a couple of hours designing your action plan.

Gather data

This may be done by answering the following questions with your line manager or mentor in order to ascertain what you need to do to achieve your chosen leadership position:

■ What are the must have experiences?

■ What mix of depth and breadth of experiences is necessary?

■ What are the nice to haves?

■ What is the golden path to my ideal position?

■ What alternative ways exist if I cannot take the golden path?

■ What is the probability of success? (If it is low, do not be discouraged – resilience and beating the odds are also leadership skills.)

■ What shortcuts are there?

■ How can I be credible in the role (technically and personally)?

■ What do people in that position need to demonstrate?

▶

▶

You can complement this exercise by investigating what kinds of pathways or experience the leaders of your organisation possess in order to pick up on any trends and patterns. When you identify those with credibility, make a point of meeting with them as this is a good way to start establishing networks.

Example: Pathways at Shell

In the Shell Finance Leadership Team, most had worked in both parts of the business – Exploration and Production, and Downstream. They had all been in business finance and portfolio finance positions. Most of them had led a change management programme of one sort or another and they had all worked in emerging markets at some stage.

Experience mapping and gap assessment

Once you have gathered and analysed your data, proceed to comparing and contrasting your findings with your own current experience and attributes:

■ Which experiences can you already tick off (only if they have been successful) and which are missing?

■ What types of experiences do you already have and what are the ones you need to put on your radar screen?

Put together your gap list

Create a list of the gaps to be filled. Avoid having an overly systematic or proactive approach to filling them, as career management is a very fluid process. The purpose of the gap list is for you to keep in mind the things you need to work on and scout for activities or opportunities that will address these. You do not have to be too scientific about what to do first or second or next – the key point is to realise what it is that you need to do.

Keeping up to date with your environment

Potential leaders commonly possess the characteristics of curiosity and impatience.

It is therefore relevant to address ways to accelerate your gaining of experience and credibility and develop a sense of what is to come while always applying rigorous self-analysis to everything you do.

Sensing what is to come

This really means keeping abreast of the changes in your environment – not only industrywise and wide but also in terms of technology or organisational theories. You need to know this as it may mean that you then need to acquire a particular new skill or skill set as a result of some development.

Here are some examples to illustrate the importance of sensing what is to come:

- General Electric very quickly realised that mastering the Six Sigma methodology[2] would have a tremendous impact on its product quality and productivity in general, boosting both customer satisfaction and financial results. The organisation heavily embraced the methodology and, as a result, any leadership position required Green Belt certification.

- After the Enron case that led Arthur Andersen to collapse, a compliance skill set became top of the skill list for a finance career.

- After the BP spill in the Gulf of Mexico, demonstrating accountability and a health, safety, security and environment (HSSE) skill set became critical to gaining any leadership position in the industry.

- In 2008, when the oil price reached record levels, risk and exposure management, paired with how to assess counterparty risk, were essential if you wanted to be seen as a credible as a businessperson.

Self-analysis

This is an efficient way to keep things in context and set you on a constant path of gaining credibility and building on this. Regularly ask yourself the following question in order to assess what is missing that you also need to factor in on your gap list:

- If I were a young graduate today looking to join my organisation, would I have what it takes? How successful would I be?

---

[2] A data-driven business management methodology developed by Motorola in the 1980s. Its aim is to eradicate any faults from the original manufacturing process by focusing on the root cause. The idea is to reach the Six Sigma: that is, 3.4 defects in 1 million. It has three levels of qualifications – Green Belt, Black Belt and Master Black Belt.

This does not mean that you need to keep changing direction. However, picking up signs and defining trends will help refine your overall strategy. It will help ensure you gain relevant experience to boost your credibility and move faster.

Exercises and action points

How to observe your environment

Sensing what is going on, being aware of the world around you, is part of increasing your knowledge and developing as a leader. When it comes to accelerating your credibility the question to ask is this:

■ How might this particular event impact my business and, as a result, which skills do I need to keep on my radar screen?

Let us look at a couple of examples to see how you might set about answering this question:

■ China's decision to let more foreign investment into its capital markets should prompt people to see how best to invest in China. It might even be an idea to ask about this at the next team meeting to gauge how your company might benefit from this decision or even to start scouting for investment opportunities there. Some people may even decide to take a basic course to learn Chinese.

■ The emergence of social, or, impact investing and venture philanthropy might prompt you to think about what your company is doing in that field or look at your corporate social responsibility programme in order to create additional value. You could start looking at investment opportunities in a different light – taking into consideration their social impact, for instance.

Dedicating some time to keeping connected with the outside world in this way is extremely useful. Keep up to date with the news every day, read industry magazines and keep an eye on the blogs of thought leaders such as Seth Godin and Tom Peters.

You may also consider increasing your ability to sense things that will add to your experience or credibility through other people. On a regular basis, engage in dialogue with your network of peers and stakeholders within and outside your company, about emerging trends (how they might impact business and organisations) or in more general philosophical debates about experience, credibility and leadership. Plan to attend conferences on topics that are of interest to you and/ or are important for your business. Make a commitment to do this on a regular basis (once or maybe twice a month).

Factor into your month some networking time with people working in different parts of the organisation, to understand their issues and perspectives and identify trends in specific skill sets that you might need in the future.

Maintaining momentum

Your credibility increases every day. It is rooted in how you behave and react in the moment to whatever is thrown at you.

The following examples or situations are classic cases that, badly managed, can immediately damage your credibility, but, if well managed, help sustain a long-lasting positive perception of your leadership:

- **A crisis** – Stay calm, assess the consequences and allocate resources.

- **A people crisis** – Stay calm, assess the person's emotional state and decide whether the best course of action is to do nothing or address the issue, involving other parts of the organisation as necessary.

- **When you make mistakes** – Be forward and up front. The minute you know about your mistake, come clean to whomever you need to. Present a clear assessment of the situation and potential corrective actions.

Approach all the infinite possibilities of what can happen in one day in the life of a leader. Increase your credibility by:

- being confident in your abilities to succeed

- making sure you are doing the best you can.

Exercises and action points

Maintaining focus

To monitor whether you are building your credibility or damaging it, it is useful to add regular checkpoints to your schedule when you reflect on your actions and experience.

On a monthly basis

Set aside 30 or 45 minutes to recap what you have done, achieved, handled or solved in the previous 10 or 20 days. Particularly, think about the following:

- Did this help increase, maintain or damage my credibility with my most important stakeholders (your team, line manager, peers)? What could I have done differently and why? Learn from this – and move on to the next day.

At other times

You may also decide to include this analysis in your natural cycle of performance evaluation, on a yearly or quarterly basis.

The four key rules of effective career management

As mentioned above, credibility is gained every day and backed up by every decision you make when it comes to your career.

The following four simple rules have proved useful for those building their careers.

Keep your sensors working

Have regular discussions with your line manager and/or your peers to find out if any opportunities for special projects or temporary assignments outside your area of expertise might be possible. For instance:

- if your line manager is going on leave, ask if you could stand in for him or her.

- ask if you could shadow one of the executives in a role you are particularly interested in, in order to get first-hand experience of what is involved

■ ask to work on a project with someone you know is challenging or very demanding

■ invite someone you do not naturally work well with to join you on a specific project.

Constantly expand your horizons

The higher up you go in any organisation, the more difficult it is to take on additional assignments. You will already have a list of cross-functional projects to work on as part of your yearly goals. Do not hesitate to think also about personal projects that could help you with your career development.

Complement your skills with courses

If you have identified specific technical skills you need, enrol for an evening class or look for a conference on those topics. At times, it can be better to enrol with a couple of other people, so that you have the opportunity to debate the ideas and crystallise what you have learned.

Regularly test your skill set and value on the market

Using external (market) validation to test your experience and credibility might seem controversial. Remember, however, that employment at just one organisation for life is a thing of the past and exposing yourself to cultural change is also a way to accelerate your learning and gain experience. It also shows your ability to take risks, adjust and grow.

Over the course of your career, dedicate some time to building and maintaining a network of human resources professionals or headhunters to help you with this process. Make sure you are always open about your objectives (for example, you might be clear with them that you are testing your value, not actively looking, wanting to go through some questions on what to do next and so on).

This does not have to be an aggressive strategy – doing so every couple of years or when you are thinking of making a move in your current organisation is generally effective. Testing your value in this way is a useful exercise. It allows you to compare, contrast and assess what level of responsibility you could aim for in an organisation.

To conclude, credibility is gained by acquiring experience and staying current. Doing this requires discipline and commitment. Credibility is only gained when there is an element of impact, tangible results or change at the personal level, arising from the experience, job or role. There is no need to become obsessed about gaining the right experience and becoming credible. What matters is that you have a clear overarching strategy, with flexibility, and commit to your personal development.

Day in, day out, it is crucial to stay focused on the expectations of your current role and the tasks at hand.

Living by your values

The process of gaining credibility as a leader will be incomplete if the questions of value and authenticity are not addressed. Being aware of what is acceptable or not in your organisation and, more importantly, what is acceptable or not for you as a person, are key elements of successful leadership. Only strong values can yield long-term business performance. Leveraging your value set to gain credibility will require you to first assess your values by means of self-questioning. It will then be important to compare and contrast your value set with that of your organisation. The more aligned they are, the more chances you will have of being able to gain credibility and be true to yourself. Finally, always abiding by your values will require discipline and the integration of regular checkpoints into your everyday life as a leader.

---

case study   ## Dealing with an ethical dilemma

An executive in the infrastructure industry was faced with an ethical dilemma at a certain point in her career. She was on the Board of a company that was shortly going to be acquired. The closing of the deal was an inherent part of the delivery for the year and would be taken into consideration for the calculation of bonuses. The valuation was also an element – the higher the valuation, the greater the bonus.

Faced with discussions about pushing the valuation up, she realised she was uncomfortable about this and decided to leave the company. She said that this was so far removed from her values and beliefs that

▶

> she had felt she would be failing herself and tarnishing her own reputation by staying and endorsing some of the proposed activities. She stated that knowing very precisely what she wanted to stand for made the decision making process easier for her. She never regretted leaving the company.

Credibility mostly comes as the result of gaining experience, but your value set impacts several parts of your leadership skill set: decision making, teambuilding and the ability to have influence. Your values are also essential when establishing yourself as a credible and authentic leader. Without personal values, there is limited business value.

The link between values and business performance

The leadership literature generally focuses on examples of good leadership and omits saying anything about 'bad' leadership, yet there is a plethora of it. It can result from a variety of causes – lack of vision, lack of innovation or lack of values.

Example: Bad leadership = poor performance

Simply open the *Financial Times* every so often to see the consequences of lack of values in different areas.

- *Financial Times*, November 2011 – about business in Asia. Olympus has revealed that it hid losses of $1.7 billion, leading to an investigation and the firing of executives.

- *Financial Times*, February 2012 – about Indian politics. Courts in India revoked 122 mobile licences. The top court ruled that the licences – which are the subject of a high-profile corruption trial in New Delhi – be cancelled on the grounds that the way they were awarded by the government was 'totally arbitrary and unconstitutional'.

- *Financial Times*, April 2012 – about business in Europe. BskyB's Board shifts pose threat to Murdoch. Mr Murdoch has come under scrutiny from the UK parliament over his role in the phone-hacking scandal that has engulfed News International, News Corp's UK arm, and led to the closure of the *News of the World*. James Murdoch has written a lengthy letter to a parliamentary committee expressing deep regret for the phone-hacking scandal, but reiterating his innocence ahead of a crucial report that could crystallise shareholders' concerns about his chairmanship.

Without proper values, businesses' credibility will suffer (Olympus), their capacity to grow and expand will suffer (India's telecom industry), they will go bankrupt (*News of the World*) or even lose critical competitive advantage (*Anti-Corruption and Anti-Bribery Act*).

Without proper values, leadership may become meaningless – even harmful. Leaders have an impact on the lives and incomes of thousands and with this comes responsibility. Leaders set the tone of their organisations and act as examples and role models. If they do not, they may put businesses at risk.

Identifying your value set

As mentioned previously, credibility is based on a mix of personal and organisational needs. When it comes to value sets, the need for alignment between personal and organisational values is even stronger than it is for credibility.

Everyone has a value system, shaped by a mixture of education, religious beliefs and experiences. Individuals' personal values are the foundation for the credibility of their leadership. However, credibility is enhanced when it is somewhat aligned with the expectations of your environment. When it comes to values, it is hugely beneficial for them to be strongly aligned with the corporate values of the organisation.

Building a strong understanding of your value set and that of your organisation is a three-step process. This will require three to four hours of your time and your feedback group's time in order to come up with a comprehensive and tangible outcome.

Self-questioning

This is the first step. The following questions will help you to discover your value set and sense what they mean for your organisation:

- **What are my core values?** Enquiring about your core values will enable you to add another dimension to your self-awareness and get a clear idea of your own boundaries. To answer this first question, think about what matters to you in your life and your relationships with others. Think back to business situations or discussions where you felt uncomfortable from a values point of view. For example, when a high-ranking person was talking to a subordinate in a demeaning tone of voice or someone was giving inaccurate information about a sensitive topic in a meeting. Consider how you felt, how you behaved and what you might have done differently.

■ **What are the perceived values of a leader in my organisation?**
This question will allow you to evaluate what it is that you want
to become. It will also cause you to reflect on corporate values and
gauge how leaders embody them. To answer this question, look for
leadership models in your organisation. Who are these people, what
values do they demonstrate, how do they live and breathe their
values and how can you emulate them?

■ **What kind of leadership values do I want to be known for?**
This question enables you to work on how people perceive you. To
answer it, consider the following list of possible attributes and pick
three to six of them that particularly resonate with you.

- Accountability
- Accuracy
- All for one and one for all, attitude
- Calm, quiet, peaceful
- Charity supported
- Collaboration
- Commitment
- Community
- Concern for others
- Connection
- Cooperation
- Democratic
- Disciplined
- Diversity supported
- Equality
- Excellence
- Fairness
- Faithfulness
- Family feeling
- Freedom, liberty, friendship
- Generosity
- Gentleness
- Giving
- Goodness

- Good will
- Gratitude
- Happiness
- Hardworking
- Harmony worked for
- Honourable
- Inner peace, calm
- Innovation
- Integrity
- Justice
- Kindness
- Love life, joy
- Meritocracy
- Oneness
- Openness
- Others' points of view, inputs valued
- Patriotic
- Peace, non-violence
- Privacy preserved
- Reliable
- Respect for others
- Responsive
- Safety paramount
- Satisfy others' requirements

- Security established
- Self-reliance
- Sensitive
- Service given to others and society
- Simplicity
- Spirituality
- Strength
- Timeliness
- Tolerance

- Tradition
- Tranquillity
- Trust
- Truth
- Unity
- Variety
- Well-being
- Wisdom

In a similar fashion to the elevator pitch exercise in Chapter 5, work on creating your value or moral statement or catchphrase and practise it as if you were in a lift. It is a good idea to spend some time comparing and contrasting your value set with the corporate value set. This gives you a point of focus for addressing matters of authenticity and analysing how well your value set matches your organisation's.

Recalibrating your value set

Values are critical to gaining credibility, mitigating any misperceptions or gap between what you think you project and what people around you actually *see*.

Consider seeking feedback to establish how you come across. As values might be a delicate topic to talk about in the work environment, it is highly recommended that you explore this with your feedback group. However, if you feel that this is too personal or too daunting, you might consider seeking feedback from those in your personal network only.

With each member of your feedback group or personal network, present and discuss:

- **the values you think you demonstrate** Ask the group if these are qualities that you demonstrate and/or whether these are traits that someone in your particular leadership position should demonstrate.

- **your value statement** Ask whether if this is truly representative of you, they would feel comfortable saying this about you and whether or not there is something missing that should be added: then integrate it into your value statement.

Crafting your value action plan

Bringing your value statement to life really comes down to actions and making the commitment to exhibit certain behaviours. It should be put into action in the way you make decisions, choices and communicate. For every attribute you have decided to include in your values statement, write down the tangible behaviours and actions that will be required to put them into practice.

Also reflect on the specific language you should start using to ingrain the message and create the right perception. Only a mix of actions and ways of communicating will make people clearly perceive your value set. Be disciplined and demonstrate this consistently to yield results.

Some examples of how to put your attributes into practice

Your value set includes respecting others

Leaders who are respectful of others will demonstrate or do the following:

- block all other sources of disturbance when interacting with someone, not checking their phone or watch
- pay attention to what the person says, listening intensely and not interrupting
- in a meeting, ensure that everyone has a chance to speak and ask for everyone's input
- demonstrate that they consider all points of view
- give constructive feedback.

Your value set includes trust

Trust is a two-way street. It is about being trustworthy yourself *and* being able to trust others. Consider doing the following to demonstrate that you are trustworthy:

- always deliver on your commitments and on time
- keep things close to your chest and do not engage in unnecessary office gossip
- keep your word when someone has confided in you
- do not hide your mistakes or errors and always accept the consequences
- use words such as 'commitment', 'expectations', 'reliance', 'we' to demonstrate that you trust others
- engage with people on different topics, asking for their opinions
- refrain from micro-managing once the expectations and the desired outcomes have been defined
- always stand by your team in meetings with others, keeping discussions or explanations for offline one-on-one sessions.

Maintaining momentum

Demonstrating your personal core values and the corporate values should be the backbone of your leadership style and your credibility. When we are put under pressure, in times of crisis or when experiencing a significant increase in workload, it is easy to slip and let performance, attitudes and behaviours slide. To stay in tune and be able to correct behaviours quickly you may consider doing the following:

■ Use your performance card (see Chapter 3) to keep an eye on the external and internal conditions required for you to perform well.

■ Factor into your routine time to think and reflect on the following.

  – Have I always lived and breathed my values: most of the time or not at all?

  – If not, what I have done wrong?

  – What should I mend and/or adjust?

This analysis can be completed in a bi-weekly or monthly session of about 30 minutes.

Experience and demonstrating a strong set of values are the fundamental building blocks of credibility. These are underpinned by one last element – authenticity.

Exercises and action points

The elevator pitch

You worked on your personal brand elevator pitch previously (see Chapter 5). Here, the idea is to adequately capture what it is you stand for when it comes to values.

As before, consider creating your value statement in the form of a couple of sentences or so that will act as your catchphrase or motto. They should summarise your value set and set out your boundaries.

This elevator pitch is to sell yourself and should be what you would say about yourself. Here is an example.

If you were in a lift with the CEO of the company of your dreams and he or she was talking about value sets, what would you say?

'I am a compassionate individual who believes in trusting in people and acting with a high level of integrity.'

Equally, your personal elevator pitch could be given by someone else talking about you.

'... is a straightforward and trustworthy person who pushes the team to excellence fairly and supportively.'

If a person who knows you was in a lift with the CEO of the company of your dreams and talked about your values, what would you like that person to say?

Authenticity and remaining true to yourself

Part 2 of this book focused on understanding who you are as an individual. It asked you to look inside yourself, understand your drivers, strengths and areas for development. Having come to know yourself better enables you to reflect on leadership in an authentic way.

Authenticity is one of the key drivers in terms of gaining credibility. It is important to your decision making when it comes to gaining experience and what you should do next. When carrying out your self-questioning and debating with others as to what would be the natural or logical next steps for you, keep the following questions in mind at all times:

- Does this resonate with who I am? What I like? What I want to do?

There is always the question of stretching yourself to consider and it is important not to shy away from this in terms of gaining credibility. You can find different types of stretch:

- **technical stretch** – moving from one function to another – say, from the position of analyst in marketing to a business development position

- **interpersonal stretch** – spearheading a function in an emerging market far from your cultural framework or getting into your first team management role

- **span of control stretch** – moving from a country-based role to a regional one.

Above all, it is important to remember that credibility comes from times when you perform at your best, and you will tend to excel in either things you have a natural ability in or passion for. Hopping on the bandwagon and listening to other people's advice might feel good at times, but also might lead to regrets. Being true to yourself will help you filter out peer pressure and popular opinion, allowing you to base your actions on your own passions, skills and convictions. It will also help you learn how to be courageous enough to act on them.

Authenticity will also allow you to assess just how good the fit is between you and your current corporate environment as well as with others around you.

Example: When the fit isn't right

One senior executive reported that twice in his career he had resigned from positions because the value gap between the corporate values expressed in the glossy annual reports and the reality of everyday life was too big. This unacceptable gap between his values and the corporation's hindered his desire to belong and his ability to perform. He simply had to take action to find a more suitable position.

The best way to take the authenticity test is spend some time assessing any gap between what your values are and the perceived values that a leader in your organisation should demonstrate. Looking at these two side by side will give you a measure of how closely the match actually is with your organisation.

This does not mean that you have to shy away from environments that do not exactly match your value set – this may, in reality, be a different type of perfectly healthy stretch. However, it is good to bear in mind the following:

- Leaders embody the values of the companies they work for. If they cannot fully commit to them due to their personal beliefs, it becomes difficult to stay the course, act as a role model and be a credible leader.

- Professional people need to be able to assess the tipping point when how well they perform and even their well-being are affected by a lack of alignment between them in terms of their values. This is soon revealed in the form of increasing feelings of inadequacy or a sense of drifting of values when completing the monthly or bi-weekly analysis of values. When this happens, it is important to pause and reflect. Eventually it will mean deciding to take the necessary steps to change course.

Summary

The corporate environment is the soil in which you plant the seeds of your success, so it is crucial to find a mix that allows you to flourish and thrive. You owe it to yourself to find the right environment for you.

Here's a reminder of some of the key points from this chapter:

- credibility comes as a result of proactively looking to gain the right experience, in terms of both technical and soft skills

- the right experience will be built on a mix of knowing what you want to achieve in your career and what your organisation perceives as building your credibility

- there are always specific events that help you to gain credibility and experience within your organisation, so find them and make sure you are proactively experiencing them – such as being accountable for a business, leading a major restructure, change agenda or transaction

- you will only increase your credibility if you multiply different types of experiences and always proactively look to step out of your comfort zone to be stretched

- stay in tune with your environment to quickly assess what skills will become useful or give you a strategic advantage in the long run – pay attention not only to technical skills but also any organisational or management skills

- you increase your credibility every day by participating in and reacting to difficult or unexpected situations or crises

- be aware that credibility and the right experiences come from doing and also reflecting

- work on a vision, your career vision as something to aim towards, not a fixed plan, as this will allow you to stay fluid and be able to grasp opportunities that come your way

- if you really want to assess how credible you are, take the acid test of seeing how the jobs market reacts to you on a regular basis – it will help you recalibrate to fill your gaps and assess your skill set

- credibility comes from living and breathing your values and the values of your organisation, so invest time in identifying them and assessing how aligned they are

- cultivate your values in the same fashion that you cultivate your leadership brand

- if your value set does not fit well with your organisation's one, do not be afraid to move on – success is built on authenticity.

7

Leading teams

'Teamwork is the ability to work together toward a common vision. The ability to direct individual accomplishments toward organisational objectives. It is the fuel that allows common people to attain uncommon results.'

Andrew Carnegie, Scottish-American industrialist

This chapter covers:

- what a 'team' looks like and how the types of teams you lead impact your leadership style
- how to balance one-on-one relationships with your team members with your relationship with the team as a whole
- tools and techniques to build rapport, enhance motivation and drive results
- trust, respect and inclusiveness – and why they matter.

The 2004 European Cup

The 2004 European Cup started with a burning question: would France retain the title? Little did France know that the team would not even make it to the semi-finals.

Greece changed the balance. Returning to the championship after 24 years, the players began by beating the host team Portugal, then made their way up to the finals, defeating the defending champions in the process, then went on to beat Portugal again in the finals.

The game plan was clear and was based on a strict man-marking strategy. They played to their strengths as solid, reliable defenders with a hard-working midfield. Despite little attacking talent, they had the winning ingredient. They played as a team, observing, supporting and helping each other. No egos, no tensions, just a bunch of guys working together towards achieving the same goal.

Teambuilding is about creating a real sense of belonging and mobilising energy in one direction. Leaders recognise the importance of this when it comes to driving change and achieving results.

Before exploring the tools and techniques required to build a team, though, it is important to clarify the following three things:

- the concept of teams and leadership – how teams are formed
- the objectives of leaders with regard to their teams
- the duties of leaders towards their teams.

The concept of a team and leadership

The model shown in Figure 7.1 represents how teams are often formed in corporate environments.

However, this is not sufficient to entirely explain the notion of a 'team'. In today's world, a number of people put together simply to carry out an activity do not necessarily qualify as a team. There are other elements required, such as having a shared vision, personal relationships, co-creation and, as an emerging trend, a sense of community, collaboration and belonging.

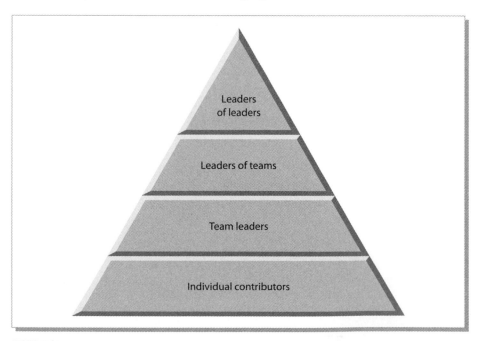

Figure 7.1   How teams are formed

In this chapter, the focus will be on leading a team as in dealing with relation to your direct reports – how to handle your peers and a team of leaders is analysed in Chapter 8. In this context, a team consists of two main dimensions – the building of individual relationships with each of the team members and the position of the leader in relation to the team as a whole.

The objectives of leaders for their teams may vary depending on the history of those teams. Is the leader inheriting a mature and stable team? In this case, the task for the new leader will be to establish him- or herself in an already formed group. Is the leader there to drive a change management agenda or create a new business? If so, it will be important for the leader to think in strategic terms about resources.

A definition of leadership by John Kotter[1] is that, essentially, leaders have two main duties: to align people in order to ensure delivery of the vision, motivate and energise them to create value.

With the above dimensions in mind, how can an individual excel in the delicate matter of building or leading a team made up of creatures as volatile, unpredictable and mysterious as human beings?

The following three cornerstones need to be considered and will be addressed in the rest of this chapter:

- **Building rapport** – commanding trust and respect or knowing how to connect with your team members.

- **Motivation and setting objectives** – aligning people appropriately in terms of what they need to achieve for themselves and the organisation or knowing how to get the best out of a team.

- **Reward and recognition** – creating sustained levels of performance or knowing how to push the team further.

Building rapport

Learning how to connect with your team can be summed up in two basic principles. The first is to invest time in getting to know them as people, to understand their drivers and their values. It requires you to hone your listening and observation skills and multiply one-on-one

---

[1] John Kotter (1990) 'What leaders really do', *Harvard Business Review*.

interactions. Getting to know your team members is particularly efficient if you are also prepared to let them know you. Creating a sense of reciprocity is key. The second principle is to aim to create an environment of trust, inclusiveness and respect that will be conducive to a productive team atmosphere. This can be achieved by paying attention to a set of attributes – being transparent and being supportive – and consistently demonstrating a certain set of behaviours – valuing difference, empowering people and righting wrongs. All of this needs to be underpinned by reciprocity and communication.

Human beings are highly social creatures who thrive on establishing emotional bonds. Anyone is more willing to deliver, push themselves and help someone they like, respect or trust than someone they do not.

According to Daniel Goleman,[2] 'emotional intelligence' is what distinguishes great leaders from merely good ones. It is the ability to understand other people's emotional make-up by means of empathy and relying on social skills to move people in the right direction.

Leaders need to heighten their ability to be inclusive, think globally and be collaborative. This is the first filter to use when building or leading a team, while the second is authenticity and being true to oneself. Everything that follows needs to be done while keeping the following two questions in mind:

- How can I demonstrate the leadership values of the future?
- How can I remain authentic with my team?

Knowing me, knowing you ... creating a personal bond

Getting to know people is a two-way process. It should be rooted in a genuine desire to get inside your team members' heads, to know them as people. It also requires the introduction of a certain level of reciprocity, letting them know you as a person, too – not only as a figure of authority – and creating a feeling of equality. The following four suggestions would make a good starting point:

---

[2] Daniel Coleman (2006) *Emotional Intelligence*, Bantam, with Richard Boyatzis and Annie McKee (2002) *Primal Leadership: Realizing the power of emotional intelligence*, Harvard Business School Press.

- invest time in understanding who they are

- invest time in interacting with them in different capacities

- create a regular schedule of diverse channels of communication

- be open to showing them your true colours and letting them know you.

Understanding who your team members are

This is about establishing their 'baseline' – discovering their main characteristics and finding the essence of who your team members are. Teams are increasingly diverse, gathered together from different backgrounds, cultures and age groups. Delivering results is highly correlated to motivation and the drivers of a 39-year-old man who is married with two children will be quite different from those of a 25-year-old woman with no children. Invest adequate time in gathering data. Using the questions and processes described in Chapters 3 and 4 can also be useful here, enabling you to understand them as individuals. Complement these with the following question, which will help you to create a list of further questions so you can answer this one:

- What do I want to know about this person that will enable me to understand, guide and get the best out of him or her?

Once the basics of an understanding and relationship have been established, a leader may decide to go one step further and enquire about the team member's personal life. Only do this if it is culturally acceptable (avoid doing so in some Asian or Indian cultures) and, as a leader, you feel comfortable doing this. Being aware and respectful of values and boundaries will guide you appropriately here.

How you go about asking these questions is a personal choice, rooted in your brand, leadership style and comfort zone. This should be built on the findings of your own self-awareness journey.

Some leaders prefer the safety of a formal one-on-one discussion in an office, where they will first present the list of questions to the team member and then engage them in a discussion about each, one after the other. At the other end of the spectrum, you may choose a less structured approach, talking over coffee and sticking to a general informal conversation where you can touch on the list of questions mentioned above but as part of general social interaction. You may also consider using Myers-Briggs type indicator (MBTI) profiling and 360-degree assessments with your team to get additional insights into how they perceive themselves.

Interacting with and observing your team members

Ongoing observation helps you to draw conclusions about individuals' inherent abilities – technically, intellectually and emotionally – based on practical examples.

Here are some things to be aware of as you interact and observe:

- **Who takes a backseat approach?** Who listens first but then, when the time is right, comes up with a statement that makes everyone pause?

- **Who is the first to talk in a group discussion?** This could reveal either courage (if the opinions are well thought through and the person regularly challenges the status quo) or insecurity (if the person opens the debate, but rapidly changes to align with others' opinions).

- **Who, most of the time, is willing to challenge or debate a solution?** This is a sign of an innovative and risk-taking individual.

- **Who comes up with practical examples?** This is indicative of an action-orientated person.

- **Who readily admits to not understanding what you mean?** This is a sign of self-confidence and thoroughness.

- **Who will systematically elevate the discussion and talk about the big picture?** This marks out the conceptual thinker from the strategic thinker.

- **Who dives straight away into the details?** This is another sign of an action-orientated person.

- **Who changes their mind if the group changes?** This may indicate conformism.

Observing your team provides clues as to how to motivate or influence its members. It can be very helpful to work out strategies as a result for the best team mix of people for any specific project. (For more on this, see Chapter 11.)

When possible, complement observations with working one-on-one with a team member. Try positioning yourself more as a peer than as a leader in order to create a different dynamic with your team member. Although this may feel slightly uncomfortable, it can help you to build a more democratic and collaborative leadership style.

Creating a routine to share and connect with your team members

Time is an important element in teambuilding. Multiplying interactions increases the chances of you being able to get inside the heads of team members and develop stronger ties.

Time should be invested in the full range of situations – formal and informal, virtual and face-to-face, one-on-one and group – addressing both operational issues and more personal ones.

Being genuine in your interactions with team members is what matters most for fostering team spirit. Keeping a log of all the information gathered about them will help with setting objectives and knowing what will aid their motivation. These actions will be instrumental in you transforming one-on-one relationships into team relationship and, also establishing your relationship with the team as an entity.

Showing your true colours to establish a certain level of reciprocity

Leadership is also about being comfortable with exposing weaknesses or fears. Good leaders make their team an inherent part of their leadership development.

It can be counter-intuitive for leaders to show vulnerability as they may fear this will be perceived as a departure from their authority and absolute wisdom. However, as shown by Robert Goffee and Gareth Jones in their book *Why Should Anyone be Led by You*? (Harvard Business School Press, 2006), it is important to appear human. It makes leaders much more approachable. Ultimately, it helps to establish trust.

'My brother-in-law is a philosophy teacher and, for some unknown reason, he always wears the oddest shoes, these old walking shoes – big, heavy, completely ruined – went out of fashion about 20 years ago, and I once asked him, 'Why on earth are you still wearing those shoes?' He smiled softly and answered, "Because the pupils always have something to make fun of me about". Regardless of your ambitions and perfection, make sure you know and show some of your weakness, to make yourself human, an imperfect being, and allow team members and other people to relate to you.'

Interview with Clara Gaymard,
President and CEO of General Electric France

However, it is important for leaders to be selective in what they show as their weaknesses. It is best not to expose anything that could be perceived as a fatal flaw in your leadership qualities. For example, if you were a finance director, it would be better *not* to reveal that you know nothing about discounted cash flow or US GAAPs. It may be safer to choose a tangential weakness instead – such as, being impatient – or one others will consider a strength – such as being persistent or driven – or think in terms of the big picture – pushing your team members to develop the ability to both use their strategic thinking to communicate with you and be able to get into the details if needed.

Beyond creating trust and solidarity, communicating a weakness also builds a collaborative atmosphere. It allows team members to feel not only needed but also able to contribute to the leader's development. This should be complemented by communicating the importance of team feedback, so you grow to become the best you can be. Relying on others and highlighting interdependencies are also important elements in building rapport.

In a nutshell, the first step towards building rapport involves taking genuine interest in others, observing your team members and sharing and being open about yourself.

Exercises and practical examples

Understanding who your team members are: hard data gathering

The purpose of this exercise is to establish a proper data-gathering mechanism to find out as much as possible about each of your team members. Gather as much of the information suggested as you can. The process should be an iterative one of mining various resources, from the human resource department to team members' previous managers and of course the obvious one of simply talking to them.

What would 'good' look like? As these people's leader, you would be able to list for each of them, accurately, what five of their attributes, qualities and pet peeves are and they could do the same for you. The following are the kinds of information you should know about your team members:

- **Date of birth** To assess what demographic group they belong to and what their motivators and values might be (as described in Chapter 2). This helps you to choose the correct sort of vernacular to use when addressing them and assess what they would expect from a leader.

- **Marital status** This helps calibrate their sociability and enables the creation of an emotional bond – by enquiring about their family, for example – once trust has been established.

- **Cultural and historical background** This allows you to gain a deeper understanding of their behaviours and stance towards authority or ability to challenge yours. It supports being able to accurately decipher body language. It is also a great way to build cultural awareness and overcome any of your own cultural biases.

- **Appetite to move and live in foreign countries** This makes it possible to gauge their attitude towards change and risk.

- **Appraisal of past performance** This allows you to position individuals on the talent curve (top talent, a solid performer or someone in the bottom 10 per cent).

- **Latest individual development plan** An example of a individual development plan can be found Appendix 1. This provides you with people's own perceptions of their strengths and weaknesses. This is useful for understanding how to motivate them.

▶

■ **Discussion with previous leaders** This can provide insights into how team members are as individuals and can be useful to calibrate your thinking. However, it could also lead to bias, so establishing rapport first is the safest option.

This is not an exhaustive list and can be enriched as you see fit. Creating a file per direct report to keep all this information handy is a good leadership discipline.

Understanding who your team members are: soft data gathering

The following questions provide you with a comprehensive way to establish rapport with your team members. They are very useful when you are beginning to do so, and convey that you have a genuine interest in them as people.

You may also choose to use some of these questions when you are performing an evaluation or giving them feedback, to ensure that you keep in tune with how they are developing and growing as a result of experience and with your help:

■ How would they define themselves?

■ What do they think are their most important beliefs and values?

■ What, according to them, are their strengths and their weaknesses?

■ What drives them? What do they want to achieve?

■ What experiences have they found most gratifying or exhilarating?

■ What are they most afraid of?

■ What do they expect from their leaders?

■ Who are they? In other words, what are their strengths, their flaws? What is their level of empathy or emotional intelligence?

■ What makes them tick? In other words how do they like to work and what drives them?

As mentioned above, it is important to store the answers to these questions and refer to them on a regular basis or when you want to either give feedback or embark on performance reviews or a career discussion.

Gaining trust and respect and creating an inclusive environment

As mentioned in the previous chapter, values do matter when it comes to your credibility. They matter even more when you are building and leading a team. Trust, inclusiveness and respect are intertwined; they build on and feed from each other. With trust comes respect, with inclusiveness comes trust and respect, and with respect come results. As a team leader, building this virtuous circle is critical.

According to Stephen R. Covey, the author of *The 7 Habits of Highly Effective People*, trust is a rare commodity in our current environment and appears significantly less prevalent than a generation ago. In an article in *Leadership Now*, Covey states that only 49 per cent of employees trust senior management and only 28 per cent believe CEOs are credible sources of information.

How can anyone lead a team, if they can't foster trust and respect? As Warren Bennis put it, 'Leadership without mutual trust is a contradiction in terms.'

There are six basic principles to be observed if you are to establish the team you want and for it to yield the results you want or need:

- reciprocity
- transparency and support
- communication and consistency
- value difference
- empowerment
- righting wrongs.

Reciprocity

You want them to trust you. Start by trusting them.

- Gain and grow trust by setting objectives in line with what you need and want and what they need and want.
- Build on their trust by being open and non-judgmental and sticking to your word.

* Make them as accountable for results as you are.

* Move from 'I' and 'them' to thinking in terms of 'we'. Now think about your personal actions and decisions as 'we'. What does this imply for the team?

Reciprocity creates a loyal and interdependent environment where all succeed or fail *as a team*.

Transparency and support

Say what you do, do what you say. Be open and transparent about your objectives, expectations, what makes you tick – even your emotional state, if you think it is important in order for your team members to understand your behaviours. For example, if you have had a pretty tough day and you know you could have a strong negative reaction to events, be ready to share this with your team if one of them comes to you with bad news or notification of a crisis. Showing your emotions will make them comfortable about doing the same.

Be there for them and support them, once objectives and accountability have been established. For instance, if an external party puts them on the spot in a meeting, step in and protect them, but make sure you address the issue less formally afterwards, too. Ask them to be there for you as well and stress the importance of their feedback for your journey.

Creating trust and team spirit implies supporting each other and presenting a united face to the rest of the organisation. Having this makes it possible to gain loyalty, too. As a leader you have an impact on your team. Set the tone and make them want to emulate your behaviours.

Communication and consistency

Talk straight, stick to your word, keep your commitments, be reliable. In other words, live and breathe your leadership brand in terms of how you relate to and interact with your team (see Chapter 5) and be consistent in how you demonstrate your behaviours.

Value difference

It has been established that inclusiveness is, more and more, an important way to accelerate progress up the ladder. Valuing difference is the first step towards inclusiveness. Purposefully build a team with members who are different from you and, if at all possible, different from each other. The team dynamics created as a result will produce enough disruptive opinions and tensions for you to steer towards and demonstrate inclusiveness.

In order to maximise the benefits of a diverse team, establish the following operating principles:

■ listen to all, engage with all, never disregard any input

■ treat everyone the same way – with respect and care – and be aware of micro-inequities

■ do not judge, listen first; attempt to understand their behaviours, building on what you have learned about them.

Be aware of your own personal biases, likes and dislikes. Naturally, you will have more chemistry with some of your team members than with others, but pay attention to your behaviour as it could have an impact on others in the team. Specifically, be aware of how your behaviour can unintentionally trigger fear.

Empowerment

A team needs space. In her book, Judy Brown[3] has a poem called 'Fire' that is particularly appropriate:

'What makes fires burn is space between the logs, a breathing space. Too much of a good thing, too many logs packed in too tight can douse the flames.'

Team members can indeed feel suffocated when they are supervised too closely. Equally destructive is a leadership style that floats on the surface of things and is not grounded in a real understanding of the issues.

Achieving the right balance between empowerment and supervision is possible:

---

[3] Judy Brown (2006) *A Leader's Guide to Reflective Practice*, Trafford Publishing.

- let them learn and let them deliver once the objectives are clear

- occasionally delve into some of their issues in detail, to provide the right level of challenge and support.

The very fact that your team knows you can and will go deeply into things will help your credibility and create respect.

The last point to be mindful of – to complete the journey from trust to inclusiveness to respect – is that you need to right any wrongs.

Righting wrongs

As a leader, never be afraid to recognise when you are wrong or say you are genuinely sorry. You will gain respect, on a personal level, and increase loyalty.

Finally Figure 7.2[4] summarises the building blocks of, and journey to achieving, trust, inclusiveness and, ultimately, respect.

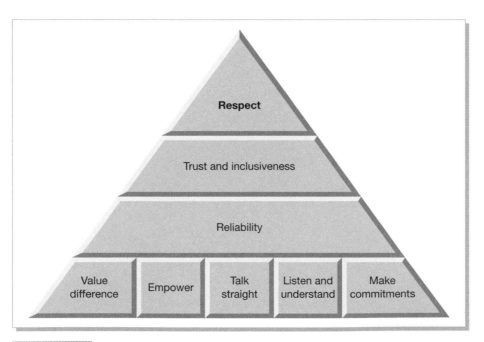

Figure 7.2 The building blocks that ultimately create respect in a team

---

[4] Based on Howard Jackson's respect model.

Trust, inclusiveness and respect should not be confused with softness. Being intelligently trustful, inclusive and respectful means that you are also conveying a strong level of expectation and sense of accountability. Delivery is the name of the game and the purpose of the team's existence.

Trust, inclusiveness and respect will contribute to fostering a safe environment in which all collaborate, contribute and yield better results.

Stretching your team members to deliver and helping them gain credibility is an important part of building rapport and motivating them.

A safe environment is one in which people feel able to show their true colours, one in which they feel valued and respected.

All of the above information is particularly useful for new leaders. Indeed, implementing it in the first 90 days of your tenure is an elegant way to create impact, establish your personal brand and build momentum towards achieving delivery.

It will also allow you to quickly grasp the overall mix of strengths and weaknesses in your team and give you an opportunity to reflect on any changes that might need to be made.

Exercises and practical examples

The trust and respect test

Trust and respect matter tremendously when establishing rapport. As noted earlier, you never have a second chance to make a first impression.

Individuals can have different views on trust and respect. Some will tread water carefully at first and, when they feel secure or safe, will give their respect and trust. Others will give trust and respect by default, until proven wrong. Each type will look for different behaviours and will judge you in different ways.

In order to know very early on which types you are dealing with – whether team members or you as leader boss – and adjust your style accordingly, the quickest way is to ask the following questions during your first meeting or even during an interview:

▶

■ Is trust earned or lost?

■ Is respect earned or lost?

While these may seem unusual questions, they will help you to frame what it is you have to do, or avoid doing, and lay the right foundations to establish rapport. Equally, you will give them some important keys to your behaviours. The results can then be translated into tangible actions:

If you are a team member and addressing the above with your boss or someone higher up than your position with whom you will have to work on a regular basis, the answers can be interpreted as follows.

■ If his or her trust needs to be earned, performing well and delivering on your commitment will be key.

■ If his or her trust can be lost, proactively communicating and coming clean straight away if you make a bad decision or a crisis is unfolding, will be the best course of action.

■ If his or her respect needs to be earned, you know that you should potentially invest time before you'll get positive feedback from this person.

■ If his or her respect can be lost, you know that you need to gauge and reflect on your behaviour on a regular basis to maintain the same level of performance.

If you are a leader, when it comes to your team members – and how to most effectively deal with them – their answers can be interpreted as follows:

■ If his or her trust needs to be earned, performing well and delivering on *your* commitments will also be key – consistency in terms of behaviours and discipline will be required.

■ If his or her trust can be lost, it will be critical that you set aside time to explain the rationale behind some of your decisions to ensure there is no doubt or misunderstanding.

■ If his or her respect needs to be earned, you know that you may need to be patient and wait for a while before that team member will naturally come to you for advice on issues. Only when he or she is personally at ease or convinced that you are a credible leader will this happen.

▶

> ▪ If his or her respect can be lost, you know that you need to gauge and reflect on your own behaviour on a regular basis to ensure you are not disrespecting people or putting them off.
>
> Make sure that you add the data resulting from this exercise to your team member's file.

Maintaining the relationship

Example: Rituals and relationships

'The next day the little prince came back.

"It would have been better to come back at the same hour," said the fox. "If, for example, you come at four o'clock in the afternoon, then at three o'clock I shall begin to be happy. I shall feel happier and happier as the hour advances. At four o'clock, I shall already be worrying and jumping about. I shall show you how happy I am! But if you come at just any time, I shall never know at what hour my heart is to be ready to greet you ... One must observe the proper rites ..."

"What is a rite?" asked the little prince.

"Those also are actions too often neglected," said the fox.'

This extract, from Antoine de Saint Exupéry's *The Little Prince*, perfectly illustrates the importance of rituals in establishing and then maintaining relationships with your team.

Establishing the rituals of regularly communicating and engaging with your team will enable you to keep your finger on the pulse of your team members' motivations, desires and needs. It will also allow for proactive corrective actions to be taken if needs be. For instance, it can allow you to sense the dissatisfaction of some at a crucial moment for the business or prevent the loss of your star performer.

There are various ways in which you can do this.

Weekly or bi-weekly one-on-ones

The purpose of these meetings is to tackle operational issues and track the development and performance of the team members.

Most of the time, these meetings will be virtual or over the phone. However, consider using Skype or video conferencing so you can create a connection by means of facial expressions and body language. Give your full and undivided attention during these meetings, shutting down your e-mail, phone and any other devices.

For face-to-face meetings, avoid checking the time and control your body language. Taking notes is a good way to stay in the moment.

Informal chats

These can be very powerful and telling. Regular calls to team members, when there are no pressing issues to discuss, to check in with them about what is going on, will make them feel valued as people.

Informal chats are useful when you sense that something is not right, as a result of previous interactions or feedback from others in the same office or region, for example. Connecting at the human level is critical to building loyalty. At times, a friendly and unexpected phone call is all it takes to reassure, motivate or simply avoid losing a team member. A chat may make someone feel special and glad to be part of your team.

Face-to-face meetings

These remain the best way to truly connect with others.

It is advisable to meet face-to-face two to three times a year with direct reports – individually and as a team. This helps break down distance and create a fair environment. Factor in proper periods of time for both business and quality time with team members (over dinner or a long lunch, for example). Engage them with social or cultural topics to show that you are genuinely interested in them.

You can record all your data as shown in Table 7.1 and add it to your team member's file.

Table 7.1 Example format to record data from meetings

Date	Team member's name
Topic 1	Problems and discussion
Topic 2	xxxxx
Topic 3	xxxx
Summary of last time	xxxxx
Actions to be taken	Xxxx by xxxx
Follow-up needed?	
Help needed?	

Motivation and setting objectives – getting the best out of your team

Being able to get the best out of your people and run a team that achieves a high standard of performance should be the goal and pride of any leader. In order to take your team's performance to the next level, two elements need to be considered. First, how to motivate your team by involving them in setting goals for the organisation, ensuring that these goals also address some of their most important needs and desires. Second, by crafting a reward and recognition system that is genuine, and addresses not only the 'what to do' but also the 'what to be'.

Before diving into the heart of the first of these, it is important to understand the documents used to monitor individual performance in any organisation.

In most companies there are two distinct sets of documents used to drive motivation and set objectives. They will be put together on a yearly basis and reviewed once or twice during the year. Though the names given to those will of course vary from company to company, they usually include the following:

- **Individual development plan (IDP)** This states an individual employee's strengths and weaknesses. It describes their personal career goals, for both the short and long term. Ultimately, it helps with crafting training programmes and potential learning experiences to enable employees to work on their weaknesses and achieve their goals. This is not part of the measurement of their performance.

- **Goals and objectives (G&Os)** This document addresses what the employees need to deliver in order to contribute to the company's goals. Their performance is based on how they have done in terms of delivering these identified goals, which they have committed to.

Examples of both these documents can be found in Appendix 1.

In most cases, these two documents are never looked at in conjunction with each other or in a compare and contrast fashion. Neither do they tend to address or factor in interdependencies or team elements. On the contrary, companies usually link team performance to company goals and promotions to individual achievements by looking solely at the goals and objectives (G&Os) document.

Leaders focus first on what is needed by the organisation and then cascade this down to their team members. This then becomes the basis for any evaluations of their performance. What may result is an averagely or even poorly motivated workforce and sometimes the sacrifice of *quality* work for *quantity* of work.

The truth? Organisations actually have limited powers to motivate employees. As human beings, most individuals are driven by intrinsic rewards, such as challenging work and the opportunity to grow. These needs are usually addressed in the individual development plan (IDP).

To build a strongly motivated team performing at the highest level, you need to enable your team members to activate their own internal motivation and deliver on the company's goals, thus aligning G&Os and IDPs while recognising interdependencies.

The following three elements need to be addressed:

- **Setting a compelling vision for the organisation to deliver on** This enhances the feeling of belonging. The notion of co-creation is an important part of this process.

- **Crafting rewarding objectives for each individual** This secures their motivation and activates their own drivers. It should also address the interdependencies to further strengthen team spirit.

- **Reflecting on a feedback process** and genuine reward and recognition.

Understanding and harnessing the virtues of co-creation

One of a leader's duties is to define a vision and set a strategy for the organisation or a particular business unit or the team they are in charge of (vision and strategy are analysed in Chapters 9 and 10). Regardless of your position in the organisation, whether you are the CEO of a company or lower down, you will always have the delicate task of bringing your team on the journey to achieving these with you. This is where co-creation can help.

Co-creation is one way to use the results of all the work you have put into establishing your one-on-one relationships and truly become the leader of your team. It is the way to create buy in and increase loyalty. It also serves to concentrate and direct efforts towards achieving a common goal. In other words, it will enable you to achieve an important part of your leadership role – aligning resources.

In the co-creation process, you may use the insights you have gained about your individual team members and their strengths and what motivates them to create positive tension and discussion.

The ideal setting for this exercise is in a one- to two-day, face-to-face meeting with all your direct reports. This allows for proper discussion, sharing and agreement.

To co-create, the following are needed:

- **sharing of information** by the leader with the group
- **questioning and reflecting** – this might be in an iterative way together with sharing of the information
- **agreement and making decisions** from the leader and the group
- **personal commitment** – mostly from the individual team members

Sharing information

The team leader is in the driving seat and communicates to the team the vision, goals and objectives that have been agreed on at a higher level, including the rationales for them. These may include the following benefits:

- **creating a sense of purpose** – by setting the context and painting the global picture, team members will feel that they are taking part in something that matters

- **creating a sense of belonging** – by being transparent and asking everyone to think together, team members feel valued and energised

- **creating a sense of fairness** – everyone feels on an equal footing in contributing to the solution.

Questioning and reflecting

The leader then takes a back seat and lets the chemistry of the team play out. Some of the following questions may be used as ice-breakers or prompts:

- What does it mean for us as a team?

- Is there anything else we feel strongly about or that needs to be considered?

- What would success look like for us?

These questions:

- reinforce the need to comply, as a part of a bigger group

- recognise the specifics of the group features, needs and so on – to allow for specific pain points or important topics

- translate words into tangible results to be delivered

- allow for measurement to take place.

Leaders will always have a personal vision to factor in and their role is also to steer the discussion towards related goals. It is important to remain open and inclusive. All inputs can result in determining goals or objectives that will yield better results than the original ones. This is therefore an important phase of the process that leaders need to facilitate and steer by:

- throwing controversial comments or ideas into the discussion

- challenging ideas – using the 5 Whys technique to fully explore the cause and effect relationships, as developed by Toyota and an important part of the Six Sigma methodology by General Electric (see Chapter 6) – or introducing some constraints

▨ fostering a culture of not interrupting and respect – an important part of creating trust

▨ factoring in formal moments to go around the room asking for every one's personal views on the discussion – this allows for the less extrovert to get an opportunity to enrich the conversation.

It is important to allow enough time for this to happen. Some of the techniques and tools described in Chapters 9 and 10, such as the entrepreneurial game and the Merlin exercise can be used in these sessions to help achieve this.

Agreement and making decisions

The leader takes back control. When everyone has been heard and the appropriate amount of discussion and reflection has taken place, the leader should:

▨ summarise what has been said

▨ acknowledge all sides of people's arguments

▨ exercise his or her leadership role and make a decision.

This approach achieves a good balance between democratic engagement (the leader is inclusive and respectful) and vertical, hierarchical decision making (the leader is the figure of authority). It also creates a strong sense of motivation and accountability.

Personal commitment

This is the critical and final element. In his book, *Conscious Business: How to build value through values*, Fred Kofman (Sounds True, 2006) states 'a culture of impeccability in commitments fosters a sense of achievement, dignity and self-worth in its members'.

Setting objectives does not mean much without securing commitment to achieving them. Such commitment comes from clarity and understanding, which are what the first three steps in the co-creation process are designed to achieve. It also results from ensuring that what is agreed aligns with people's values.

Language is important in this process – use words such as 'personally', 'engage', 'commit', 'accountable'. You could consider mirroring some of the language used in the oath a new president makes in taking office, as it crystallises the leader's accountability and responsibility when representing values and commitment. Expressing commitment in front of others also gives some solemnity to the exercise and can be a powerful way to create a positive sort of discomfort.

Once the objectives have been set, ask for team members to state their personal commitment to act to deliver the co-created agenda.

For the most efficient outcome to co-creation and goals and objectives, two simple rules are helpful:

- Keep it simple – avoid complexity. Set a reasonable number of straightforward targets for the team as this creates a culture of execution.

- Ensure that the targets are clearly defined and focus on *what* needs to be achieved, not *how* it should be achieved. This should be left to the team members to work on so that they can bring their own ideas and personality to the task. This is part of the empowerment and trust process.

Figure 7.3 summarises a co-creation process.

Aligning individual and organisational goals

Building rapport is the first step in motivating people. It shows a will to connect at the personal level and a commitment to investing time in them.

Setting team objectives in the process of co-creation is the second step – albeit an important one. Co-creation is a powerful way to recognise the intrinsic value of each and every one of your subordinates. Additionally, it builds positive team dynamics and contributes to creating a trusting and safe environment.

To truly motivate team members to deliver for you, merge the following:

- the insights gathered about your team members – their motivations, needs and dreams

- the co-created goals to develop these individuals' objectives. Figure 7.4 summarises the process.

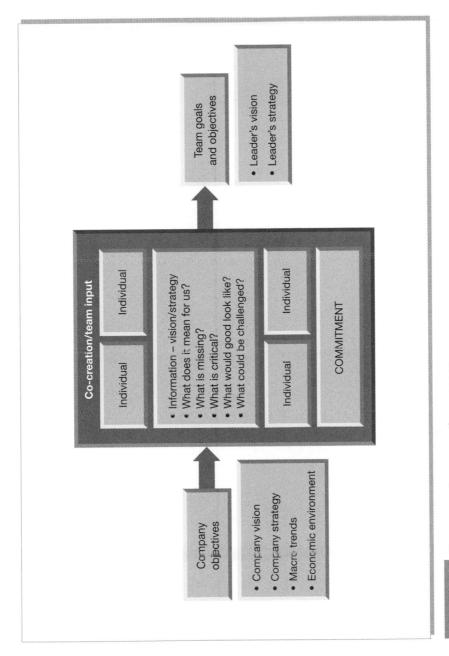

Figure 7.3 Summary of a co-creation process

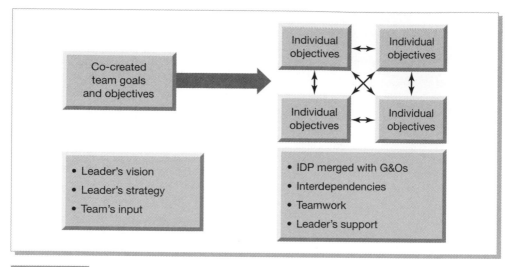

Figure 7.4 How to increase motivation and alignment

In doing this, leaders demonstrate that they are taking into account individuals' needs and wants. This gives team members a sense of empowerment and control over their own destiny and yet, at the same time, the company's goals are also being worked towards. Essentially, this meshes individual and organisational needs.

To ensure that this is the outcome leaders should invest the necessary time in setting adequate objectives with individual team members. Consider doing the following:

- Take the time to hold two comprehensive sessions of one or one and half hours per direct report – this is the foundation of a winning delivery strategy.

- It is recommended that you do not schedule these at the end of a busy day or week as you will need to be in a listening and problem solving mode. From a personal branding perspective, poor scheduling can send the wrong signal about your priorities – that the team and people are the last thing on your agenda.

- Holding all the sessions in the same week can present you with the global picture, enabling you to then draw up an action plan having a clear vision of how everyone in the team can contribute.

For a fully comprehensive, individual, co-creation goal-setting exercise, follow these three steps:

- **Preparation work** Individual needs are reviewed and the leader creates a mental picture of what might be beneficial for both employees and the organisation.

- **Hold two meetings** In the first, the team member expresses his or her views and needs while the leader listens and decides on areas of agreement. In the second, the team member and leader compare thoughts and settle on co-created objectives.

- **The handshake** This happens at the end of the session – the moment when the terms of the contract between the leader and the team member are crystallised, including what each will deliver. The right balance needs to be struck between what the team member needs and what the company or the leader needs. What is agreed has to be compelling.

The above can be complemented by also systematically ensuring that team members enjoy job enrichment. In his *Harvard Business Review* article 'One more time: How do you motivate your employees', Frederick Herzberg (January 2003) presents job enrichment as a sophisticated way of factoring employees' desires and needs into the crafting of meaningful goals and objectives. He states that if you:

- empower individuals by removing controls, you will increase their accountability

- stretch people constantly, you will increase their sense of belonging and self-worth – for example, by giving them responsibility for a complete process or unit of work, letting them take on new or more difficult tasks or encouraging them to become a subject matter expert for the group

- communicate and share information directly with individuals, not their managers first, you will enhance their motivation and sense of achievement.

Herzberg also states that it is desirable for leaders to be self-confident and master their fear of not being needed. Leaders need to embrace what they are really there to do – develop people.

While engaging with your employees, make sure that you also address the ways in which you will be working – that is, how you will interact with them. Keep the concept of job enrichment in mind and express your commitment to them as well. Over the course of the year, or when you are reflecting on your own behaviour, ensure that you are delivering on or behaving in a way that complies with this commitment.

This creates a virtuous circle and enhances the company's performance, too.

Although it is not an intuitive or common practice, crafting team and individual objectives by means of the co-creation process is a highly efficient way to ensure that there is alignment of goals and motivation, as the objectives come out of dialogue and respect. This helps to generate a greater sense of commitment and accountability as a result of the feeling of community and shared success generated.

Figure 7.5 summarises these new ways to create high-performance teams, meshing all the critical dimensions – the company's objectives, leader's vision, individual members' needs and team interdependencies.

Exercises and action points

How to handle co-creation of personal objectives with team members

Preparation work

■ Review the IDPs of all direct reports *vis-à-vis* the agreed team goals and objectives. This helps the leader to create a mind map, identifying which are the natural pairings for achieving maximum results and assessing what goals are most or least likely to build on the team's strengths. For example, if one team member needs to develop his communication skills, another needs to work on his listening skills and strategic thinking, and one of the team's objectives is to foster business partnering, pair these two members to work on presenting a business plan to the sales team.

First meeting:

■ The direct report is in charge of this meeting. The leader's role is to steer the discussion and keep in mind the team's mind map and company's objectives, while listening to the team member's needs.

▶

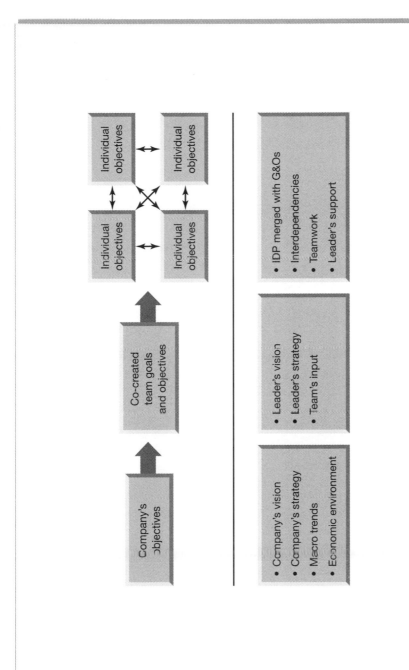

Figure 7.5   Co-creation – How to create high-performance teams

▶

- Start by reviewing the direct report's individual development plan. Compare and contrast *vis-à-vis* the team's goals and objectives.

- Discuss with the team member, translating his or her needs into actions that address the team's goals and objectives. This may feel uncomfortable at first, for your subordinate to feel so empowered, so ease the process by asking the following questions.
  - What do you want to achieve or develop in the coming period?
  - How do you see the company's objectives matching your needs?
  - What do you think is missing?
  - What do you think you need or who do you think you need?
  - What should we factor in to help you grow? How could we stretch you?

- Make sure that you adjust the style of the meeting and the questions asked as required to suit team members' cultural backgrounds and take into consideration what you already know about them.

- Address and discuss interdependencies relating to goals and needs, as identified in your preparation work. This strengthens the spirit of collaboration and the sense of being a team.

- Communicate how you will personally support and, at times, challenge the team member in reaching his or her objectives.

- Close the discussion by asking him or her to reflect on the questions above and propose G&Os that resonate with him or her and are aligned with the team's objectives.

Second meeting, gaining commitment and the handshake

- The purpose of this meeting is to review a subordinate's G&Os, assess them for relevance and accuracy and gain his or her personal commitment. To ensure commitment, it is important to take care over the language used. Employ strong words such as 'personally', 'engage' and 'commit'. It may also help to ask your team member to state, 'I personally commit to ...'.

- Finally, shake hands to reinforce the commitment made.

Giving feedback and recognising and rewarding performance

Motivating a team is an on-going process and one of the key parts of what a leader does. It is achieved by being constantly aware of the levels of motivation of your team, providing regular feedback and developing mechanisms to reward and recognise people's efforts.

Taking the pulse of your team's motivation

The rhythm of communication presented in the section 'Maintaining the relationship', earlier in this chapter, gives three practical and effective ways to keep your finger on the pulse of your team. For instance, make one of your weekly or bi-weekly meetings with them, about them. This is beneficial for your personal brand and increases trust and respect. More generally, setting up a quarterly meeting to discuss each team member's motivation, needs and progress is highly recommended.

Providing regular feedback

Giving feedback is not easy – leaders need to show empathy, yet also be able, at times, to convey difficult messages. Feedback can be given via a mix of structured sessions and ad hoc.

In a formal feedback process, the purpose is to reassess goals and objectives, the individual development plan or a co-created hybrid document resulting from the goal-setting exercise described in the previous section. It helps to measure progress and potentially recalibrate behaviours. Refer again to the exercise above, 'How to handle co-creation of personal objectives with team members'. The same principles may be applied here, as well as factoring in the following:

- include an external stakeholder's feedback for a balanced view of their performance
- gather specific facts – feedback is only useful if it is precise and tangible (especially negative feedback) and is not based on impressions or hearsay (this is why observing your team members in situ and taking notes is useful)

- providing *positive* feedback as much as areas for improvement will support positive reinforcement, as described in Chapter 3

- take the opportunity to also elicit feedback about yourself via these sessions, as this will reinforce the reciprocity of the process and help to establish the value of the interdependencies of success (leaders and teams).

Complement formal feedback sessions with regular on-the-spot feedback. This might involve debriefing team members on their performance after a meeting or a presentation. It helps them relate their behaviours to real-life events.

Feedback plays an important part in any individual's motivation, showing that you care about their growth and development. Negative feedback, if delivered in a constructive way, is also beneficial. Leaders are role models for the individual's development.

When uncertain as to which approach to take or behaviours to demonstrate, holding up a mirror to yourself and thinking about the following might help:

- How would you like to receive negative/positive feedback?

- How would you have reacted to how the feedback was given?

Giving negative feedback is definitely something that most leaders or managers dread and, at times, shy away from. Some will argue that there is a strong correlation between tolerance of conflict and the ability to give negative feedback. Others correlate the sense of accountability (or lack of) in any corporate culture with the ability to give negative feedback and handle consequence management.

There is no doubt, giving negative feedback is difficult. As a leader, you need to find the right balance between getting your message across and preserving your employees' motivation.

It can trigger and/or resonate with your own insecurities. It can even send you into a spiral of self-doubt – the 'Is this person really that bad or is it me?' moment. Also, it can have an emotional impact on you, facing and handling others' reactions – especially if the person is in denial.

The following techniques have proved particularly helpful when it comes to giving negative feedback – even more so in the extreme cases of firing someone or making them redundant.

Follow a process

Negative feedback cannot come out of the blue – it is important to provide enough signs of your discontent previously to prepare your team member for what is to come and alleviate the risks of an emotional reaction.

When, say, the performance of one of your team members is below par, make a point of addressing it in ad hoc comments or even by having a friendly warning conversation. You can frame it in an 'I am concerned about your performance lately – is everything OK? Do you want to talk about it?' way. Showing concern and enquiring about the person's well-being will defuse aggressive behaviour. It will also provide a chance for him or her to turn things around.

If things do not improve, it is highly recommended that you log specific situations when performance or behaviours were not up to standard (poor-quality work, not meeting deadlines, for example) before moving to the next step. Then arrange a formal meeting with a telling title – feedback session or performance discussion – so there is no misconception as to what the meeting will be about.[5]

Data

Negative feedback can only be valid if it is well documented and presented with as much objectivity as possible. Also, as mentioned above, it is critical that you are able to substantiate the whys of your negative feedback with concrete examples and situations – dates and details of situations, indicating who did what, are very helpful.

Additionally, quietly enquiring about the person when you are talking with peers and other major stakeholders is also recommended. This will be useful in terms of presenting not only a documented but also a balanced view of the negative feedback and alleviate the risk of claims seeming to be purely personal.

---

[5] It goes without saying that you would not use a title such as 'Firing meeting' or 'Redundancy meeting' but something more subtle: 'Feedback' or 'Career discussion' would be good.

Preparation

Being well prepared is critical when giving negative feedback.

It will help to clearly articulate what you have to say and find the right rhythm.

It is also wise to enable yourself to create some mental space while in the meeting and be able to stay in tune with the other party – by means of body language and so on – so you can gauge if you have to stop the meeting or reconvene.

It will help, too, if you create a certain emotional distance from the situation, as this will help you to keep calm.

Consider investing some time preparing with someone from your feedback group, perhaps role-playing the scenario. That way you can test your flow, vocabulary and rhythm. Try it both as you and then as the recipient of the feedback to get an idea of how it can sound and feel, and adjust what you do accordingly.

Timing

Given that negative feedback sessions can become emotional events, it is preferable to schedule them in the morning, when you are likely to be in a good mental space and able to handle any reaction.

If this is not logistically possible, make sure you have enough time to regroup after completing your previous meeting, quieten and focus before starting the session.

Equally important, is to gauge the emotional state of the person receiving the feedback (or being fired). If you sense that he or she is too stressed or tense (perhaps fidgeting, avoiding eye contact and so on) feel free to reschedule the meeting.

Conducting the meeting

The most important thing is to make sure you tune into the other person.

If you feel that he or she is not receptive any more – perhaps crying, agitated or in a state of shock – it is highly recommended you stop.

You can, for instance, say, 'I can see you are in a state of shock' or 'I believe it is better you digest the information before we continue.'

It is important to ensure that you do not give in to anger and emotion. Also, try as much as you can to stick to the script.

In the case of firing an employee, you do not have to conduct the meeting alone and can choose to ask for support from someone from the human resources department or have that person on standby.

If the meeting goes badly, it is important to ensure that the person gets home safely. A member of your team could look after him or her and enquire how he or she is the next day. If the person does come in to work, make sure you liaise with the human resources department.

Finally, be familiar with the five-step process that individuals go through when confronted with traumatic situations:

- denial
- anger
- bargaining
- depression
- acceptance.

This is also known as the Kübler Ross model and it can help you make sense of and/or reframe the situation.

Giving negative feedback is part and parcel of being a leader and, unfortunately, firing or managing out employees is part of the bank of experience that you need to become a credible leader.

Reward and recognition

Reward and recognition are critical constituents of motivation and should not be overlooked. Rewards have a financial impact while recognition has more of an emotional one. Both are equally important for sustaining a team's motivation and both can be used at the individual or team levels to maintain healthy competition and foster collaboration. Both are also usually discretionary and decided by leaders.

There are seven key principles for establishing an efficient reward and recognition programme:

- **Make it genuine** Reward and recognise achievements above and beyond the call of duty – not people just doing their jobs. Then you will push people to excel.

- **Recognise both doing and being** Reward and recognise both results and behaviours. For instance, achieving quarterly targets is great, but preventing a highly strategic customer from walking away is equally great, as is showing a high level of integrity (even if it has a negative impact on someone's results). It needs to address the entirety of people's skill sets.

- **Ensure it is aligned with core values** Reward and recognise based on the leader's values and those of the company. This strengthens a sense of belonging and shows consistency.

- **Account for individual and team dimensions** Leaders need to keep both in mind.

- **Know when to reward and when to recognise** Leaders need to use what they know about their subordinates to properly employ reward v. recognition. For example, if one person is impaired by a sense of failure, public recognition might be a better way than financial reward. It will increase your brand of being an inclusive leader.

- **Foster friendly competition** The idea is to encourage the team, make its members want to be the best they can be. Leaders need to inspire excellence, to drive higher levels of business performance.

- **Make it personal and special** If it fits with the leader's personal style, it can even be fun. Carefully crafted, it will convey that you know your team and care for people.

A comprehensive reward and recognition programme might look something like that set out in Table 7.2.

Table 7.2 Example of a comprehensive reward and recognition programme

	Rewards	Recognition
Individuals (ongoing)	• Financial compensation • Night on the town with partner • Day off to compensate for long hours	• Personal handwritten 'thank you' notes (with financial reward, after successful completion of big project, at year-end, etc.) • Thanks for a job well done
Team (quarterly)	• Propose your team for leaders' awards (CEO, CFO, business units, etc). • Financial compensation	• Quarterly announcement of highest achievements or performance (webcast and/or e-mails) • Includes friendly competition in teambuilding

One powerful exercise to consider doing with your team is to co-create a reward and recognition programme for the entire business unit/function you are responsible for – this has the potential to add a lot of value to the company's performance. As a leader, you have less and less direct control over delivery. Investing time at the beginning in building solid relationships, co-creating solid objectives and reflecting on how people will be rewarded will translate into increased performance.

Aligning, inspiring and motivating is what leaders do. Being collaborative, inclusive and empathic is what excellent leaders of the future are.

Exercises and action points

How to prepare for a formal feedback session with team members

The following questions can be used as pointers for a feedback session with team members. They can be answered and analysed in advance of the session:

- What do you think were your biggest achievements this quarter and why?

- What do you think were your shortcomings and why?

- What do you think you could have done differently?

- What do you want to start doing?

▶

- What do you want to stop doing?

- How do you think you have performed?

These questions act as a performance self-assessment for team members and give pointers to the things that motivate them and the things that derail them. They help to locate and calibrate perception gaps and establish how best to handle the session.

In the session itself, it is important to keep the following in mind:

- Do not hold the meeting if you are not in a balanced emotional state.

- Pay attention to the atmosphere in the room, especially if you are about to give negative feedback to someone.

- Listen, listen and listen.

- Stick to facts as much as you can, without emotion.

Summary

Building a team is as much about building the different members of the team as it is about focusing on the team itself. It takes time and requires passion and investment. Successfully built and led teams are like ecosystems where members feed off each other's energy, build on each other's strengths and, to some extent, counterbalance each other's weaknesses. However, it is important to recognise that teams are fluid and people change and evolve.

For a leader, it is critical to keep track and take stock. It is also important to renew and replenish energy with celebration and recognition, as successful teams perform at a high level and deliver.

'If a leader is a person who inspires and motivates his/her team to do things proactively and to think by themselves, then I do not find many around me. I would like to see leaders mobilising their workforce around a purpose, an objective, and stop giving too much direct guidance or actually trying to consistently micromanage.

I would like to see a leader drawing from a wide array of experience in the team, not imposing a view. I would like to see leaders taking chances with people to help them grow and develop. I have also observed that inspiring and motivating is not seen as a must have in some corporations, whereas to me it is at the essence of leadership, a natural ability to unleash people's potential.'

Interview with Sherene Metwally, Downstream LNG Finance
Manager Europe and Global Support for Royal Dutch Shell

A good analogy for great teambuilding and leading is that of an orchestra conductor. The conductor's primary duties are to unify performers (build rapport and know teams), set the tempo (be a role model and use co-creation), execute clear preparations (set objectives and deliver) and listen critically (give feedback).

This is what all should aim to become on their road to leadership.

Here's a reminder of some of the key points from this chapter:

- invest time in knowing your team members as people, with desires, needs, emotions, backgrounds and dreams

- observe, learn and spend time with them – increase both formal and informal interactions, where you can also let them know the person you are above and beyond being their leader as this creates a beneficial reciprocity and, in the long term, ensures loyalty

- trust, respect and inclusiveness is the name of the game – develop systems and questioning, complemented by your demonstration of certain behaviours, that will lead to fostering the right environment to produce a high-performance team

- advocate and practise co-creation – it will help you get strong commitment from your team members, as they will have a purpose and feel empowered

- make sure the individual dimension is catered for in your goals and objectives – again, it will further strengthen loyalty and accountability. 'What is in it for them?' is the question to keep in mind

- feedback is the breakfast of champions – craft a system that mixes formal and informal, structured and ad hoc feedback

- reward and recognise your team and team members on a regular basis – be present and engaged and make sure you give praise for what matters and what is above and beyond the call of duty; doing *and* being are both needed to foster what will add value to the business.

8

The art of influence

'The greatest ability in business is to get along with others and to influence their actions.'

John Hancock, American politician

This chapter covers:

- what influence is and how it relates to power and authority

- the attributes of influential leaders

- group dynamics, alphas and the underestimated power of body language

- the importance of stakeholders and how to manage them efficiently to reach desirable outcomes

- the importance of multiple and diverse networks to sustaining performance and creating value for the company.

Rasputin and Olympes de Gouges

Gregory Rasputin was a nineteenth-century Russian mystic. The self-proclaimed holy man schmoozed his way into the Romanov Court at a time when both the empire and the Church were looking to rekindle their divine authority. He played on the Empress' sense of guilt at having introduced haemophilia into the Russian imperial family line and benefited from the Russian family tradition of seeking the intervention of holy men for different purposes.

Having apparently managed to heal the infant heir to the Russian throne from haemophilia, he established significant influence over the Romanovs. When Emperor Nicolas decided to lead the army personally in the war with Germany, leaving the Empress to rule the country, Rasputin became the decisive influence in internal affairs. It led to the appointment of one of his protégés as Minister of War, at a critical time during the war against Germany and subsequently to thousands of deaths. This was followed shortly afterwards by the abdication of Tsar Nicolas and the assassination of the Russian reigning family. Rasputin's influence brought to an end 300 years of history and took Russia into communism.

▶

▶

Olympe de Gouges was an intellectual of the French Revolution and is often seen as the founder of feminism. She became fascinated by the ideas and the passion of the Revolution and began to write about politics. She denounced extremism of all kinds and promoted human rights. Her profound belief in the complete equality of all human beings and rejection of social conventions made her a prominent figure in the newly formed feminist circles. She wrote the 'Declaration of the Rights of Woman and of the Citizen', which was published in 1791. The document was written in a language similar to the Rights of Man and called for the rights to be extended to women, including freedom of speech, the right to vote and the opportunity to be elected.

She advocated a complete legal equality of the sexes to the newly formed French National Assembly. Although she was sent to the guillotine in 1793, she opened the doors for a public conversation on the subject of women's rights. She fought to broaden the definition of a women's role in society and planted the seeds of modern feminism.

What conclusions can be drawn from these examples? Influence is irrational and somewhat unexplainable. It may have a negative effect when it plays on people's fears or is not exercised in line with values. Equally, it may help to bring about changes for good and have a positive impact on the world. It is rooted in charisma, inspiration and credibility.

Increasingly, businesses need to develop sustainable alliances and competitive advantages in order to survive and succeed in highly competitive and globalised markets. Corporate structures face increasing numbers of interdependencies, which can lead to conflicting or competing priorities.

What does influence mean when applied to the corporate and business environment?

It can be defined as the ability to reach desired outcomes for your sphere of control when dealing with areas or individuals outside of that sphere or being confronted with resistance within it.

Influence is, first and foremost, founded on the intrinsic values of the individual, but is enhanced by two key elements:

■ **The capacity to assess the environment** How can leaders quickly grasp group and stakeholder dynamics? How can they then transform the dynamics in a group to their advantage?

■ **The capacity to build diverse and long-lasting networks** How can leaders increase their strategic and operational influences over time?

Stakeholders, group dynamics and you

Leadership is never exercised in a vacuum – it involves observing and 'playing' the environment. Establishing long-lasting influence comes from a deep understanding of your stakeholders and crafting specific strategies to manage them – ranging from looking for involvement to endorsement to merely informing. Influence is also built on an ability to quickly assess who are the leaders in any group – formal or informal – paired with the skill to play different roles, in different group dynamics. Finally, developing the ability to 'read' people by means of body language can create a competitive advantage by providing an innovative way to influence others.

Understanding how to increase and when to exercise influence is a powerful way to achieve faster decision making, enhance motivation and, ultimately, pave the way to more effective delivery.

Stakeholder management

Who will make the decision to promote me in the future? Who do I need to gain agreement from for this project to go smoothly? Who do I need to watch and manage to alleviate all the risks of delay or failure for this particular project? These are the questions that are prevalent in stakeholder mapping and require you to exercise your role of gaining agreement from people. This will show how efficient and effective you can be as a leader.

To undertake stakeholder mapping you need to understand who your stakeholders are, analyse them and then craft an adequate strategy to manage them.

Understanding who your stakeholders are

Take stock of the different layers of stakeholders and always remain aware of the less obvious ones. A 'stakeholder' can be defined as anyone with a form of decision making power or whose endorsement is needed or opinion is important for any effort undertaken.

In order to spot your stakeholders, keep in mind the following:

- stakeholders have some accountability in terms of what needs to be achieved
- they may differ or overlap depending on your objectives and deliverables
- they can be internal or external.

Consider systematically setting aside time to have a stakeholder mapping session whenever you are starting a new project, establishing yourself as the new leader of a team or any time you feel you need a clear understanding of politics in order to achieve quicker delivery.

The best way to gain full benefit from a systematic stakeholder mapping session is to reflect on the following questions:

- Who would be primarily accountable for the project?
- Who could have the biggest impact on the project – positive or negative?
- Who would most benefit from the project?
- Who would the project impact the most – positively or negatively?
- Who could derail delivery and execution of the project?
- Who could be the best endorser or supporter of the project and why?

Think about the answers to these questions from all possible angles – economic, social, regulatory, impacts and so on – to ensure that you are looking at it as broadly and completely as possible. For example, imagine you are the leader of a business unit and you want to change its strategic direction to comply with a change in the legal system. The window to perform the change is very short and execution is key. Your stakeholders will be:

- your own boss – he or she has the ultimate responsibility for the business unit's profit and loss
- head of the legal department – a key person, who will allocate proper resources to explain the change

- head of investor relations – could be key if the change has a material impact on the results or if it triggers a new reporting structure that will be scrutinised by analysts

- if the latter is the case, the finance and controlling function and, potentially, your customers – they would need to be informed if the change has consequences on processes or costs.

Here's another scenario: you are the CFO of the business and have been tasked with outsourcing 20 per cent of your workforce by the end of the year. Your stakeholders in this case will be:

- your team members – they will need to accept the decision and progress the necessary actions to make this happen

- the human resources department – it will need to be informed of the headcount changes and where the people are located to help plan potential consultations or redundancy processes and provide adequate information for recording of impending liabilities (redundancy provisions, retirement elements and so on)

- the legal department – in case of litigation.

Performing this exercise will lay solid foundations that will enable you to quickly grasp and navigate your environment.

Analysing or mapping your stakeholders

Once you have identified who your stakeholders are, it is necessary to 'map' them by looking at their:

- **influence and power** – this helps you identify who matters and who will be listened to

- **interest** – finding common interests enables collaboration and faster solutions or delivery.

Managing your stakeholders

This means being able devise strategies for what to do with different stakeholders to progress towards the desired outcome.

Once you have identified who your stakeholders are, using the previous questions to categorise them and draft a strategy to proactively manage them has proved to be useful. The ultimate outcome and purpose of the mapping and strategies that follow are to manage your time and effort so that you spend it on what will yield the best results in the least amount of time.

Figure 8.1 illustrates the four different categories of strategies there are and which ones to implement depending on stakeholders' level of power and influence in combination with their interest.

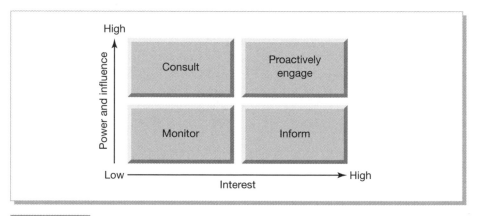

Figure 8.1 Which strategies to use depending on stakeholder factors

For stakeholders with low levels of power and influence

These stakeholders do not have a critical say or real decision making power in relation to any initiatives. However, they can end up blocking or derailing a project if they have no interest in the decision and are not managed properly. Equally, they can turn into great advocates and may even prove to be an additional source of influence over other stakeholders if they do demonstrate interest in the topic.

It is important to either monitor (assessing if there are any potential roadblocks) or inform them to create a positive perception. Monitoring can take the form of ad hoc meetings to understand how they are personally with the change resulting from the initiatives and what actions they are taking. Informing could be a regular status report on important milestones in the project. This will ensure that they are aware of progress and know how they can support you if need be.

Monitoring and informing do not require a lot of time to be invested, but they help to position you as engaging, a good communicator. They are also useful for building consensus.

For stakeholders with high levels of power and influence

These stakeholders are the real decision makers and can make or break ideas, projects or initiatives.

If they have a high level of interest in the project, it is critical to pro-actively engage or even co-create with them to get their commitment early on. This will enable you to communicate to others that they are on board if any issues arise or for them to act as sponsors. If, however, they show limited interest in the process, using them as a sounding or advisory board by consulting with them will secure their support. They can also act as endorsers.

- **Proactively engaging with stakeholders** This can take the form of weekly or bi-weekly meetings, aiming to first present the strategy and action plan, then inform them of progress and issues. It should also address your needs or issues.

- **Consulting with stakeholders** This can be done on a more ad hoc basis or if a crisis emerges, in the form of a consulting board. It should focus on getting an independent view or advice on actions taken or problems that need to be solved.

Both engaging and consulting require some investment of time, but enable the speedy execution and fast resolution of issues. They also allow you access to proper sponsorship and endorsement if and when they should be needed. At the personal brand level, this adds to your credibility as trust and respect are developed in the process.

When and how to use stakeholder mapping

Stakeholder mapping may be used for a wide range of projects and situations, including:

- **internal projects** either for business units or cross-functional situations

- **strategic or customer-facing projects** when the definitions of your stakeholders take on an external dimension (for example, government officials, regulators, business partners)

- **customer negotiations**

- **deal making** so the mix of internal and external stakeholders to take into consideration is clear and, if necessary, the public relations department can be involved to create a fit-for-purpose monitoring or informing process

- **creating a new business or strategy**.

As business environments and circumstances are evolving so quickly, consider recalibrating your stakeholder maps on a regular basis. Consider reviewing them when:

- some key milestones have been achieved

- critical changes have taken place in the external environment – for example, changes in government regulations, management of a customer or future business partner, government officials or political regime

- something has changed in the company – such as a strategy or there has been a promotion, demotion or the departure of previously identified key stakeholders, which could lead to changes in the balance of interest and influence.

Undertaking comprehensive stakeholder mapping, including crafting your stakeholder management strategy, will probably take around two hours. Thereafter, it is a good idea to proactively set aside times with your different categories of stakeholders in order to ensure that the strategies consistently deliver the desired results.

Using stakeholder mapping in a systematic way for every significant project is a valuable exercise, as it helps in the achievement of your objectives or to gain experience or increase your credibility. It helps crystallise key relationships and transforms thinking by means of tangible actions. It helps you to stay abreast of changes in the organisations you are working with, to keep up the momentum and quickly make adjustments for maximum and efficient delivery.

Additionally, pairing this session with a co-creation session can prove tremendously efficient and has a great impact. It allows you to align everyone's objectives with your team while proactively identifying what and who are critical to the delivery of a project. It can lead to pairing team members with critical stakeholders (those in the high levels of power and influence category) to increase their visibility and exposure. Finally, it reinforces the feeling of community within the team.

Exercises and action points

Run a stakeholder mapping session with your team

If you do this as part of a team co-creation exercise, consider running it as a full-day meeting with three distinct sessions as follows.

First session

Brainstorm by inviting all your team members to voice their thoughts in relation to all the questions listed in the earlier section in this chapter entitled 'Understanding who your stakeholders are'. Make sure everyone is contributing by watching and monitoring everyone else's actions in the room. Your main role is to focus on these questions:

- Who else are we missing or overlooking?
- What else are we not thinking about?

Second session

Rationalise your stakeholder lists and decide which factors shown in Figure 8.1 apply to each and, therefore, which of the strategies is appropriate.

The purpose of the session is to challenge what has been said and discuss the factors of power and influence and interest. What do they mean in your context? It is also about letting the team's dynamics play out. Your role in this session is to push for a bit of controversy and manage tension if some arises. You will also have the final say about which strategy is used for which stakeholder.

Final session

This is an accountability session. It is about deciding jointly who will be specifically in charge of handling which stakeholders, almost marking each as you would in a game of football. As leader, keep in mind the relevance and interpersonal skills of your team members, and what their areas for development should be to ensure good matches. In some cases, direct them to pair with others who have different styles of working and are not a natural match for each other so as to develop the positive quality of inclusiveness in the team.

Making the most of group dynamics

'Group dynamics' are any group boundaries, differences in power, emotions, understandings and leadership behaviour and how they impact individuals' behaviours. Gaining and exercising influence in groups (team meetings, external meetings, conferences to name a few) has proved to be effective in establishing yourself as a leader.

Group dynamics is a huge subject in itself, but the two main points to focus on when applied to leadership and influence are the ability to spot the alphas and informal leaders.

What alphas are and how to influence them

One of the quickest ways to increase your own influence is to be perceived as an influencer of the alphas (male or female).

The term 'alpha' is inherited from the animal kingdom, where it is used to describe the physical dominance of some males over other males. In their article 'Coaching the alpha male' in the *Harvard Business Review* (May 2004), Kate Ludeman and Eddie Erlandson define the modern and corporate human alphas as highly intelligent, confident and successful people. They are bright, quick in their assessment of people and situations and do not change their minds easily. Both alpha males and females are truly happy when they are the ultimate decision makers, feel accountable and hold a high level of responsibility.

Identifying who are the alphas in group meetings is rooted in observation. They will always surface as the driving force of a group and demonstrate:

- a high level of energy and self-confidence
- eagerness to express their opinions
- self-confidence, bordering on arrogance
- unawareness or insensitivity to people's emotions
- a focus on the flaws in others' arguments
- curiosity about business challenges and data
- a lack of fear of conflict (or even a tendency to stir up conflict) – in the case of an alpha male
- a tendency to adopt a more collaborative approach and avoid clashes – in the case of alpha females.

Generally, the alphas are the formal leaders of any group – they will be easy to spot as they are the ones everyone naturally gravitates towards during breaks. However, this is not always the case, so observing who everyone naturally defers to for approval or endorsement is a good indicator of who the real alphas are. Other signs will be:

- the quality of listening in the group when some individuals speak – a sense of respect or deference will indicate the presence of an alpha

- how often the 'formal' leader of the group will address or ask for the opinion of another team member – if one person stands out, that person will probably be another alpha

- the impact of alphas on the body language of other people (see later in this chapter).

A beneficial approach is to define a strategy to manage and influence both formal and informal group leaders.

The basic principles for establishing rapport with team members (see Chapter 7) are equally useful for doing so with alphas. However, the following points need to be added when it comes to communicating with them specifically or attracting their interest in team meetings:

- Get straight to the point and be action orientated. Focus on the solution and come prepared to substantiate your recommendations as you will, more than likely, be challenged.

- Master 'report talk' as alphas are sensitive to establishing facts and gaining power. Deborah Tannen, author of *You Just Don't Understand: Women and men in conversation* (Virago, 1992) came up with this term. Her research shows that men feel more comfortable with 'report talk' that focuses on status, independence, advice, information, orders and conflict. Women prefer 'rapport talk', which focuses on support, intimacy, understanding, feelings, proposals and compromise.

- Sound confident and authoritative – you want to be taken seriously.

- Sound in control of your team and actions by using active sentences.

- Engage their egos using approaches such as, 'Have you considered …?' This is a great way to get commitment and make the idea 'theirs'.

- Be passionate – passion conveys power and power engages alphas.

What informal leaders are and how to influence them

Groups tend to rely on informal leaders to both influence members' thinking and progress decision making and actions. They are not necessarily alphas, though they are well respected due to their personalities, specific expertise or simply perceived status in the organisation. Informal leaders are usually the quiet ones who everyone listens to in the end.

To spot who the informal leaders are, follow the same strategy as for the alphas, observing and taking mental notes. Who is the one who can swing opinion in a discussion? Who is the one to whom everyone defers when some smoothing over is required in any situation?

Also pay particular attention to who it is the alphas will naturally turn to for ad hoc checks or to see reactions, such as when something controversial or innovative is said. One common trait of informal leaders is that they are often the last to speak.

---

12 Angry Men – a classic example of increasing influence

An interesting example of how to increase influence is demonstrated in Sidney Lumet's film *12 Angry Men*.

The plot is that a dissenting juror in a murder trial slowly manages to convince the others that the case is not as clear cut as it seemed in court. In the course of the film, this juror comes to establish a bond with every one of the other jurors, to understand their motivations and bias, and, thus, manages to change their minds using credibility and rationale.

Try watching the film, analysing it and keep in mind the following:

- Who appears to be the alpha?
- Who is the informal leader?
- What types of techniques are used to change jurors' minds? Fact, emotions, values, and so on.
- How long does it take to work on each one and when does the need to comply start kicking in?

This is not an exhaustive list but gives you some pointers.

To influence informal leaders, it is critical to develop enough rapport with them to cultivate their behind-the-scenes support. Their commitment is vital if grass-roots support is to be generated for an idea – they can be relied on to sell the ideas to other team members.

The notions of alphas, informal leaders and how to influence are equally valid when you are in a group of leaders. Recognising these types of leaders will help you increase your own credibility as a good leader or a person with a lot of potential. This skill is equally useful when you are in a meeting with the team you spearhead. It is also a very useful skill when dealing with customers, suppliers or any external organisations. Furthermore, it can be a great help when playing the game of office politics.

Exercises and action points

Hone your abilities to sense group dynamics

To master group dynamics, you need to develop your senses, mainly by means of observation. It can prove to be an interesting exercise to be 'in' the meeting – in other words, to focus 100 per cent on what is being said and participate while at the same time be 'above' the meeting to observe its dynamics. The best way to manage this is to stick to three simple rules.

Be prepared

This is particularly important when you are a new member of a leadership team or a new leader of any team. Invest time in gathering data from your networks, your feedback group or even your predecessor to get a high-level picture of the team's dynamics. You can be open and honest about it and ask the following three questions:

- Who would you say counts as the heavyweight in the team and why? They may choose on the basis of the mix of expertise, scope of responsibility and so on.

- What do you need to know about these people? How do they operate?

- Who is the biggest influence on the leader? Who does he or she listen to? The corollary to that question is, who has the power to counter that of the leader?

Be selective

During meetings, you will naturally have more interest in or impact on some topics than others. When preparing, select which topics you will use to switch from participating to observing your environment. When observing, pay attention to changes in atmosphere, body language, side conversations, even who sits where are all very revealing of team dynamics. Take as many notes as you can.

▶

▶

Use the break

A useful tool. During breaks, observe who congregates naturally with whom, how social groups form, who is the loner, who moves from group to group and so on.

Make sure that you record all your observations and factor in any other activities, such as stakeholder mapping, project endorsement, ensuring agreement before decisions are made and so on.

Fulfilling a clear role in meetings

Increasing your influence is about having an impact in every meeting you go to. It helps with leadership branding and credibility (see Chapters 5 and 6 for more on this). It is important to keep in mind the bigger role you serve in the meeting, above and beyond your job title. The role you want to play will change depending on the type of meeting you are attending.

Choose an angle and make sure you act in accordance with the approach you have selected. This will definitely help you to have a greater influence in meetings. To test how efficient you have been, ask for feedback on how you came across in a meeting *vis-à-vis* the role you chose to play – this is also a good way to measure your level of influence.

Exercises and action points

The key to establishing yourself as an influencer

Preparation is key to adequately fostering your influence. Before any meetings, ask yourself the following question:

■ What am I personally bringing to this meeting that no one else can bring? What is my angle or my edge?

You can choose to be the challenger of the status quo or the one asking the difficult question.

You can choose to be the visionary, reflecting on the global impact for the organisation or the industry of what is under discussion.

▶

You can choose to be the ideas person, systematically throwing new angles of thinking into the conversation.

You can choose to be the voice of the team or practicality, pushing for simplicity or cutting through complexity.

You can position yourself as the functional expert and provide a specific perspective on, say, finance or marketing.

During meetings, keep demonstrating the attributes of the role you want to play and be consistent, even if sometimes you choose an alternative one. This all helps to develop your leadership brand.

Using body language to influence

'When my current CEO flexes his eyebrows, I know I will not get him to agree with me, so when I am discussing with him I look for that very cue and know when it is time to back off. Interestingly enough, this helped me establish myself as a great influencer of our leader. People come to me for help and I am perceived as an important stakeholder to have on board when important decisions, even outside my area of control, need to be taken. It helped me move ahead'

Interview with Estelle Clark,
Group Business Assurance Director, Lloyd's Register

Research suggests that approximately 55 per cent of the way human beings communicate is non-verbal. Regardless of emotional state, culture or gender, some key universal principles underpin body language.[1] Generally, we leak information about our emotional state in our body movements, making the body a more honest indicator of our state of mind than the face.

Being able to adequately read other people's body language is key to being able to influence them. It helps to quickly establish trust with business peers, anticipate attitudes and behaviours and adequately adjust to other people's signals.

---

[1] Desmond Morris (1995) *Bodytalk: The meaning of human gestures*, Crown.

There are four key principles to grasp in order to gain a basic understanding of how to use body language to influence people:

- understand an individual's baseline
- freeze, flight and fight
- comfort and discomfort
- mirroring and matching.

Understand an individual's baseline

This baseline is the default attitudes of an individual. We all have our own body language behaviours. These encompass facial expressions, hand gestures and body positioning. They appear when we are relaxed or in comfortable settings.

Establishing an individual's baseline is the first step towards being able to read that person's behaviour, by identifying any deviations from it. The best way to establish any baseline (for team members, peers, customers and so on) is to observe them.

It is also recommended that you work on establishing your own baseline in order to consciously control and use your body language effectively. Having one of the members of your feedback group specifically observe your body language while in different settings and subsequently debrief you is a good way to build this awareness and create an appropriate action plan.

Freeze, flight and fight

These are our primal reactions when we feel threatened or attacked. They translate into specific body language reactions you can look out for:

- **Freeze** involves restricting movement to avoid detection, so generally manifests as restricted or limp arms and/or a closed or stooped posture.
- **Flight** is characterised by blocking – in other words, protecting the front of the body, by crossing the arms, turning the torso or leaning away.
- **Fight**, naturally, presents as aggressive gestures, such as prolonged staring or leaning forward to invade others' personal space or puffing out the chest.

Once you have established an individual's baseline, looking for the above cues is a great way to detect when an individual is in a state of stress or emotional distress. Sudden changes in the baseline are highly telling of changes in emotional states.

Comfort and discomfort

A person's level of confidence or ease can be assessed by how comfortable or uncomfortable they appear to be.

- **Comfort = high level of confidence** This usually translates into relaxed and expansive movements and the natural tendency to mirror those we are most comfortable with – in other words, to naturally replicate their body positions, hands, arms and legs. Displaying this kind of body language is a way to establish trust and understanding.

- **Discomfort = low level of confidence** When feeling discomfort, the body tends to restrict movements and engage in pacifying behaviours, such as touching the neck and face, stroking, soothing, whistling, and hugging the body. As levels of stress increase, so may the amount of neck and facial stroking. Males and females exhibit different pacifying movements. Females will particularly cover their neck dimple (indentation just below Adam's apple), play with their earrings or a necklace and stroke their hair, hands or arms. Males will play with their tie or cufflinks, touch their face and engage in robust cupping of the neck beneath the chin.

Mirroring and matching

When someone displays body language similar to our own, it creates a sense of similarity and hence, trust. Mirroring is the act of getting in tune with another person by subtly echoing his or her movements and is a powerful way to alter the signals and, thus, the feelings of others.

Mirroring can be applied in different ways:

- **pace of your speech** – to create a sense of trust, adjust the pace of your speech for a short while, then change it again and, usually, the other person will follow suit

- **vernacular** – using the words said by another person is also highly effective

- **tone of voice** – even when a person is yelling at you, staying one tone below his or her level of voice will help establish rapport, then allow you to calm him or her down

- **body positioning** – if a person leans forwards towards another, generally the other does the same, but if, on the contrary, he or she leans back and relaxes, the other tends to do likewise

- **gestures** – if the other person crosses his or her arms or leans his or head on one side, reciprocate

- **facial expressions** – if he or she smiles or laughs, do so, too.

To be effective, mirroring needs to remain unconscious and subtle – obvious mimicking will create mistrust or a lack or rapport. Matching is based on the same techniques as mirroring, but a delay is introduced to the change of position.

Mismatching is also a skill that it is useful to master if you want to create some distance or end a conversation. You can do this by:

- breaking eye contact
- turning your body so it is at an angle to the person
- breathing faster or slower than them.

Being able to quickly grasp the emotional states or reactions of your peers or subordinates gives you a competitive advantage as you work to increase your influence.

A lot of elements can be considered or used, but the following seven are a good start:

- Feet do not lie. As human beings we are inclined to control what is clearly on display – face and upper body. As feet are generally hidden, they will be 'truer', naturally pointing to people we like or moving away from people we dislike.

- People lean, point or adopt open postures towards people or things they like (torso, head, arms). So, turning your head towards someone, not crossing your arms and so on are signs of comfort.

- Significant and/or abrupt changes in posture, leg and feet or hand movements and so on indicate a negative impact – that there has been a change in the comfort level for the person.

- Dominance is expressed by occupying a lot of space, so, standing straight, making a lot of arm movements, spreading out in a chair and so on are associated with alphas.

- Hand movements increase credibility and make people respond strongly. Steepling – palms together but apart, tips of fingers touching – is the most powerful gesture of confidence.

- Acting as a barrier to the other person or not expresses the level of comfort a person is feeling. The more someone angles him- or herself towards something or someone else, the more comfortable they are. The more discomfort is felt, the more obstacles he or she will put in the way, crossing his or her arms, leaning or turning away.

- Greeting a person with relaxed arms and open, palms visible, will communicate that you mean no harm. This posture conveys openness and being on an even keel.

These seven pointers can be used for different purposes and in different situations, such as the following.

To establish trust, pay attention to the following:

- mirror and match those you are in conversation with

- when greeting them for the first time, lean towards them and use a firm handshake, make good eye contact, then take a step back

- if they take a step closer, this means that they are favourable towards you

- if they step back or turn slightly away, they probably want to be somewhere else.

To influence your peer's behaviours, the most efficient way is to first identify their baseline behaviours by spending some time observing how they carry themselves (arms, torso, hands), then match this, behaving as they do in terms of the positions of your hands, arms, angle of your body, then slowly introduce your own body language for them to respond to you.

To enhance communications during a meeting, follow a similar process as above, but stop short of mirroring the angle of their body (called blading) – just match what they do with their hands, head and gestures. This will create a feeling of trust as you will be perceived as 'one of them'.

To improve negotiations, you can use body language to grasp the underlying power structure in the other team.

- Identify the leader by noting that when the leader shifts position, the followers will naturally match it after a short delay.

- Identify the 'different' one – the one who does not react in the same way or at the same pace. This person will not alter his or her behaviour when the leader does. Knowing this can be useful as it may be helpful to work with this particular individual in some other way.

- Create a sense of comfort and ease with your feet, voice and an open posture.

- Then recalibrate once you have observed other people's reactions.

Reflecting on your own body language and learning to either control it or project what you want to are usually untapped techniques for influencing people that any leader might want to consider developing in order to become influential without others realising how it is done.

Exercises and action points

Establishing individuals' baseline behaviours

Observe people in different settings, both when they are not aware that they are being observed and when they are in one-on-one meetings with you. Pay particular attention to when they are:

- at their desks – note how they position their legs, hands, arms

- at the coffee machine, when interacting with work colleagues – how they position their feet, torso, if they cross their legs, lean forwards or not

- in meetings – whether or not they take a lot of personal space, stretch out their legs, lean back in their chair.

(See Appendix 2 for explanations of the common body positions and what they might indicate.)

▶

If you want your baseline for an individual to be accurate, it is probably a good idea to take notes rather than just rely on memory. If you are specifically observing your team members, you can complement what you notice with the information you gathered on building rapport in Chapter 7. This will give you everything you need to know to adequately motivate, manage and influence your team members in one set of documents.

If you use the following exercises to practise, they will greatly help you to become more aware and astute at picking up on the cues people give.

Exercise 1

Read and absorb the information included in Appendix 2 so you will have the knowledge you need to be able to interpret body language well.

Sit down in a public place (a restaurant, coffee shop or public transport) and observe the interactions of couples or groups of friends around you. Observe how they position the various parts of their bodies and move when they talk or interact. Do they match or mismatch? How do they adjust to each other or not?

Be aware of sudden changes of position and what these trigger in other people.

Compare and contrast what you have observed with the information in Appendix 2 and draw your own conclusions.

This exercise will help you familiarise yourself with what matching and mirroring demonstrate in everyday situations.

Exercise 2

Practise matching and mirroring with your partner or a friend

Introduce one element after the other – eyes, hands and posture – to make the process smooth and subtle and assess the impacts they have.

The best way to measure how well this technique works is to engage in a slightly controversial conversation and use matching and/or mirroring to control the outcome.

Building networks and alliances[2]

There is so much you can do on your own to increase the influence you have. Leveraging links with others around you by building networks is a critical step towards enhancing your efficiency. It requires time and patience to build a long-lasting network. It also entails the integration of three specific dimensions – operational, strategic and personal. Finally, it involves a mix of endorsers, allies and advocates. Establishing a network is based on one principle: unattached reciprocity. A network helps you to be better known, better equipped and better connected. It is an ongoing good investment of your time.

Aristotle taught us that, '*Man is by nature a social animal.*'

In an increasingly virtual, fluid and complex corporate world, one other thing also remains universally true: being successful as a leader requires you to invest in a proper networking strategy.

Example: The value of networks

Lord Alan Sugar, who, despite calling networking a 'waste of time', told the following story about receiving a referral in his book *What You See is What You Get* (Pan, 2011).

Rupert Murdoch contacted him out of the blue to ask him to manufacture satellite dishes on the advice of Lord Weinstock, the Chairman of GEC, who had said, 'Go and see Sugar, he's the man who can bring a consumer electronics project to the market faster than anyone else. In fact, while Sony and Philips are still thinking about it, he will have them in the market for you.'

Networking is about having the ability to contact or put people in contact with each other to solve a problem fast or create value. It allows you to create a rich ecosystem of personal contacts, ready to provide support, feedback and resources to get things done.

---

[2] With the contribution of Andy Lopata who was described by the FT as 'one of Europe's leading Business Networking Strategists'. He is the author of three highly recommended books on networking including and *Death Came Third* (co-authored with Peter Roper) and *Recommended: How to sell through networking and referrals*.

To fully benefit from networking, having a well thought out strategy is critical. You need to:

- have the right attitude

- build the three required types of network

- invest time and effort to ensure long-lasting positive effects.

Developing the right attitudes towards networking

Regardless of whether it is internal or external to an organisation, networking is often perceived as a way of using people, of being manipulative, but this is not the case. 'I started to understand the power of networking the day I stopped calling it networking and personally renamed it advice consulting – that is, seeking and giving', recalls Venetia Howes, former Shell executive and Head of the Worshipful Company of Marketors.

It is important to grasp the real value of networking. It is about the inherent ability to see, attract and put together unique qualities to create tremendous value. Networking harnesses and leverages the power of diversity for the greater good. It helps you to know where to go to yield maximum results.

The best way to understand networking and build sustainable relationships is to, first and foremost, look at it as a way to connect with people for who they are and not for what they may bring to you. What you need to keep in mind is what *you* can *give* to your network, how you can help those in it reach *their* goals. When you meet people in different capacities in different settings, always ask yourself:

- What can I do for them?

- What can I bring them?

Think of it in terms of a balance sheet. Build your asset side first before your liabilities. This is good housekeeping in networking. One easy way to do this is to rapidly assess every person you meet or interact with in terms of the factors shown in Figure 8.2.

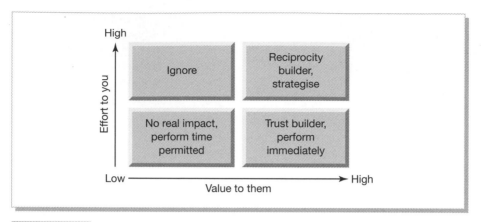

Figure 8.2   Assessing the networking potential of people you meet

If you assess someone to be in the lower-right hand corner of Figure 8.2 on meeting, take action immediately. This might be by way of making an introduction or an ad hoc investment of time. It is a great way to call on your 'unselfish gene'.[3]

The upper-right hand corner is where the value of your network will sit and will help you accomplish great things as this is where others will naturally reciprocate.

Networking can be considered the ultimate form of social sophistication. It requires you to be socially savvy and help and support in a genuine spirit. It also asks that you immediately assess where you are on the trust ladder. Building great networks is about true genuineness in the giving, regardless of it being reciprocated. It is absolutely not about keeping score. It is important to keep this distinction in mind if you are to succeed and build sustainable networks.

As building a network takes time, it is never too early to start. Take a look, you may not realise how much of a network exists in the communities you are already a part of – alumni groups, sports clubs and so on.

[3] Yochai Benkler (2011) 'The unselfish gene', *Harvard Business Review*, July.

Exercises and practical examples

Overcoming a fear of networking

Basic principles

- Have a strong intent.

- Make a point of systematically engaging in conversations with people around you.

- Be clear about your intentions and silence the doubts in your head.

The objective

- To part ways after meeting a person either knowing two or three things about them or having been given a business card or a promise of another meeting.

The process

- Engage the person in conversation. It is important to assess the right moment and way to do this. You might consider using the body language techniques described earlier in this chapter (mirroring or matching him or her) to create the right environment.

- While in conversation, decide what you want to learn about this person. You can also decide up front what you want to know or, if preparing for a networking event, ask for the list of attendees and research them.

- Assess what you think you could do to help the person and start to bring it up.

The frequency

- Repeat this process as often as possible until you feel you no longer feel uncomfortable with it.

Good places to practise networking

- Plane or train ride.

- Parties or other social settings.

- Shopping, gym sessions and so on.

- Formal, scheduled networking events.

The point of this exercise is for you to become at ease with the process and develop your ability to connect.

Working with the three types of internal networks

Building networks takes work and requires an important investment of your time, so establishing which is the right type of network to ensure your success is critical.

A professional network can be defined from two different angles:

- Intention – what intention will the network serve?
- Outcome – what problem will your network help you solve?

A network that serves an intention

Internally, a leader mainly interacts at three different levels – with his or her:

- superiors
- peers
- subordinates.

Every one of these levels plays a specific role and serves a specific purpose (see Figure 8.3). It is important to integrate these three dimensions into any networking strategy.

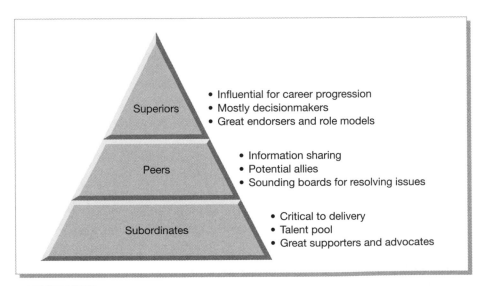

Figure 8.3   Leaders interact at three levels

The role of advocate should be part of the equation at every level, not only the subordinates level. Advocates are people who will promote you, who you are and what you do because they want to, because they relate strongly to you.

Always keep all three dimensions in mind while building your network.

A network to help solve leader's core challenges

Every leader juggles three main types of challenges.

Operational

These can usually be defined as short- or medium-term challenges and are highly correlated with the delivery of specific targets. For instance:

- identifying potential new talent to join the team or ensuring a smooth transition when one of its members is due to move on

- understanding the implications of Internal Accounting Standard 17 on capital expenditure to ensure that the budgeting process is accurate

- getting to know the sales lead before a strategic planning exercise starts.

A strong operational network ensures that the work is done efficiently.

Personal or ad hoc

These are for solving ad hoc problems and may be linked to particular situations, needs or circumstances. For instance:

- joining a new team and needing help to establish yourself in it

- needing to understand the current legal framework in a new territory for an upcoming joint venture negotiation

- wanting to develop proficiency in dealing with tax in order to have more impact in your role.

Strategic

Most of the time these have long-term implications and can be either personal – what you want to achieve as a person – or related to the company's vision – what you want to achieve as a leader. For instance:

- wanting to make a switch from a finance function to general management and needing to find a strong sponsor for this

- embedding innovation into the team's way of working to foster stronger business strategies.

The value of networks in solving these three types of problems

A rich strategic network helps you to figure out future priorities and challenges while at the same time identifying who are the right stakeholders to support your plans. It will make you a better-known, better-equipped and better-connected person.

Developing the three separate categories of network will enable you to work on the three dimensions necessary to be a credible leader and increase your influence. These dimensions are:

- depth – strong working relationships

- breadth – having a wide range of contacts who might be useful in terms of referrals or to solve issues fast

- leverage – the ability to translate what you learn to what is needed for your business, yourself (thinking outside-in).

If you focus on the intention and the purpose of your network and include the internal and external dimension you have a solid basis for an efficient and bulletproof network.

The most critical network in terms of accelerating the development of your leadership is the strategic network. The ability to plug into circles of people with different backgrounds and different perspectives will only strengthen your strategic thinking and open your eyes to new perspectives and new business opportunities.

Exercises and action points

The five people exercise

This exercise is geared at helping you establish strong relationships within any of your three types of network. It will also help you to see the different elements in your network that you could add value to by bringing them together.

For five people in each area of your network, do the following.

Ask them:

■ What do you need most right now?

Then ask them:

■ Who would they benefit from knowing right now?

Finally, ask yourself:

■ Who could I introduce them to?

Then, assess the five people in relation to the factors in Figure 8.2 and take the associated actions.

Establishing and maintaining the right types of networks

As mentioned above, there are three main categories of challenges that leaders need to address in their career – operational, personal or ad hoc and strategic. Each of them benefits from contacting specific communities for support and help. Consequently, to build an effective network, a strategy that takes into consideration several dimensions needs to be devised.

At different stages in your career, you will have to rely more heavily on one particular part of your network than another, so the ability to quickly activate whichever network is required to reach the person you need will definitely prove to be a useful competitive advantage.

To build an effective strategy, consider setting aside some quiet time to reflect on the following questions:

- **What is the purpose of the network I am trying to build?** This will crystallise for you if you are thinking in terms of strategic, operational or personal networks, as they serve different needs.

- **Where are the best places to find adequate people to join this network?** This will help you map the different avenues to and pools of help available to you. Reminisce about your education, family background and previous work experience.

- **How do I go about it? What actions should I take?** This will turn your thinking into action and articulate how you allocate your time and commitment. It is this that will make the difference in the long run.

Table 8.1 summarises the elements of the most effective strategy to follow when building a network.

The strategy in Table 8.1 is underpinned by five key principles.

Practice, practice, practice

Not everyone is at ease with networking. What matters is establishing rapport and getting to know people.

Some of the exercises on building rapport in Chapter 7 can usefully be applied to networking. You can also try to identify a person you respect who networks ethically and effectively and observe how he or she does it – even ask, 'How do you do it?' You could also ask him or her to be part of your feedback group. If developing your networking abilities is one of your desired areas for improvement, factor it into your improvement plan.

Create reasons to network

To develop a network, you need to find occasions to network. Leaders need to use and create opportunities to interact with others, both within their organisations (other departments or business units) and externally.

Table 8.1 The optimum strategy for building a network

	Operational networks	Personal or ad hoc network	Strategic network
Purpose	• Deliver what needs to be done	• Personal or professional development, useful information and referrals	• Enable to keep abreast and think of potential priorities and challenges
How to identify actors?	• Stakeholder mapping • Specific focus on internal contacts • Mainly subordinates and peers	• 'Life' mapping • Specific focus on external based on own experience and history	• Stakeholder mapping • Mainly superiors and peers • Includes external contacts based on long-term future goals
How to find network members?	• Prescribed by organisational structure • Prescribed by tasks	• Investigate alumni association • Investigate professional associations • Investigate personal-interests communities • Clubs or specific profession (head hunters, coach etc.)	• Investigate lateral and vertical relationships • Investigate professional associations • Key is to keep it diverse

How to build and maintain a network?	• Refer to building rapport (Chapter 7)	• Reflect on your personal history and design a 'getting back in touch' strategy:
		  – use LinkedIn, Facebook, etc. to reconnect
		  – factor in 'regular catch-ups, two or three times a year (for people living abroad, do so when travelling)
		  – make quarterly phone calls or check e-mails
		• For associations:
		  – ensure regular and consistent attendance
		  – develop one-on-one relationships
		  – always ask for and propose introductions
			• For internal stakeholders:
			  – monthly or quarterly meetings
			  – have relevant topics of conversation
			  – ask for advice or opinions or share experiences
			• For external stakeholders:
			  – increase memberships
			  – ensure regular and consistent attendance
			  – develop one-on-one relationship
			  – always ask for and propose introductions

Take advantage of your social interests, too, to set the stage for your strategic concerns.

Put yourself at the centre of your networking activities. For instance, if you are a music fan, consider sharing this with your stakeholders and customers, so you can learn things about them and use this subject to keep up to date with their thinking.

When you meet people, consider recording their names, professions, companies, interests. Specify how you met them and how often you have seen them. At a later stage, you can record other details, such as their birthdays. Indeed, record anything that will help you maintain genuine and respectful relationships with them.

Find connectors

Who you choose to include in your network may have a significant impact on how fast you can create and leverage it. In his book *The Tipping Point*, Malcolm Gladwell defines what elements are necessary to create a pandemic effect for a product, concept or even a person. Among the seven key ones presented in the book, the connectors concept is particularly relevant for building networks.

Connectors are typically highly social people who usually interact with different types of groups with different interests. Their own networks usually stretch into a range of industries or areas of interest. Others will often come to them when they need something.

Connectors are particularly important when establishing a network as they are able to contact a wide array of people to solve problems or discuss issues. They are also able to broadcast important information to their larger audiences.

Maintain the relationships

Networking can be thought of as a different form of friendship and it works if you follow the same principles. Friendship is based on trust and care – we expect our friends to communicate with and care for us and not only when they are facing difficulties or need help.

As a leader it is important to give and take continually – do not wait until you need something from someone in your network to contact them. It is important to build into your schedule proper time to call other network members and to meet or interact with them (see Table 8.1).

Revise your strategy on a yearly basis

As you evolve or change roles, your needs – as well as those of your contacts – will also evolve, so keeping up to date is critical. Additionally, reviewing your strategy like this will ensure that you factor your prospective needs into how you develop your network. For instance, if you start to work in a new industry or shift from one type of environment to another, proactively developing your network in that field can accelerate your path.

Exercises and action points

How to handle the 'How can I help you?' question

When faced with this question, there are three things that it is important to keep in mind:

- do not shy away from it – any opportunity is good if the person is genuine: shying away might be perceived as arrogant

- be careful what you ask for – think about the two or three top critical things for you and make sure they are reasonable.

Be sure to ask how you can reciprocate and, if you are able to, act on it.

Summary

It takes lot of research to develop a network as you need to understand what the environment looks like. You need to get to know who people are and what they need. Thinking, observing and listening are key.

It also takes a lot of patience and effort. You need to practise, invest time, be patient and be consistent in your interactions and strategy.

Networks also need to be maintained. You need to give and take continually to keep the relationships you have established alive and healthy. In the words of the twentieth-century English writer Elizabeth Bibesco, '*Blessed are those who can give without remembering and take without forgetting*' (Haven, 1951).

Here's a reminder of some of the key points from this chapter:

- influence comes from observing your environment and managing it, understanding your stakeholders and creating and using networks

- identifying clearly your stakeholders in everything you do via stakeholder mapping will give you a clear head start when it comes to projects or teambuilding, as well as helping to establish your leadership brand or credibility

- implement a strategy to manage your stakeholders – depending on their interests and influence, they can act as leverage, accelerators or blockers

- decide who you want to be in every interaction or meeting – whether an expert, decision maker or the challenger, make sure you have an impact

- observe your environment to find the alphas and informal leaders and invest time in getting to know them – building rapport with them will help you to create and expand your area of influence by association

- networking helps you become better known, better equipped, better connected, so it is important to craft a strategy to develop the three main types of networks needed

- three different types of network are necessary – operational, personal or ad hoc and strategic – they need to operate at different levels – superiors, peers, subordinates, bosses – and internally and externally, so a comprehensive strategy is needed to ensure this happens

- delivering your network strategy involves identifying its purpose, places to network, as well as require investing time in it and being disciplined

- networking is based on 'unattached' reciprocity – you are not in it for what you can get out of it, but what you can do for others, which then means you do get something out of it.

Building and executing your vision – from ideas to results

'Excellent firms don't believe in excellence – only in constant improvement and constant change.'

Tom Peters, author of In search of excellence

When times are tough, disrupt

By Glen Manchester

Received business wisdom talks about how innovation plays a pivotal role in leading economies out of recession. But, all too often, untargeted R&D spend is instead only promoting further stagnation. Business owners, large or small, should instead consider the possibilities for disrupting their markets when facing a tough economy.

A wake-up call came in July with the announcement of a 2012 Innovation Index Nesta, the innovation foundation. According to Nesta, investment in innovation by British businesses has been in decline over the past decade, with a fall of £24bn since the current recession began.

These are sobering numbers. Yet the report, again, confirms the vital link between innovation and economic growth. As an entrepreneur, what I particularly like about the Nesta index is that it recognises that traditional research and development is only part of the innovation picture. It also measures the downstream co-investments needed to bring new ideas to market, such as design, software development, innovative training and organisational development. In fact, on the latest numbers, R&D represents a meagre 13 per cent of innovation investment.

When I launched my company in the customer communications market in 2001, I looked to use the uncertain times as an opportunity to disrupt the status quo and create a new market. Amid the fallout of the dotcom bubble, we designed and built an enterprise software platform that is today used by 14 of the world's 15 largest investment banks and some of the world's largest energy and commodity trading companies.

Anyone familiar with the 'innovator's dilemma' theory, a phrase coined by the book of the same name by the Harvard Business School professor Clayton M. Christensen, will recognise the patterns. Firstly, our innovation which leveraged new disruptive technologies created a new market in the downturn. This was followed by years of sustaining innovation, with incremental improvements to our technology to meet the evolving needs of our customers.

The cycle has now gone full circle. Although we now have hundreds of employees rather than a handful, I've opted to disrupt the business once more. Keeping a watching eye on technology and consumer trends – especially with the impact of social media and mobility – we saw that we needed to change.

Two years ago, amid the global economic turbulence of the times, I made the decision to invest in a new disruptive innovation strategy. We have invested heavily, tripling the size of our engineering teams. Once again, we're setting out to create a new market rather than focusing our innovation investments on small iterative product improvements.

Thinking this way can help a business avoid a troublesome 'Kodak moment'. For a century, this company based its business on silver halide film and paper, but when faced with the market disruption caused by digital technology, could not respond, opting instead for sustaining innovations in its core business and not diverting enough focus to digital imaging. We all know what happened next.

Don't be afraid to keep your start-up flair and instincts as your business grows. Consider how much profit should be diverted to sustaining innovations, and how much on a future moment of disruption.

Every chief executive needs to ensure the balance of innovation investment is right. I know from my own experience that it can be daunting to invest in innovation when belts are being tightened, but times like this should be seen as great opportunities. Economic pressure forces markets to look for cheaper, more effective solutions. Leveraging this opportunity to disrupt and innovate should give British companies the drive to succeed and come out the other side of the recession stronger.

As the UK's double-dip recession sharpens once more, it's time to be bolder with British innovation.

Source: Manchester, G. (2012) When times are tough, disrupt, *Financial Times*, 7 September.© Thunderhead.com 2012.

Being a leader is about changing things from the way they have been happening. When you are a leader, something different happens because of you, because of who you are. Leadership is rooted in a set of attributes ranging from self-awareness to the ability to influence.

Leadership is the act of a leader. It encompasses everything from gaining credibility, to managing a team, to building a network.

Parts 1 and 3 reflected on and presented techniques so you could examine, first, yourself and, second your environment. Also highlighted have been the importance of the team and the concept of co-creation, both of which should remain at the forefront of your mind for this final part.

Part 4 focuses on the bigger picture and looks at how you can have an impact on the world around you, from the following angles:

- **Vision and innovation** A widely recognised skill of leaders is their ability to craft a vision, to give a purpose to their organisation in the medium to long term. Different ways of crafting a vision and reasons to do so are explored in Chapter 9. This is paired with some reflection on whether or not it is necessary to be innovative.

- **Strategic thinking** Once the vision has been established, translating it into concrete action is the next natural step. Leaders play a critical role in that translation process, by reflecting on effective communication processes and ensuring that their vision is always in tune with an ever-evolving environment. (This is explored in Chapter 10.)

- **Execution** The true test of a leader is execution. How do you deliver your strategy to deliver your vision? Various skills are required, such as the ability to lead change, make decisions and progress and monitor results. (This is the topic of Chapter 11.)

Building your vision

'Vision is not just a picture of what could be; it is an appeal to our better selves, a call to become something more.'

Rosabeth Moss Kanter, Professor, Harvard Business School

This chapter covers:

- the differences between ideas, mission, strategy and vision
- the key elements to keep in mind when building your vision
- why and how innovation fits into the vision building process
- the key criteria for unleashing innovation – both in you and in your team members.

The case of the State of Singapore

In less than three decades, the State of Singapore moved from being a developing country to the emerging financial power in Asia. From mosquito-ridden island, just about leaving behind its colonial past, with no proven model of self-management and no natural resources, Singapore became an economic success, a model of efficiency where it is easy to do business. More importantly, it – at least on the surface – presents a model of successful integration, where diverse communities live harmoniously with one another.

Lee Kwan Yu, the leader of the People's Action Party, provided the impetus and led the way for almost 30 years. He had a sense of what would be required for this relatively small country to become an important player in the world's economy: political stability, an English-speaking community and business-friendly ways. He systematically tackled these three elements. He freed the country from colonialism, even cutting ties with neighbouring Malaysia, imposed English as the business and administrative language and created a fiscal and regulatory environment that appealed to corporations and individuals alike. Success came as a result of having a very strong social framework, which may not appear to be a true model of democracy – he was several times tagged the 'benevolent dictator' – but it has worked.

Lee Kwan Yu had a fierce sense of purpose. He knew what he wanted to achieve for his country and, over 30 years, he systematically worked towards it. He crafted a compelling vision of putting Singapore on the map of the global economy. He possessed a certain clarity and purposefulness and succeeded in his mission because of his rigorous execution of that vision.

Successful vision building cannot be left to chance. Thinking things through and defining the intention is the safest way to reach the vision. The vision itself is vital – to inspire, trigger action and, ultimately, ensure there is a reaping of the rewards.

Mission, vision, ideas and strategy: making sense of the melting pot

Vision is the mountain to be climbed to get closer to the mission of your company. It is a new definition of the future. It should be inspiring, compelling and unique. It should channel everyone's energies in one direction. It is built with ideas and turned into action by means of strategy.

In the corporate mind, the mission statement, strategy, vision and ideas can appear, at best, intertwined and at worst, blurred and generally confusing. It is critical, however, that the definitions of each of these elements and the logical flow from one to the other are fully understood.

Defining 'mission'

'Mission' may be defined as the ultimate purpose of an organisation. It represents what the organisation is and what it does. It should be ingrained and seen as everlasting.

Example: Some mission statements

- Google's mission is to organise the world's information and make it universally accessible and useful.
- Apple is committed to bringing the best personal computing experience to students, educators, creative professionals and consumers around the world via its innovative hardware, software and Internet offerings.
- General Electric has a relentless drive to invent things that matter – innovations which build, power, move and help cure the world.

All mission statements have one thing in common: they are never reachable and will never be completed. A mission statement should represent the star on the horizon that the organisation is constantly aiming at.

Defining 'vision'

'Vision' is more concrete than 'mission' – it is what the organisation is aiming to become in the near future. It includes an element of the dream and permits a certain freedom of thinking. It requires the ability to see above and beyond the now and the real.

> **Example: Some vision variants**
>
> - Google's vision is to develop the perfect search engine.
> - For General Electric under Jack Welch's management, it was, 'To become the most competitive enterprise in the world by being number one or number two in every business in which we compete.'
> - Some 45 years later, the vision for General Electric under Jeffrey Immelt is to make things that very few in the world can, but everyone needs.

Vision acts like guidance. The purpose of it should be to answer the following question:

- What is the future I want to stimulate progress towards?

A vision has a timeframe and should evolve to stay in tune with what might be possible in the future. A vision should be convergent, crystallising energies towards one single point of focus that makes sense and is compelling.

The connections between mission, vision and ideas

A vision should be rooted in the mission of the company and its core values. As we have seen, a mission is everlasting, but a vision is evolving and should change over time. If a mission is indeed the star to be reached, a vision is the mountain to be climbed to get closer to it. Once climbed, then it is necessary to move to the next-highest mountain.

In the past decade, there has been much emphasis in leadership on the generation of ideas, with increasing pressure being put on executives to develop their creativity. Leaders of the future, however, will have to work not simply with problems but also with dilemmas – unsolvable problems – in a more and more complex and fast-moving environment. Ideas will be readily available, but turning them into a vision will be what counts.

Does a vision come from ideas? Yes, but with a caveat. Ideas are the fertile soil for vision building, but, at a certain point, vision building needs to cut through the plethora of ideas, rationalise and ultimately focus on one idea, translating it into strategy and actions. Vision is the relentless exploration of one direction, by researching and having a deep understanding of it.

'Thinking outside the box' is a great way of describing the generation of ideas. If we apply it to vision, we might talk about 'building a new box'. Vision aims to change existing paradigms.

Finally, ideas, when applied to problem solving, can appear culturally neutral. However, visions are not. They are deeply rooted in a clear aspiration for a new world and reflect the personal culture of the thinker.

Defining strategy

Strategy is the next natural step. It is the necessary move forwards from ideas and goals to ultimately create impact.

Strategy sits close to vision, but further away from the mission statement. A strategy finds the best paths to enable the vision to be achieved, taking into consideration any likely changes in the environment. A strategy should be fluid and partly reactive, partly proactive. It should have one purpose only – ensuring the adequate delivery of the vision.

Example: Some strategies

- For Google, developing the perfect search engine requires:
  - the core competence of the company to be the ability to develop search engine programs and so on
  - a steady revenue stream, resulting from advertising
  - that an eye be kept on privacy issues to avoid regulatory risk
  - the development of market-changing products (android tablets and so on).
- For General Electric, in 2012, its strategy is based on insourcing, innovation and strong growth in emerging markets. The company is refocusing on what it does best – manufacturing, with a specific interest in leading global trends, energy and healthcare and being an American workforce company.

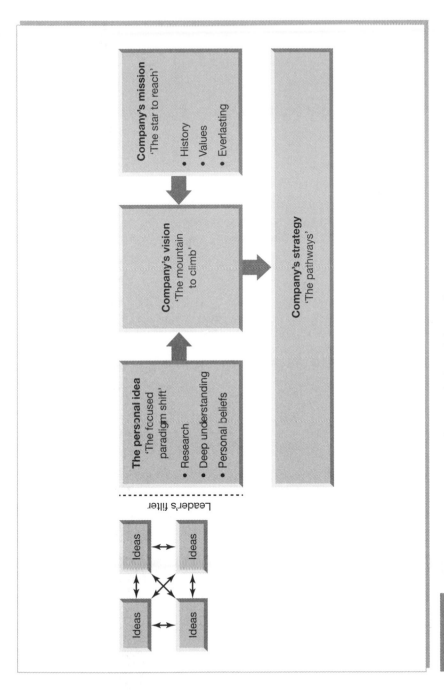

Figure 9.1   The relationships between ideas, mission, vision and strategy

Being clear on all the key concepts and existing interdependencies allows for the vision to be developed and communicated effectively. Figure 9.1 represents the flows between the different concepts.

How to create your vision

Vision building is an exciting *and* daunting exercise. It involves taking into account several elements, such as your own vision-forming abilities, the organisation's core ideology (values and purpose) and leader's personality. It also entails establishing either a series of bold goals or a picture of a better, brighter future, articulating what is in there for everyone. The role of innovation in the vision building process needs to be defined and the line drawn clearly between incremental progress and breakthrough. Vision building is not a solitary exercise – involving your team in co-creation is key.

Vision is an inspiring tool, depicting an exciting future for the organisation. In the same way that you have established a personal brand for yourself, transitioning from your current state to your desired future state, vision is the equivalent of applying personal branding to the company, business unit or department.

Finding the visionary leader in you

Before delving into how to create a vision, it is important to first assess your visioning capability by reflecting on the following questions:

- Do you believe that your work involves managing an endless series of crises?
- Do you often wonder 'Why am I doing this?' or 'Does it really matter?'
- Do you feel that you have a sense of a long-term purpose?
- Do you remember the last time you talked about your job with excitement?

Generally, if you are more inclined to reply positively to the first two questions and negatively to the last two, your visioning abilities are not being activated or challenged or, more fundamentally, you are not the visionary type. If, alternatively, you reply negatively to the first two questions and positively to the last two, you have sustained visioning abilities or have found a vision that is both compelling and exciting.

It is important to invest time in working on your vision, both for your own sake and because of the impact the lack of it will have on your organisation. If you do not believe in your vision or have lost sight of it, the chances are that this will be felt by your team. Another key thing to learn will be how to leverage your team's diversity to co-create your vision.

To define your leadership brand, decide how you want to be perceived by the organisation. This builds on your observations of the behaviour of the role models you identify in the organisation (see Chapter 3) and how your core values match the organisation's (see Chapter 6).

Vision building needs to emanate from the two dimensions mentioned above. Asking yourself the following question may be useful:

- In line with my leadership brand and my core values, what do I want to create that will have a long-lasting impact on the organisation?

This should be the one of the building blocks of your vision building process.

Establishing the building blocks

If you take a step back, creating a vision involves answering the following macro question:

- What's next, better or new for the organisation?

This needs to be asked while applying different filters or looking at things from various angles. The goal is to come up with the most compelling answer by capturing the following:

- purpose and values
- personality
- impact
- cohesion.

Purpose and values

This requires that you look inside your organisation. Your vision will be most compelling if it resonates with the environment you are operating within. It needs to address the core values (what the company stands for) and the core purpose (what the company's reason for being is) to create a feeling of consistency and inspire action.

The first step in vision building is to conclude what the essence of the company is. To be powerful, it needs to be decided on by individuals within the company who have the relevant value set. It also needs to be deeper than simply the pursuit of outstanding financial results.

Example: Some companies with purpose and value vision

- 3M defines its purpose as the perpetual quest to solve problems innovatively rather than the production of adhesives and abrasives. This always leads them into new fields.

- For McKinsey & Company, its purpose is not management consulting, but to help corporations and governments be more successful. It is leaving itself open to opportunities to move into other activities, such as developing an outsourced innovation company or think tank.

- Walt Disney did not conceive that his company's purpose was to make cartoons. He defined his purpose as making people happy. This thinking resulted in the Mickey Mouse character, Disneyland, the EPCOT Center and the Anaheim Mighty Ducks Hockey Team.

Personality

This requires you to look inside yourself.

Example: Darcy Winslow's vision

Darcy Winslow – one of Nike's most prominent leaders – had a passion for the environment. She always wanted to reconcile her passion with her purpose in the company. She came up with the idea of ecologically intelligent product design. By analysing the environmental impact of chemicals used in the making of Nike's products, she aimed to replace the most toxic with less or non-toxic ones. She had to work with several stakeholders to bring her message home, as the impact was that the manufacturing process would have to be significantly altered.

Darcy talked about her vision with passion and enthusiasm. Her message resonated with her personal commitment, which was also in line with global and societal needs. It was a massively inspiring vision. She managed to convince all the relevant stakeholders and the changes she proposed were subsequently implemented.

The ultimate purpose of a vision is to trigger action. This is easier if you root it in something that you deeply care about which will also bring benefits to the organisation.

Impact

This requires you to look beyond the current state of the organisation.

Being forward-looking, being able to envision exciting possibilities and enlisting others to join in a shared view of the future is the attribute that most distinguishes leaders from non-leaders, according to their followers.

Example: Look to the future

James M. Kouzes and Barry Z. Posner, in their article, 'To lead, create a shared vision' (*Harvard Business Review*, January 2009) surveyed tens of thousands of working people around the world and asked them, 'What do you look for and admire in a leader?', followed by 'What do you look for and admire in a colleague?' An average of 72 per cent said that they were looking for the ability to be forward-looking in their leaders, the percentage reaching 88 per cent when the question was asked at a more senior level in the organisation.

Some schools of thought state that 'forward-looking' means having a vision depicting a sustainable and compelling future, built by means of big hairy audacious goals (BHAGs).[1] BHAGs typically have a lifespan of 10 to 30 years and are grounded in an understanding of current reality, enabling the projection of a desirable future.

BHAGs can be driven by:

- quantitative or qualitative targets, such as Wal Mart's becoming a $125 billion company by the year 2000
- role models, such as Chinese company Taobau's of becoming the eBay of the East – these are usually effective for up-and-coming organisations

---

[1] The term 'Big Hairy Audacious Goal' (BHAG) was coined by Jim Collins and Jerry Porras (1994) in their book *Built to Last: Successful Habits of Visionary Companies*, HarperBusiness.

- common enemies, such as Honda's statement in the 1970s, 'We will destroy Yamaha' or, more recently, the Apple/Google battle over the 'Don't be evil' mantra

- an internal transformation, such as General Electric's drive in the 1980s to 'Become number one or number two in every market we serve and revolutionise this company to have the strengths of a big company combined with the leanness and agility of a small company.'

Cohesion

This requires you to look inside the people in your organisation.

A leader or a leadership team needs to craft goals that are compelling for the organisation and which appeal to the employees. Creating enduring, visionary companies is 1 per cent vision crafting and 99 per cent alignment. The alignment part is linked with the employees – they need to be part of the equation, to have a voice. The stronger the alignment, the higher the chance of empowerment and execution.

Building a shared vision by understanding their human condition and articulating how the vision will, to some extent, help them fulfil their hopes and dreams is critical. In simple terms, your vision has to 'do something for them', so listen to what they find exciting and important.

In his tribute to Steve Jobs at the Silicon Valley Bank's CEO Summit in October 2011, Guy Kawasaki crystallised this:

'We rose to the occasion because we were presented with the biggest challenge ever. If you ask employees of Apple, "Why do they put up with the challenges of working at Apple?" "Because Apple enables you to do the best work of your career", is what they would answer.

You will not find anything related to pushing yourself towards excellence in Apple's vision statement. However, people go above and beyond the call of duty at Apple because they inherently know it makes them better professionals. There is a strong pull for them to align themselves with that idea and make it true of them.

Exercises and practical examples

The random corporate serial killer – how to find your company's purpose

The purpose of this exercise is to move away from a purely financially focused vision and towards one with a real purpose. It engages your team in finding the real reason for the company's existence.

Perform this exercise as the ice-breaker for your vision building. It will enable you also to gauge the commitment of your team and their understanding of your organisation's history.

Set the following scenario for your leadership team.

Imagine you could sell the company to someone who would pay a price that everyone inside and outside the company agrees is more than fair.

Suppose the buyer will guarantee to keep the workforce (although not necessarily in the same industry). In other words, it will provide for everyone. However, the buyer will literally 'kill' the company. Products or services will be discontinued, the brand name shelved forever. The company will cease to exist.

Ask the team the following questions:

- Would you accept the offer? Why yes or why no?
- What would be lost if the company ceased to exist?
- Why is it important that the company continues to exist?

The feedback gathered will allow you to put together a descriptive statement, such as the one below:

The company is manufacturing the most effective components to be administrated safely to people suffering from prostate cancer. If it was to disappear, this would potentially affect millions of people and will not be conducive to finding a cure for a devastating illness.

The Mars group – how to extract your company's values

The aim of this exercise is to extract what the core values of your organisation are, keeping in mind that:

- core values are not related to strategies or the environment
- there should be no more than a handful of them
- they should stand the test of time.

With your leadership team imagine you have to recreate the very best attributes of your organisation on Mars, but you only have a limited number of seats (five to seven) for people to send there to do it. Ask, 'Who would you send from our leadership team?'

The people you and they choose should embody most of the core values of the organisation and have the highest level of credibility with their peers and/or top level competences.

Once you have all decided on the group to send from your leadership team, ask them to reflect on the following questions and report back:

- What core values do you personally bring to work?

- If you had enough money to retire, would you continue to live by these values?

- Would these values stand the test of time? Would they be valid 50 or 100 years from now?

- If you had to start a new organisation tomorrow – in any field or industry – what core values would you want to bring to it or build on?

If they come back with more than five or six, they might be confusing core values with operating practices or business strategies or cultural norms. Challenge them by asking them this question:

- 'If the circumstances changed and holding this core value would hurt our competitive advantage, would we still keep it?'

If they can't honestly answer 'Yes', then the value is not a core one. It can take a couple of sessions to go through the process and discuss what has been reported back.

The ultimate purpose is for you to settle on a handful of core values. These identified values should be at the forefront of your thinking while building the vision.

It is recommended that both this and the Merlin exercise below are run on the same day.

The Merlin exercise – how to decide on BHAGs for your organisation

The purpose of this exercise is to come up with a couple of BHAGs for the organisation to achieve, starting with defining a compelling future. This can also be used as the first step in strategic thinking (see Chapter 10).

How to run the exercise

This exercise is best worked through face-to-face with your leadership team. It generally takes a day to a day and a half for comprehensive vision building to occur. You can complement this work by beginning with one of the exercises on values.

For big groups, consider dividing up into smaller groups working independently and hold a presentation and challenge session at the end. For smaller groups, the outcome should be achievable in one day. In either case, it is recommended that a facilitator comes in to guide the process.

The exercise can be hugely valuable for aligning the goals of teams, so you might also like to consider bringing different parts of the organisation into the process.

Because leaders are increasingly needing to be collaborative and inclusive, using technology and internal social media while performing this exercise can be powerful. Asking people to tweet or instant message while the session is in progress will provoke reactions and instantaneous feedback. This could be paired with a communications campaign or a specific blog for the vision building exercise.

The process

Start by asking the group to depict the future, using the following question:

- What will the company look like in 15 years?

Take them deeper into the process to get a real look and feel for the outcome by suggesting these questions:

- What would we love to see?

- What should it feel like for us?

- What will the organisation have achieved?

- If journalists have to write an article for a major business magazine about this company in 20 years' time, what will it say?

This will induce a highly participative conversation, which should be recorded on flip charts or via computer groupware. The ideas expressed may be contradictory, they may build on each other or they may bring in different possibilities. The key is to allow a fluid conversation in which all can freely participate and express how they see their organisational future. The idea is to capture the full diversity of their thinking.

Use the tips and techniques explored in Chapter 7 and factor in the time needed for challenging and questioning.

Once you have explored all the possible angles, regroup to find patterns and key themes, then reorganise and extract what will become the one invented future or vision. It is important to pick the elements that are the most convergent in order to create one image, one future.

You can then assess it using the following questions:

- Does it get our juices flowing?
- Do we find it stimulating?
- Does it spur forward momentum?
- Does it get people going?

This process will help to not only test the solidity and completeness of your vision but also crystallise what it will be important to communicate to others about it.

The 5 Whys – how to crystallise your company's purpose

The aim of this exercise is to identify the purpose of the company and its reason for being. On completion, you will have generated a purpose statement. It can take several hours to create a purpose statement for the organisation.

You can either first play the Random corporate serial killer game or simply start with a descriptive statement such as:

> We make X or Y products, or deliver W or Z services or, using the example above, we manufacture the most effective drugs for curing prostate cancer.

Present the descriptive statement, then ask the team this question:

- Why is this important?

Ask this question five times in a row, taking a deeper look each time. Ultimately, the fundamental purpose of the organisation will emerge. Allow several hours to go through this process in order to capture all the ideas of the team and allow co-creation to take place.

The role of innovation in vision building

It is interesting to compare and contrast vision and innovation. In the past 20 years, the imperative to be innovative has been paramount for executives. It is important to assess why innovation can help vision building, understand the difference between incremental and disruptive innovation and be acquainted with the three elements that will turn you and your teams into better innovators.

Why innovation can help vision building

These two fundamental questions need to be asked:

- Do you have to be truly innovative to build a vision?
- Is a vision good enough if it is *not* innovative?

The answer to the first question is 'No'. If you look around you, how many companies are actually really innovative in their vision building? What matters is the ability to differentiate and create some additional value by having a compelling vision. Can it be qualified as innovation, though?

Example: The vision of the Standard Chartered Bank, Singapore

This is a good example of a vision that differentiates this bank from others.

'We have a key role to play in stimulating economic and social development through the services we provide and by being a force for good. The success of our business depends on this.'

It plays on the current trend for social and impact investing and the crisis in values. In some ways, therefore, this could be seen as innovative. However, its main strength is that the bank differentiates itself from its competitors by having a very strong responsibility angle.

The answer to the second question above is probably 'Yes'. There is no right or wrong vision. There is only a vision that resonates with the core ideologies of the company and predicts a future that you as a leader want and will be compelling and motivating for the whole staff.

The point here is that innovation – both the incremental and breakthrough types – is not a necessary requirement for vision building. However, its role is that of an enabler for leaders to make a vision entirely theirs. It is their way of expressing their own creativity in and through the vision – their mark, their brand.

Incremental or breakthrough innovation?

The difference between the two is an important one to keep in mind. As a leader, you may have different views on innovation and different approaches when it comes to how to best use it.

You may take what could be defined as an evolutionary approach in your vision for your organisation. This would imply a reliance on integrating innovative ways with BHAGs to create your vision. You would be looking for improvements big or small from your current internal base. These could be applied to products, as much as processes or organisational or business models. For example, Gillette made an incremental product innovation when it moved from one-blade to two-blade razors, and up to five now. Also, the Apple iPod initially came out only in white and was only able to store and play MP3s. Now we know it as a colourful device that also stores videos and pictures. The concept of shared service centres that has led leaders to rethink organisational structure in terms of functional processes and value-adding activities is also an example of incremental innovation at an organisational level.

The aim behind all these examples is to attain a vision of excellence, creativity or productivity.

One way to revolutionise a company is to practise what might be called 'entrepreneurial vision building'. Such as vision is built on pure innovation and some kind of breakthrough. This can be brought about by addressing gaps or current problems in the market or, alternatively, projecting a reality of your own creation and desire – not by attempting to succeed in an existing market, but by creating a new one.

> **Example: Entrepreneurial vision building**
>
> Henry Ford aimed his business towards a future when everyone would have access to a car and, by so doing, he changed the automotive industry.
>
> > 'I will build a car for the great multitude. It will be large enough for the family, but small enough for the individual to run and care for. It will be constructed of the best materials, by the best men to be hired, after the simplest designs that modern engineering can devise. But it will be low in price that no man making a good salary will be unable to own one — and enjoy with his family the blessing of hours of pleasure in God's great open spaces.'
>
> Steve Jobs is another example of an entrepreneurial visionbuilder. His vision for Apple was even more entrepreneurial than Ford's. His mantra was to challenge life around him and he strongly advocated thinking about building your own things that other people can use, regardless of what others say or want. Apple revolutionised the computer, music, telephone and film industries in an unprecedented fashion. Its vision was not built on what customers needed or wanted, but on what its leader (Jobs) could present to the world, regardless of rules or the status quo.

Innovation is, in the end, very 'personal' to the leader – and the organisation. Incremental innovation may be appropriate and relevant in one company while breakthrough innovation will suit another.

How to become more innovative or foster innovation

As Disney's CEO Robert Iger stated, 'Innovation is the balance to tradition to keep things moving forward.'[2] Developing a sense of innovation, becoming innovative or building on your natural abilities is what matters.

You need to be aware of what skills are required to make innovation possible and you and your team more innovative. Consider the following three activities:

■ **Questioning** This requires you to constantly filter and challenge business models, issues and, vision – in other words, challenge the status quo. Think in terms of 'Why?', 'Why not?' and 'What if?' Enrich a vision building exercise by systematically introducing constraints that could jeopardise the future you want to bring to life. This will help you to find innovative solutions or even lead to breakthroughs. The name of the game is to challenge, challenge and challenge.

---

[2] Robert Iger (2011) 'The HBR interview: Technology, tradition, and the Mouse', *Harvard Business Review*, July.

- **Observing** Keep your sensors open. Observe the environment as a whole, both inside and outside your business. Look for pain points and frustrating situations. One way to do this is to spend time with your customers and suppliers to understand how your company fits into their own value chains. Observe and make notes. How do they differ from how you had perceived them? What was interesting, better or worse than what you had imagined? What does this mean for your business and how can it be enhanced or changed?

- **Networking** This allows you to develop a wide frame of reference. Connecting with others will feed you intellectually and allow you to compare and contrast viewpoints. (More on networking can be found in Chapter 8.)

Ultimately, these three activities lead to developing one skill, which is the ultimate skill of the innovative thinker – the ability to associate. It is this skill that Guttenberg used when he created the printing press. Guttenberg attended a social gathering at one of the local beermaking families' houses. He took a tour of the brewery and, when he saw the pressing mechanism, he experienced an epiphany. He applied this idea to book printing.

Similarly, Charles Merrill created the first retail bank by associating banking services with what could be defined as the key characteristics of a supermarket. This was to address the increasing need of a vast new middle-class market, adopting low-cost high-volume merchandising and the concept of chain outlets with a great variety of products.

Mark Zuckerberg associated the concept of a virtual community with the traditional university or school yearbook to create Facebook.

You can integrate either incremental or breakthrough innovation into your vision building. As a self-aware leader you will know whether you naturally lean towards the evolutionary way of incremental change or the revolutionary way of breakthroughs.

Exercises and action points

How to become more innovative

The purpose of the following exercise is to develop your innovation skills by performing the three activities of questioning, observing and networking.

Set aside some quiet time on a daily or weekly basis to purposefully work on your creative and innovative capabilities. If you focus on one skill only, prioritise working on your ability to question. This will trigger the most significant change in your innovation skills.

Questioning

To improve your ability to question, practise daily.

Write down the top five to ten questions that would challenge the status quo in your organisation or revolutionise its set ways of doing things.

Regularly use your feedback group to discuss these questions.

In everyday situations, make a habit of challenging and asking 'Why?', 'Why not?' and 'What if?'

When facing a strategic decision, systematically come up with questions that will both impose and eliminate constraints.

Observing

To enhance your ability to observe, think about the following (note that leisure activities can also be used to develop yourself).

- In work settings
  - Schedule days to spend with your customers and your suppliers. This will help you gain a deeper understanding of what it is they are trying to achieve and how they get their jobs done.
  - Stay neutral in your approach.
  - Observe and make notes about what you liked and how things differed from what you expected.

- Settings outside of work
  - Attend conferences on topics outside your area of expertise.
  - Explore the idea of shadowing the most innovative person you have ever met, to understand how he or she innovates.

- Keep an ongoing reading list concerning emerging trends or processes.
- Make a point when travelling to fit in museum visits or any activity that will help you to observe and learn about different local behaviours.

Julia Cameron's book, *The Artist's Way* (Tarcher, 1992), gives useful pointers on how to rekindle your creativity, which may lead to innovation.

Use your network and your networking skills to develop your vision and strategic thinking.

■ Consider using your strategic network to exchange ideas.

■ Hold or attend breakfast or lunch meetings monthly or so to meet different people as well as current contacts.

■ Look specifically for creative mentors. Identify three or four of the most creative people you know (inside or outside your organisation). Ask them to think about and share with you how they fuel their creative thinking and hold ideas discussions with them about potential business models or emerging industry trends.

Be:

■ curious

■ open

■ receptive.

The entrepreneur game

The purpose of this game is to mirror the thinking process of an entrepreneur coming up with business ideas. The best way to increase opportunities is to interact with entrepreneurs themselves. Here are some options.

■ Take an advisory position in a start-up company to experience first hand entrepreneurial and innovative spirits.

■ Implement a Google-like model in your organisation. Agree on a certain number of hours a week or month when you can work on your own business ideas, but in line with the company's core mission.

■ Create a vision session for yourself. Consider writing a fictitious business plan to answer the following two questions.
- What is needed in the industry?
- Why is it needed now?

Saying what you've got to say

A vision can only become a good one when it acts as a trigger for bringing about a new future, above and beyond what it says in the vision statement. It needs to have an impact and, to do that, being able to communicate with passion, conviction and emotion in any medium, orally and in writing, is critical. As the world today is highly connected, using modern means of communication, such as videos and social media, is a sign of a leader of tomorrow.

Example: How not to make a vision a reality

In 1993, George Fisher took the helm at Kodak. He soon realised that the greatest opportunity about to come along was the digital camera. He envisioned a different future for Kodak: 'We are a picture company, not just a film company.' Despite his best efforts, the firm never quite embraced his vision.

The strategic direction of his vision proved to be correct as digital photography took over the world and Eastman Kodak filed for bankruptcy in 2011. However, Fisher failed in terms of one key element regarding the endorsement of his vision: communication. The '*not* just a film company' part was lethal. As a newcomer to the company, he failed to understand the cardinal rule: respect the past. He would have been better integrating the new vision with both the history of the company and the emotional attachment the long-serving employees had to it.

So, what are the important points to take away from this?

Vision statements can be powerful, but a vision needs to be cascaded down through the organisation. It needs to spread, almost virally, so all understand and get behind it. Engaging people with the vision and drawing others in by means of adequate communication is the last (but not least) element to consider in making a vision a reality.

Effective spoken communication

Oral communication is the most efficient way to broadcast your vision, but language matters. Words, your words, matter in getting the people around you to buy into your vision.

These words can happen in small settings – one-on-one or team meetings – or in front of big audiences. You can choose to simply stand up and talk or go through accompanying slides.

Anyone who is knowledgeable about the art of public speaking will mention the three following attributes as being essential to bringing your vision to life:

- **passion** – because it is this that will most certainly trigger a reaction and subsequent action

- **emotion** – people need to establish emotional bonds, so if you create a feeling of belonging and make your listeners believe in your vision or make your vision personal to them, they will deliver for you (remember the example of Apple earlier in this chapter)

- **conviction** – because you need to believe in what you are saying before getting others to believe in it.

These three attributes help to make the vision vivid and so have an impact on people.

Use images, metaphors and stories to depict the future and why it matters. Do not worry about articulating the 'how we will get there' – this will be dealt with by your strategy. If the vision is compelling, the people around you will find the paths to get there.

Example: Effective communication

General Electric's new vision is a good example:

'Make things that very few in the world can, but that everyone needs.'

Underlying this message is the history of the company and even the history of the USA as the real founder of General Electric was Thomas Edison. It also alludes to the innovative spirit of the USA and its traditional position as one of the key players in the global economy. This vision statement is therefore emotionally charged and a call to action, for people to put the USA back at the forefront of the world's economy.

It can be daunting to express emotions and passion while addressing a large number of staff or even talking to individuals. The following are some pointers and tips to help you overcome this discomfort:

To communicate an emotion

- Reminisce on a particular personal situation that was emotionally charged, good or bad. For instance, you might think about a conversation with your boss when a lot was at stake, having an important discussion with your teenage offspring or preparing for a break up. This will allow you to reconnect with and fire up your emotions. You can then hold on to this feeling as you speak.

- Think in terms of colours. What is the colour that would best describe the emotion you want to feel? What words, sounds or situation will best describe your emotion?

- Put yourself in the picture by linking the situation to and telling a personal story.

To communicate with passion and conviction

- If the subject is of personal interest to you, then just show that and let the energy light up what you say.

- If you have to fake it, then imagine you are talking about one of your hobbies, a favourite activity or something else you are particularly interested in. Project what you would say about these things and how you would say it on to the topic in question.

Practise and practise again

- Think about what you want to say and how you want to say it. Practise by speaking out loud, standing and occupying the space in front of a mirror, alone or with some members of your feedback group.

- Come at it from different angles, practising to feel the emotion, for example. The best way is to do this is to picture yourself giving this speech to someone dear to your heart – your partner, spouse, children.

- Practise to test that the vocabulary and rhythm of your presentation are right.

- The benefits of practising are twofold. First, you will be able to control the flow of your presentation and the accuracy of it much better than if you don't. Second, it will allow you to observe and sense what is required in the room, adjusting your rhythm, personal examples or even data as necessary to keep your audience with you.

- Consider enrolling in poetry, debating or acting classes or a toastmasters group. Any of these will help you develop your communication skill set, particularly communicating your vision, public speaking and negotiation.

Winston Churchill was the master of communicating with emotion, passion and conviction. The following is from the address he made in 1938 after Austria fell to the Nazis:

'We should lay aside every hindrance and endeavour by uniting the whole force and spirit of our people to raise again a great British nation standing up before all the world, for such a nation, rising in its ancient vigour, can even at this hour save civilisation.'

He did not simply say, 'Beat Hitler', he made it personal to everyone, drawing on people's national pride and their sense of destiny. He made everyone feel that they were about to make history, regardless of the outcome. More importantly, he made people *want* to be part of that history.

New times, new media. Churchill's lessons are timeless when it comes to *crafting* a message, but leaders must be in tune with their own time when it comes to *delivering* their messages. In a world of video and instant messaging, any communication strategy that doesn't include these and other media is incomplete.

Example: Using video to communicate and engage

A team of Shell executives had a radical vision to be implemented in the next five to ten years. The company was embarking on significant change and a heavy restructuring agenda, which were needed to enable Shell to be more competitive in its market. The vision that needed to be articulated was reconnecting with growth via a leaner organisation. The vision needed to be clearly understood by everyone to enable fast progress.

The team members debated a statement that would express the new vision. After a couple of brainstorming sessions, they realised what really mattered was to mobilise energy and personal commitment was the way. Commitment to deliver on the vision regardless of the consequences.

The team decided to put together a video in which every member articulated in 30 seconds what success would look like for them personally and how they would commit to it. The theme and the goal were the same, but each leader made it personal and related to their own leadership style, region and team. The video was sent to the entire organisation as part of the leaders' end of year message. The following year, this particular division had the best leadership score in the organisation.

Effective written communication

It takes time to personally present the vision to every member of an organisation. Some leaders are not at ease with being recorded using any media, so the next best way to communicate your vision is in writing.

This requires you to be able to mirror the attributes of effective spoken communication mentioned earlier in this chapter – passion, emotion and conviction – without the benefits of an immediate feedback loop that is the audience's reaction. It has to be interesting and have impact right away as there is no guarantee that your target audience will read the piece and you can't gauge how they will react to it.

Expressing your vision in writing is probably going to be a difficult exercise – some are naturally gifted when it comes to words, others are not. The principles that follow, however, should help to make the process a little easier. They can be applied to any important communications addressed to teams or peers.

Write from the heart

- The best way to trigger interest is to establish an emotional 'hook' that 'catches' the invisible audience.

- Whenever possible, start your communication with something the audience will easily relate to, that will 'talk' to them.

- Starting with words such as, 'Our company', 'business unit' or simply 'We', or opening with a controversial, witty or personal story can also act as powerful hooks. The 'I have a dream' opening of Martin Luther King's speech or the 'It was the best of times, it was the worse of times' start to Dickens' *A Tale of Two Cities* are great examples of this.

- Because, you need to appeal to different people with different backgrounds, cultures and histories, your hooks will need to be different each time. Consider having tailor-made introductions and conclusions to cater for different regions and cultural backgrounds. You can even consider having the entire vision document translated into different languages. It may sound like unnecessary work in a business world still largely dominated by English, but it can guarantee a heightened commitment from the employees concerned. You will not only show your cultural awareness, but also engage with them at a more profound level.

Structure and clarity

■ Construct your communication so that it has a clear start, middle and end. Apart from the emotional hook at the beginning, the audience needs to believe in the vision, so make it compelling and achievable by adding facts and figures or any relevant hard data to support your case.

■ Clarity is also important – clarity of language and clarity of message. Focus on a few themes using concise and simple vocabulary – it will read better.

■ Identify and stick to your purpose – what do you expect from the communication?

■ To secure commitment to your vision and trigger action, it is preferable to end on an inspiring note, depicting what the future will look like or how one person will feel in that future.

■ Words expressing achievement, legacy or a sense of accomplishment can be valuable as endings (for a supreme example refer back to Churchill's words above).

Work and rework

■ Finding the right structure, length, balance, imagery and rhythm takes time.

■ You can choose to write everything that comes into your head without constraints. This is usually best achieved by imagining that you are talking to yourself about your vision. Write as much as you can, until you feel that there is nothing more you have to say.

■ You can choose to repeat in your head what it is you want to say and how you want to say it, just as if you were preparing for a speech. When you feel ready, sit down and put on paper or screen what will sound like an already largely structured piece.

■ Either way, dedicate an adequate amount of time to editing what you've written. The best questions to ask yourself while editing are these.

    – Does it flow?

    – Is it logical?

    – Is it interesting?

- What does this particular part add to the argument?
- What do I really want to say here?

▨ Consider reading your piece out loud during the editing process. You will very quickly identify the good and the not-so-good parts, the elements missing or the unnecessary or irrelevant ones this way.

▨ Finally, test the impact and clarity of your statements by reading what you have written to a person in your feedback group and ask him or her to read it to you, so you can slip into the audience's shoes and gauge that the impact is what you would expect. Consider letting it rest for a couple of days and revisit it cold, to measure if the impact is still the same. You will then be ready to print and post it or press the 'send' button.

Timing

▨ *When* to communicate is as important as *what* to communicate.

▨ Your purpose is to have an impact, gain commitment and inspire action. Make sure you publish your words when the circumstances will be ideal for achieving the desired impact. Typically, avoid Monday mornings as people are barely back into work mode. Friday evenings may or may not work – on the one hand, people are more relaxed towards the weekend, but on the other hand they might have already switched off. Midweek is generally a sensible time to send e-mail messages.

Some final pointers

It takes practice to produce effective written communication, so it is important to increase the number of times you do so – send messages to your team and others above and beyond your vision statement. Establishing a schedule of written communication that mirrors announcement cycles for financial results (quarterly, twice a year) or your reward and recognition cycle (see Chapter 11) can prove efficient and maintain the bond staff have with your organisation. Consider, too, communicating with them when there are major events in your organisation or industry. The bottom line is, communicate when you have something interesting to share or important to say.

Exercises and action points

Tell me your vision

The purpose of this exercise is twofold:

■ to ensure that you can articulate the vision in your own words

■ to test if it is compelling and inspiring.

Without rewriting it entirely, this exercise asks you to interpret and project your vision statement. In other words, it involves you telling someone else what the future organisation or business unit would look or feel like.

What is the process?

Think about how and what you would tell people to make them excited about your vision of the future. Keep it as concise and clear as possible. Test it either on your feedback group or gather a random selection of five to ten people from different layers of the organisation.

If you can't communicate your vision in five minutes or less and are not sensing understanding or interest in your audience, go back to the drawing board.

Example: Finding the right words

One of the prominent French banks was working on redefining its approach to recruiting for the next five years. A new vision was needed to engage the entire human resources department with the change to come. After a couple of sessions, the team was not satisfied with the statement. It lacked impact and inspiration.

The Chief Human Resources Officer then got involved and, after listening to the team's reasoning and what they wanted to achieve, simply said, 'What you are really pushing is an organisation where we recruit for profile not for résumé.' It was this that enabled everyone to embrace the project.

Write to me about your vision

Developing your writing skills is nothing more than becoming increasingly at ease with language. It comes from reading different types of material – from literature, to business books to newspapers.

Consider putting together a reading list on a quarterly basis, being realistic about the time you will have to read. It is recommended to stick to two or three books per quarter, plus daily newspapers and one to two monthly magazines. You can add to this if you are travelling or on holiday.

To benefit as much as possible from your reading, ensure that you have the right mix of the following:

■ Business books – so, if you are not already, you become acquainted with business terminology and concepts. An extensive vocabulary and the ability to use the right words will make your writing impeccable. You will also be able to mirror good sentence structure and rhythm.

■ Great writers' work from different times. They will provide you with wit, imagery and great stories to refer to or quotes to use in your own writing. You will be exposed to a wide range of writing styles, which will enable you to develop your own.

■ Poetry, to reinforce your understanding of sounds and rhythm. It can help you to see how to recreate sensations, translate emotions and so on just using words.

If you are keen to develop your skills further, consider investing time in:

■ writing on a daily basis – two or three pages every day on anything that you feel like writing about will soon make any writing less daunting

■ keeping a list of your favourite words and, in your spare time, play with associating, opposing or combining these words

■ taking a creative writing class

■ adding writers or journalist to your network to get first-hand information on how they write, their techniques and tips.

Summary

Successful vision building is not simply a matter of the vision statement appearing on the front page of the annual report. It happens when the vision becomes part of the essence of the organisation.

If you can see that anyone joining or entering your organisation for the first time feels the sense of purpose in the people around them, then you have done a magnificent job with your vision building. A vision needs to also change and evolve. Never be complacent, always keep trying to reach for the mission and find the next mountain to climb.

The following quote from leadership guru Peter Drucker[3] perfectly sums this up:

'One day a traveller, walking along a lane, came across three stone-cutters working in a quarry. Each was busy cutting a block of stone. Interested to find out what they were working on, the traveller asked them what they were doing.

The first stonecutter replied: "I am making a living."

The second kept on hammering while he said: "I am doing the best job of stone cutting in the entire country."

The third stonecutter, when asked the same question said: "I am building a cathedral."'

Here's a reminder of some of the key points from this chapter:

- mission feeds vision and vision feeds strategy and each is a distinct concept to be clear about – mission is the star to reach, vision is the mountain to climb, strategy is the route to take

- the purpose of vision building is to prompt actions towards achieving a certain future – it needs to resonate with the purpose and values of the organisation and the leaders and address the question, 'What's in for me?' for the staff

- innovation is an important aspect to keep in mind when vision building as it will help push the boundaries of what it is the organisation can achieve, but it is not essential

- the ability to be innovative can be developed by means of questioning, observing, curiosity, openness and networking, increasing the number and types of experiences you have and building and maintaining a wide frame of reference

- a vision can only be successful if agreement and passion for it cascades down to all teams, which can result from co-creation and communication using a wide variety of tools, including video or even social media

---

[3] Peter Drucker (2008) *The Essential Drucker: The best of sixty years of Peter Drucker's essential writings on management, Collins Business Essentials*, HarperBusiness.

- effective communication, both oral and written, that draws on emotion, passion and conviction and can articulate what is in it for the staff will win their commitment to it

- how the vision is communicated can be left to the direct leaders of the teams, using storytelling techniques, cultural references and so on, to create emotional bonds with their audiences.

10

Cultivating your strategic thinking

'The real challenge in crafting strategy lies in detecting subtle discontinuities that may undermine a business in the future. And for that there is no technique, no program, just a sharp mind in touch with the situation.'

Henry Mintzberg, Cleghorn Professor of Management Studies,
McGill University, Montreal

This chapter covers:

■ what a leader needs in order to spearhead the strategic thinking process

■ how to use traditional strategic tools

■ the best ways to develop your strategic thinking abilities

■ the role of trend spotting in strategic thinking.

LAN Chile and the ant colony

In 1994, the Cueto family acquired part of the Chilean national airlines, LAN. Their core expertise was in the cargo business and they had limited experience in the passenger business. While looking at the different value drivers and pain points of each of the business models, they decided to merge both activities and develop an independent low-cost offering. The main rationale was to maximise the different demand cycles of cargo and commercial flights. They also saw this as an innovative way to increase profitability (due to the reduction in their break-even point on routes) while using their physical assets to the fullest. By doing so, not only did they multiply their share price by 15 between 1998 and 2010 but they also made entry into the market in Latin America very difficult for other low-cost airlines.

In an ant colony, each individual ant has a decision maker role. It must choose between patrolling, looking for good opportunities to find food or cleaning up debris. The ants themselves have no sense of the global system and, equally, it is not possible to understand the concept of an ant colony by only looking at an individual ant's behaviours. The individual role and the total system are highly integrated. Ants are able to solve complicated and challenging problems with no strategic plan. An ant colony is a typical example of a complex yet adaptive system geared to getting results.

What lessons can be derived from these two examples?

First, business success comes from innovative ways of approaching strategic thinking. Looking beyond the obvious, finding new and different angles, taking risks (in terms of business models) and not contemplating only the easiest and most obvious ways – these are all ways to increase power. The owners of LAN Chile did this. They used their knowledge of cargo and, by associating the risk–reward equation of a known business model with one they did not know, they created a new model and a solid base for success.

Second, efficient problem solving comes from the ability to immediately react to fast-changing circumstances, as demonstrated by the ant colony. Ants constantly adjust to reassess their priorities based on what results are necessary. They think independently and react in the moment to maximise results.

Most companies have a formal strategic process that will run its course over the year. It will typically start with strategy formulation or reformulation and end with the operational plan. The strategic process is or should be the top priority for all leaders as it is the key translation process from vision to action. Once the strategy has been set, it is cascaded down to all levels of the organisation and measured in different ways. However, it is increasingly important for strategic thinking to be rooted in the here and now while at the same time constantly addressing and adjusting to the immediate future.

From vision to strategy – a translation exercise

Strategy building is the link between vision and execution. It requires the ability to look both inside and outside of the organisation to articulate both what is needed for and what could prevent the vision from being realised. Strategybuilding also means to identify and secure long-lasting competitive advantage by means of a fluid, albeit rigorous, questioning process. Finally, it is a balancing act between short-, medium- and long-term thinking. The translation exercise is only deemed to have been completed when the strategy has been communicated to the wider organisation.

Vision has been previously defined as the 'what'   what does the company want to achieve in the long-term future? In turn, strategy is there to answer the following two key questions.

- How are we going to reach this vision?

- How are we going to build long-lasting competitive advantage?

There is a handful of key elements to understand and make the translation process easier:

- the value equation of your company and how to test it against traditional strategic tools

- the strategic process.

In the same fashion as the vision, the strategic thinking is then to be communicated.

Working on the value equation of your organisation

Before being able to build or articulate your strategy, it is essential to understand the value equation of your company – in other words, how your organisation, company or business unit actually makes money and/or creates value.

Drawing up and understanding the value equation forces you to:

- identify the key interdependencies – internal or external – and crystallise what the success factors are – again, internal or external – for your organisation

- take into consideration the different forces that are playing for or against you – they may come from different functions, customers, suppliers or competitors

- create business models efficient enough to establish or sustain competitive advantage

- decide on your best course of action.

These are the real foundations of successful strategic thinking and strategy building. As an add-on benefit, they allow you to create fit-for-purpose metrics and support and track the execution of your strategy.

How to create and understand your values mind map is explained in the first exercise at the end of this section. Appreciating and using traditional strategic tools are also examined. This is a way to improve your abilities in assessing and deciding on the best strategic directions for your organisation. There are several strategic tools that you can use, but the most widely used remain the following.

Porter's five competitive forces

Porter's model focuses on understanding and coping with competition by defining it as broadly as possible. The model asks you to think in terms of the value chain and takes into consideration different elements of potential competitive pressure. It encompasses obvious and less obvious elements such as the following:

- **The bargaining power of customers** They have the upper hand for when it comes to setting price. This power comes about when there is a plethora of offers for a product, there is hardly to no differentiation between one product and another, the customers represent a big part of the turnover or margin of the company (concentration) and there is hardly to no cost for changing suppliers.

- **The bargaining power of suppliers** The suppliers have the upper hand regarding settings prices. This power is usually associated with highly differentiated products, very high demand or concentration of production or constraints.

- **The potential for substitution of products** Can the product be easily replaced?

- **The possibility of new competitors competing for the same or even a different part of the value chain** In other words it is easy to enter the market because there is, for example a low level of investment in the infrastructure to start with, low loyalty from a customer standpoint or low government regulations.

This model helps to create a common framework for any industry. It also helps to identify long-term creators of **value**. You will gain a complete view of the major players, too, and be able to craft a comprehensive action plan to help either protect or gain the profitability of the company.

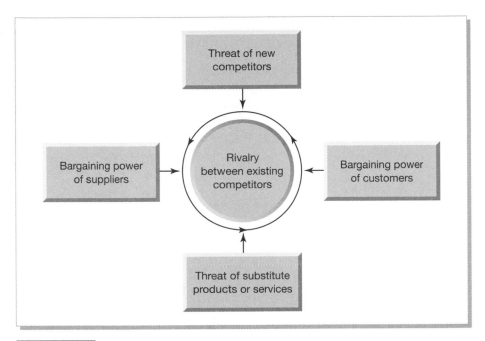

The five forces that shape competition

Porter's analysis can be used in any phase of a company's lifecycle, from start-up to traditional player to leader in an industry. It helps you understand where you stand and what you need to do to be more competitive. It is a must do in any strategybuilding session (see Figure 10.1).

McKinsey's 7S model[1]

This model is usually used with the aim of improving the performance of a company, assessing the effects of future changes or helping in the formulation of strategy. It represents a good questioning framework and allows you to quickly grasp interdependencies.

It is based on the premise that there are seven key aspects that need to be aligned for an organisation to be successful. Both internal and external factors need to be studied. There are hard aspects that are easily identifiable and directly controllable:

[1] Developed by Tom Peters and Robert Waterman while working for McKinsey and further explored in their management book *In Search of Excellence.*

- strategy (statements)
- structure (organisational charts)
- systems (IT system and processes).

There are also soft aspects, which are more difficult to assess and influence, namely:

- skills
- staff
- style
- shared values.

The model highlights interdependencies and helps to show how changes in one aspect trigger change elsewhere (see Figure 10.2):

- **Strategy** In this case, this is the means by which the plan is to be maintained and/or competitive advantage gained.
- **Structure** The organisational structure.
- **Systems** The process – what the daily activities and procedures are that are undertaken to create value.

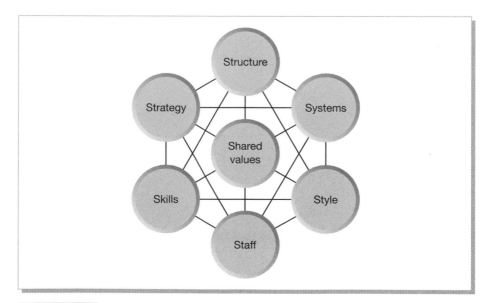

Figure 10.2   McKinsey's 7S model

- **Shared values** The core values of the company. Out of these the company's mission and vision are developed.

- **Style** This means the style of leadership in action.

- **Staff** The workforce (of a particular department or the entire organisation).

- **Skill** The actual skills and competences of the employees working for the organisation.

To use the McKinsey model effectively, it is recommended to assess all the elements in the model independently by means of a thorough questioning process. This exercise is best performed as a team to benefit from other diverse perceptions and expertise.

It is preferable to start by questioning the shared values, as they are at the heart of the system. Ask if they are consistent with your structure, strategy, investments and if they need to change?

Then move to the hard and soft elements – debating how they support one another or noting if they should be changed.

Once you have gathered all the information, look for gaps and inconsistencies in the different elements to draft an action plan.

The 7S model is a very iterative process as it is built on interdependencies – if one piece moves all the others will be impacted.

The model can be used in a variety of situations (team, project and so on) when the main focus is alignment, and is particularly helpful when embarking on a major change management programme.

The Boston Consulting Group's matrix

The matrix is based on one principle – that market share and market growth are strongly correlated with profitability. If you have been active in a market for a while and have built market share, you should know how to be profitable and have started to realise what economies of scale can be formed. The market growth element is used to assess the market's attractiveness and help justify investments.

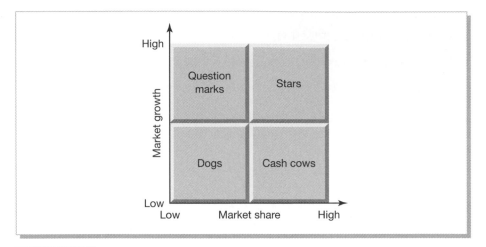

Figure 10.3   The Boston Consulting Group's matrix

The Boston Consulting Group's matrix works as follows (see Figure 10.3):

- **Dogs** Companies with low market share and low market growth. These will require a lot of hard work to improve the situation. An exit strategy could be used to generate cash to be reinvested elsewhere (in stars or to push the question marks).

- **Cash cows** Companies with high market share and low market growth. These are usually nice and profitable businesses that should be 'milked', typically they require a low level of investment to keep their market share stable.

- **Stars** Companies with high market share and high market growth. These benefit from a strong presence and can grow with the market. The best course of action here is to think hard in order to fully transform the opportunity with a view to outperforming the market.

- **Question marks (problem children)** Companies with low market share and high market growth. They usually represent a pool of opportunities and can call for different types of strategies. They can lead to a turnaround if there is a significant advantage to be gained from them and the effort–results ratio is acceptable. It may be decided to do nothing and observe external factors in the market to gear the decision towards a turnaround or an exit at a later stage. Alternatively, an exit strategy may be called for – in other words, the business, organisation or asset may be either sold or closed down, depending on what matters to you and what is a reasonable timeline.

The question marks group should be the core part of your strategic thinking as you craft and monitor an action plan. They actually represent your possibly good strategic bets and may require investment and effort in terms of redefining what business models and alliances are needed.

The Boston Consulting Group's matrix is particularly beneficial if you are thinking in terms of a portfolio of products and/or geographies. It is instrumental in articulating the best cost–benefit ratio, screening opportunities and helps in the allocation of resources. It helps in the process of deciding where to invest in your business or, similarly, where to divest when in a cost management or productivity mindset. The different strategies are typically action orientated.

SWOT analysis

This is used to help identify a sustainable competitive position in your market. Looking at your strengths and weakness and assessing both the opportunities and the threats that are attached to them helps with crafting differentiated strategies for your market. It can be used at different levels, from corporate strategy to specific product lines or markets. To be effective, it has to be rigorous and driven by facts and figures.

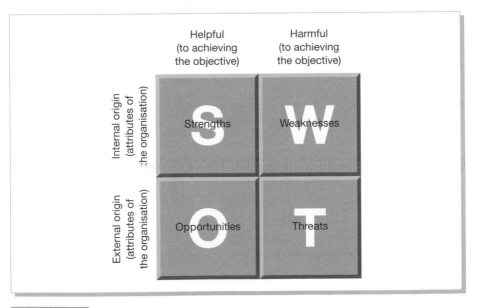

Figure 10.4 The SWOT analysis matrix

- **Strengths** These need to be considered both from internal and external perspectives – that is, asking what the customers see and what the competition says. The identification of real strengths will come from comparing your organisation with the competition and asking how you differ from the rest. If an identified strength does not differ from your competitor's, then it is not a real strength.

- **Weaknesses** These also need to be assessed both internally and externally. Weaknesses might be born from a complex organisational structure or a slow decision making process. Try to be as realistic as possible in order to devise the best ways to overcome them.

- **Opportunities** These should emerge from observing your environment and paying specific attention to the emerging trends and changes in your consumers' behaviours. You will need to think in terms of technology, the regulatory framework, your growth path and geographical expansion, to name just a few. Ask yourself how you can differentiate from or take advantage of what you know, or mitigate and overcome.

- **Threats** These should also result from observing the same parameters as for opportunities, but asking yourself what risks are they posing and how it is possible to mitigate or overcome them.

Using the strategic tools

The above tools are useful for building your awareness in terms of your competitors, organisational design strategy, strategic prioritisation and strategy formulation. They are best worked through with your team as part of preparing for a big strategic session, but they can be used on your own as well to help with a wide array of situations.

It can be tricky to know what to use when, so Table 10.1 will help you to navigate the strategic landscape.

Table 10.1 Which strategic tool to use when

Potential issues/problems to solve	Preferred tools
• Investment decision (technology, infrastructure or product development)	• Boston Consulting Group's matrix • SWOT analysis • Porter's five competitive forces
• Market entry or exit	• Boston Consulting Group's matrix • Porter's five competitive forces
• Organisational change	• McKinsey's 7S model
• IT system change	• McKinsey's 7S model • SWOT analysis
• Company valuation for an acquisition strategy	• Porter's five competitive forces
• Integration in case of merger	• McKinsey's 7S model • SWOT analysis

In order to come up with the best strategic outcome, always consider using a mix of tools. After a certain period of time, you will naturally switch from one model to another, even creating your own model by cherry-picking the different parts of different models that are most suited to your needs.

---

case study   Shell Downstream's strategic review

In 2008, the Downstream leadership team decided to focus only on core or highly strategic markets.

The Downstream strategy team looked at a list of different criteria that included items, such as:

■ current market share

■ current aggregated turnover

■ projected GDP growth in different countries

■ projected turnover in different countries

■ current and projected aggregated operating costs and yield

■ current and projected aggregated return on capital employed

■ current and projected demands in the country

■ potential asset maintenance or investment requirements for different countries.

▶

> The team used several timeframes and complemented the study by looking at factors such as political stability and the impact of mega trends such as renewables and sustainability.
>
> The result was a list of countries produced that either needed to be exited from or entered over the next few years.
>
> Inherently, a mix of the Boston Consulting Group's matrix, SWOT analysis and Porter's five competitive forces analysis was used to reach a conclusion.

Before moving on to the translation process itself, it is important to note that this strategic process can be carried out in two specific ways, which present opposite forces in strategic thinking.

Top down v. bottom up

Top down usually refers to leaders viewing things from the top and assessing the bigger picture. This approach does not necessarily take into consideration all the nitty-gritty implications of any one strategic direction. It can also at times suffer somewhat from the tendency towards oversimplification and overlook the difficulties of execution.

Bottom up refers to the activity of piecing together subunits' needs to reveal the bigger picture. It can at times suffer somewhat from the tendency towards an overly conservative strategic approach or some level of complacency. However, this approach does help to shed light on the realities of a business.

It is important, instead, to engage both the top and bottom of the pyramid when formulating strategies. Doing so while at the same time, in either a dual or parallel process, undertaking a high-level analysis using the strategic tools described, complemented by some sensing carried out at several levels in the organisation, will result in a much more reliable and workable strategy than would either a solely top-down or bottom-up approach.

Traditionally, strategic thinking has been the remit of the leadership team and what has been produced has then been cascaded down through the rest of the company. Today, being able to adjust quickly and stay, as much as possible, close to the reality of the business is the best way to build long-lasting competitive advantages. Consequently, it is highly recommended to engage and gather input regularly from all levels and parts of the organisation.

Translating vision into strategy

At the core of effective strategic thinking is cutting through complexity. You need to eventually crystallise your direction into a handful of themes. These, in turn, will be broken down into smaller pieces and turned into tangible, concrete actions.

Using the different strategic tools presented above will give you much information to sift through, different pieces to keep in mind and a variety of potential outcomes. How do you then simplify your strategy choice and decide which course of action to take?

The best way is to keep the following three questions in mind:

- What does this strategy mean for the organisation?
- What will get us closer to reaching the vision? Can it potentially do so faster?
- What is required in order for this to become a reality?

These questions need to be assessed using the following filters:

- short term v. long term
- proactive v. reactive
- global v. local.

Short term v. long term

This is the most recognisable source of tension when it comes to formulating strategies – the best analogy is the marketing budget discussion between the finance and marketing parts of an organisation. The former will typically push for tighter controls on the marketing spend to preserve the current bottom line, while the latter will argue, 'What is planted today will be harvested tomorrow', wanting to increase the budget.

What to do? Make a point of thinking through the interdependencies and the impacts of each decision on each dimension. Keep in mind that any decision will be imperfect as the future may be shaped but is not known.

Proactive v. reactive

The most traditional way to approach the formulation of strategies is based on proactively trying to assess what could and could not happen. However, no one can ever predict the future and, in a fluid and increasingly volatile environment, reactivity or even agility is what will help you prevail.

In his book *Loose: The future of business is letting go* (Business Plus, 2011), Martin Thomas presents the argument that it is time to recognise the limitations of long-term thinking and slow motion and promote the need to operate in real time and immediately adjust to the circumstances.

Always leave yourself space to improvise and change due to unforeseen yet critical events. Ensure you have some leeway, never be too prescriptive[2] and empower your team to deliver.

Global v. local

This is the biggest source of tension when it comes to the moment of simplification. There is always a healthy tension between the need for consistency and conforming to a global strategy and the need to adjust to local realities.

Remember that people based locally have a much better understanding of how things are there than you and so have insights that will be valuable for you. Constructively challenge all potential deviations but be open to adjusting to take account of local specificities. What really matters is being able to deliver the vision, which can still happen even when such local adjustments are made.

---

[2] An interesting article to look at in relation to this is 'Strategy as simple rules' by Kathleen Einshenhardt and Donald Sull (2001) *Harvard Business Review*, January.

Translating your vision into strategy should not be a one-off exercise, but be factored into and part of the organisation's essential way of operating. Make sure you hold sessions throughout the year to help you constantly recalibrate your thinking.

It is also very powerful and somewhat innovative to use social media while engaging in your strategic thinking. You may decide to tweet while in the strategy planning session or even broadcast live while it is underway and allow for everyone to participate in a virtual co-creation exercise.

Keeping in mind the three filters – short term v. long term, proactive v. reactive and global v. local – will enable you to create a flexible strategy, based on deep thinking about potential scenarios, and systematically integrate the unexpected.

This exercise is one of the most challenging yet interesting parts of a leader's job as it demands that you think from the outside in (from the environment in to the company) and inside out (from the company to the environment) at the same time, plus have a Janus-like face to absorb the past while also looking to the future.

Communicating your strategy – the art of pitching

Chapter 9 covered communicating your vision. More generally, as a leader, you will engage in a variety of activities and situations that will most definitely require you to make some form of presentation (also called a 'pitch'). Presenting your strategic plan to the Board is one of these, and an important one, as it carries the fate of the business for the coming one to five years.

How do you master the art of presenting your business strategy – or making any other kind of presentation for that matter?

You will find lots of dos and don'ts for how to prepare to make an effective strategy presentation and different opinions about what is appropriate in terms of length, structure, look, feel and so on. However, it can all be boiled down to the following simple set of parameters.

It is a story

As with a speech or when writing about your vision, your presentation needs to tell a story – the story of the business at a certain point in time, now or in the future – and articulate how you will get there.

Keep the following two questions in mind:

- What is the story you are trying to tell?
    - Is it a growth story? If so, it will require a lot of details on the how, qualitative details on market opportunities and action plan.
    - Is it a cost-reduction story? It will require hefty financial information, headcount data paired with a timeline on execution or the main actors to engage with.
    - Is it a run and maintain story or an innovation story ... the list can go on.
    - What matters is that you find the angle you are going to use and articulate your story about the strategy around that.
    - Your presentation will have to be of interest to the other parties and address some of their concerns or needs.

- What do you want to achieve by giving this presentation?:
    - If it is to simply inform the attendees, once the strategy has been agreed, particular attention needs to be given to the contexts and fit-for-purpose data (numbers, percentages, statistics).
    - If it is to get commitment and agreement to the strategy, it is critical to articulate fully what specific benefits will be gained and clearly present risks and opportunities.
    - If it is to reach a decision on which potential strategic direction to follow, add information on the alternative solutions, potential lost opportunities or even the cost implications of each. Integrating a decision tree can also be useful.

Focusing on these two questions will guide you as to what level of detail and which content to include.

It is a structured story

A pitch requires a start, middle and end. An effective presentation will definitely include an introductory slide (usually an executive summary or an overview slide) and a summary slide – this can be at the beginning or the end of the presentation or both, to articulate the logic.

Include key points on every slide and pay attention to the titles of the slides as they will help you to locate where you are in the flow of the presentation and make it easier for your audience to follow, too.

It is a visual tool

This is a very important point to keep in mind. A presentation of a strategy – any presentation – has to be very visual. Use graphs, images, pay attention to the aesthetics – the size, colours and font matter. Also, minimise the number of words on your slides. The best presentations not only sound great but actually look great, too.

It is only a support tool

The minute slides are put up, the audience's attention shifts from you to the slides. A presentation is there to act as a support tool for you, so you should be the centre of attention, not the slides. Most of the story will be told by you, so stick to two or three key messages per slide, complemented by supporting data to aid understanding. What matters is that you talk around and about the visuals and make the story come to life, not just read the slides.

If we had to sum up the art of putting a presentation together in one sentence it would probably be:

> *the ability to translate business challenges into visuals.*

Putting a presentation together will require some amount of rework (see also the advice about editing in Chapter 9), so plan accordingly. It is important to make sure that it is as simple, concise and clear as possible, so:

■ fight the tendency to use complicated words – if a sentence or a bullet point is not clear, ask yourself, 'What is it I am trying to say?' and write down your answer.

■ fight the temptation to put too much on the slides or have too many slides by asking yourself, 'What does this add to the story?' or 'Is this relevant?' – if the answer to either of these questions is 'No', either take it out or consider moving these slides to an appendix section

■ give the presentation to someone who has not been involved in the process to ask for feedback on its clarity, logic and how interesting it is

■ learn to let go and stop fiddling with your presentation – there is no benefit to be gained from endlessly reworking the same presentation.

When it then comes to actually giving the presentation – about your strategy or something else – the three principles of conveying emotion, passion and conviction (developed in Chapter 9) need to be applied.

At a certain point in your career, you will have to guide others on how to deliver a high-quality strategic pitch. Training them at an early stage and guiding them to follow these same principles is a great investment.

Exercises and action points

The checklist exercise – how to build your values mind map

The aim of this exercise is to extract the key process or relationship that will allow your company to make money and establish very quickly the key interdependencies. It will help you to create a mental checklist of these interdependencies.

When to use it?

It is recommended that you undertake this exercise when you arrive fresh at a new business. It will very quickly help you to understand the value equation of the company and create your strategic checklist.

The process

You will need to spend some time with different parts of the organisation and/or the regions. It is a good idea to gather this knowledge via face-to-face interactions. A series of one- to two-hour

▶

meetings will be needed, each leading to a series of other meetings with the top two or three critical partners, functions and so on. The meetings should address the following five questions so that you can come to understand the value chain:

- How do you make money? What different business models are used?

- Where do the products, information or values come from? In other words, what are the inflows and who do you rely most on?

- What do you do with these inflows? What are the processes and what do you take into consideration as critical success factors?

- What happens next? Who gets the final products? What are the final outcomes? What are the outflows and who relies most on them?

- Who are the key two or three people you rely on in case of crisis? What are their functions?

The final outcome

At the end of the process you should have a mind map of your business with the key salient points and the two or three elements that are critical to its success. This will allow you to perform a strategic stakeholder mapping and also to establish a filter for any trends, information or events. That in turn will ensure you quickly assess the impact of any events on your value equation. You will end up with a powerful mental map.

The Merlin exercise, Part 2 – how to develop your strategy

In Chapter 9, the Merlin exercise was recommended as a way to enable you to define a compelling future for your company. It can also be used to help you develop your strategy. The process is the same, the exercise being carried out face to face with your leadership team. Take the same approach for small or bigger groups and consider having a facilitator present.

Process

In Chapter 9, the following key question was used:

- What will the organisation look like in 15 years?

To create one compelling 'invented' future that is exciting and challenging. In order to move the exercise on to building your strategy, the following question threads have proved useful.

▶

■ In order for the organisation to look like this in 15 years, what should it look like in 10 years' time?

This should address but not be restricted to the following:

- In which markets should we be players?
- What types of business models should we have implemented?
- Where?
- What types of strategic alliances should we have built?
- What types of acquisitions/divestments should have taken place?
- Which organisational structure should we have adopted to most efficiently support it? (This includes both workforce and system structures.)
- What could be the barriers to us achieving this at a macro level (GDP growth, political environment, market trends, regulatory changes), micro level (competition, suppliers, customer presence, positioning) or operational level (human resources strategy, desired metrics, organisational structure)?
- How could we overcome these barriers? Could we do this via products, processes, people or technology?
- How should we measure success?

This list of questions is not exhaustive. The questions you should use need to be relevant – to your industry, business unit, organisation – and have impact:

■ In order for the organisation to look like this in ten years, what should it look like in five years?

Repeat the questions you used above to create the next level, then finally ask the following question:

■ In order for the company to look like this in five years, what should the company look like next year?

By using this iterative process of sequential futures, the participants will break through the here and now, shifting their perspectives from the conventional feasibility of an idea to jointly assessing what to do both as individuals and together. This process also delineates clear measures for accomplishments, which will then be easier to cascade down to the rest of the organisation. The exercise provides a lot of opportunities to challenge, debate and build on each others' ideas.

▶

The Merlin exercise is a very powerful and creative strategic thinking tool. It can also incorporate some of the more traditional tools described earlier. For example, you could hold this as a two-day session, starting with a brainstorming session using a set of strategic tools (Porter's five competitive forces and the Boston Consulting Group's matrix, for instance), referring to some research and analytical data, then move on to this exercise.

The entrepreneur game, Part 2

You will recall that, in Chapter 9, the purpose of this game was explained as being to mirror the thinking process of an entrepreneur when coming up with a business idea in order to aid your vision building process. Consider complementing that vision session with a strategy building session. Simply address the following questions on strategy using the same fictitious business plan as in Chapter 9:

- Why am I the best one to do this? Who are my competitors and how do I differentiate myself from them?

- How will I make money? How does the product work and what type of business model will I need?

- How will I go to market? What types of strategic alliances or endorsements will I need?

- What are the risks and the opportunities for my business? How will I mitigate or take advantage of them?

- If I were to invest in this business, what would I want to change or make stronger? What questions would I want to ask?

This exercise can be done on your own if you are wanting to test potential ideas before taking them to a group setting to be challenged and recalibrated.

When using this exercise, in a group setting, it is a good idea to form two distinct groups. One group to play the role of the company's executives and be responsible for developing the strategy. The second to take the part of an independent body, which might have a different purpose or view. This could be a potential investor or a regulator for example. The purpose of the second group is to challenge and push the thinking in any potential direction with a view to creating the best strategic outcome possible.

The pathway to superior strategic thinking

In a world that is becoming increasingly complicated, modern strategic thinking needs to go above and beyond the translation exercise – from vision to strategy. Becoming an 'integrative thinker' is the name of the game. This skill can be developed by building on a solid understanding of traditional tools, constantly challenging ideas by embracing complexity, being in tune with fast-changing circumstances and promoting cognitive diversity.

What is an 'integrative thinker'? In layman's terms, this is someone with the ability to hold and explore two opposite thoughts at the same time and, using the resulting creative tension, come up with a superior third option. Integrative thinking requires a frame of reference or knowledge framework that is rooted in accepting complexity, pushing innovation and looking for cognitive diversity.

Embracing complexity and thinking in 'ecosystems'

In business terms, 'complexity' has a multilayered meaning. It alludes to the number of functions and activities in business increasing, each moving with its own dynamics. This causes difficulties when it comes to predicting how one element will react to a specific event and suggests that the same starting conditions may at times yield different results. Complexity also means that, contrary to what we can perceive, unplanned or unusual events are more frequent and have more impact than we can comprehend.

Consciously embracing complexity is the first step towards becoming an integrative thinker. How so? Because it pushes you to look for and assess the entirety of the business universe. In other words, it requires you to look at any question, business model or function to proactively identify recurring or singular events. At the same time, you need to stay grounded in the here and now and be fully aware of your own inability to measure the impact of any decision.

To develop tolerance or the ability to embrace complexity, focus on the following key skills:

- the ability to look at a problem from every angle

- see issues within their context

- agile decision making.

The ability to quickly change perspective

Systematically apply different lenses to the same problem. This could mean applying different functional lenses (marketing, product, finance, consumer, regulator). Some questions that might be useful to keep in mind are, 'What would it mean to me if I was a marketing person/analyst/chief finance officer/consumer? How would I react to this products/line/strategy/idea?'

Another way to approach this would be to methodically take the opposite view in relation to one specific strategy then apply the 5 Whys technique described in Chapter 9.

---

case study   ## American Express v. Google

American Express is a traditional credit card issuer. Amex makes money in two main ways: payments from vendors that accept the cards and annual cardholder fees. With the increasing development of mobile apps for making payments, all the big technology giants, such as Microsoft or Google are now entering the payments market. Google's income stream is still heavily dependent on advertising so making money from payment can appear a relatively immaterial additional source of income, not core to its profitability. This gives Google the ability to give much better pricing conditions to customers using its apps and can have negative consequences on Amex's profitability. This then prompts Amex (and others) to react and innovate.

Taking the example of American Express v. Google, if you were in the credit card industry and you knew your competition was going to be the Amexs or Visas of this world, what could you do?

If you adopted a traditional strategic thinking approach, you would decide to compete by means of differentiation. However, how much could you realistically differentiate yourself from the competition? You could do so a little, by adding benefits to being a member or increasing your vendors' database.

Another option would be to not compete but collaborate in innovative ways. You could choose, for instance, to create an enhanced value proposition with some of your competitors and for the market. You might consider jointly developing an app for your members to download free of charge. It would enable them to pay not only with their cards but also with their mobile phones and other mobile devices.

You can change perspectives by creating different scenarios, in a 'What if?' chain of questions. For this, it is important to have a clear mental picture of what the value equations are and, of course, who the main actors in the market are. Do not overlook the less obvious ones as they may present interesting opportunities.

In order to practise your ability to change perspectives, try the following.

Choose the top three critical elements of your strategy and, for each one of them, play or draw up different scenarios, taking into consideration positive or negative impacts. Assess the impacts of events on each one of them separately, then look at the interdependencies with the others.

If, for example you identified regulators and health and safety regulations as key elements in your strategy, you could do the following.

Contemplating how the regulator is going to move in a particular country and how this could impact the health and safety part of your equation may lead you to make certain decisions or act in certain ways. In a highly regulated market, you may decide to not to grow much or develop a lobbying strategy to have an impact on the regulators. In markets relatively immune to regulation, however, you may decide to move quickly to give yourself a chance to shape the regulatory framework.

> ### Example: Shell's scenario methodology[3]
>
> Shell has been using its scenario methodology to enrich its strategic thinking for over 40 years. It recognises that the future landscape in which its investments need to prosper is neither certain nor random.
>
> Shell applies a dual approach, looking first at the 'predictability' of the world by considering predetermined mega trends that it knows can and will have a direct or indirect impact on the industry in all plausible outlooks. This is complemented by a review of critical uncertainties that may lead to very different feasible outcomes. These are often the result of choices made – political, social or consumers' – as well as more technical uncertainties.
>
> Shell runs through unpredictable events that would have an impact. These might be as wide-ranging as the deployment of technology, or the Eurozone crisis. It identifies, analyses and keeps a finger on the pulse of these events by means of a pool of experts within and outside the company to promote cognitive diversity.
>
> Shell uses the scenario methodology to test the strategic thinking of the company, prepare leaders to respond to uncertain developments and, at times, create breakthroughs and gain competitive advantage. For example, it contributed to Shell's choice to invest in bio-fuels and increase its presence in Latin America to do so. Shell's significant involvement in the natural gas sector is also consistent with this work, as is its early concern with the issue of greenhouse gas emissions.
>
> Following the Macondo crisis in the Gulf of Mexico, the scenario methodology encouraged Shell's leaders to be on the front foot regarding transparency, standards and constructive relationships with regulators. This may have contributed to Shell being granted new exploration licences in the Gulf of Mexico, as well as guiding its approach in other frontier areas, such as the Arctic.

By moving quickly from a constrained to an unconstrained environment and looking for different angles, you will strengthen your strategies.

The ability to think in terms of an 'ecosystem'

That is, 'ecosystem' in the biological sense of the word. It means that all organisms living in a particular area interact with each other to, ultimately, create a sustainable and mutually beneficial environment.

Applying the notion of an ecosystem to strategic thinking means that you firstly identify communities, functions or units that share the same ideas about goals, objectives or impacts. This will enable you to identify the sharing and exchanging mechanisms between them and

---

[3] By Jeremy Bentham, Vice President Global Business Environment and Head of Scenarios Team, Royal Dutch Shell

strengthen the model or assess the relevance of it. In other words, thinking in terms of ecosystems will push you to address the 'Does this make sense?' question.

Developing your ability to think in terms of ecosystems is mainly achieved by broadening your terms of reference by learning and constantly using your strategic networks (as described in Chapter 8). Complement this by systematically thinking in terms of a value map when presented with different or new challenges or areas of knowledge.

The questions to ask to develop this way of thinking and analysing are these:

- How does this impact my value-creation mechanism?
- What are the interdependencies?

Your innovation skills developed by means of the exercises and practical examples given in Chapter 9 will also be helpful here.

Example: The Wine Source Fund

In 2009, a successful, high-profile executive decided to match his business skill with his passion for wine and create a wine fund. As any mindful entrepreneur would, he started to gather information on the value system, competition and critical success factors for this idea.

He soon realised that the best way to alleviate most of the risks related to a wine fund was to create a two-pillared model or an ecosystem, so the entry and exit risks would be adequately mitigated. He created an independent merchant company located in the best-in-class wine-producing country and another independent distributor company, again in a country with a tradition of selling wine.

These two distinct companies allow not only easier access to products, but also first-hand, prime information on price, habits and consumer behaviours – all extremely important to correctly valuing a fund.

This ecosystem is one of a kind and now established as a solid and tangible platform on which to develop the financial product. The pilot profitability of the fund has reached a healthy 21 per cent in the past year.

The ability to be agile in your decision making

There are natural human limitations to our ability to understand all aspects of one given business. Keeping that in mind will clearly ground you in the now and push you towards building a healthy observe–assess–adjust rhythm into your strategic thinking process. Keep the following mantra in mind to help you:

I do not know what I do not know, and
what I know today may be obsolete tomorrow.

Figure 10.5 illustrates how we should all be careful about our perceptions of our knowledge.

A useful way to address the perception of knowledge is to systematically conclude any strategic thinking session with the following two questions:

- What do we think we have forgotten?
- If the world changed tomorrow, how much of this would still stand?

Ask for answers to these questions from everyone in the room to capture all potential angles.

In brief, uncertainty is the word to reflect on. Each organisation has an almost infinite number of possible futures available, all resulting from the current situation. Some may be anticipated as a result of certain events and trends. Others are not yet on the map or their beginnings are unnoticed in the present. Finally, there are some possibilities that do not exist because they have not yet been invented.

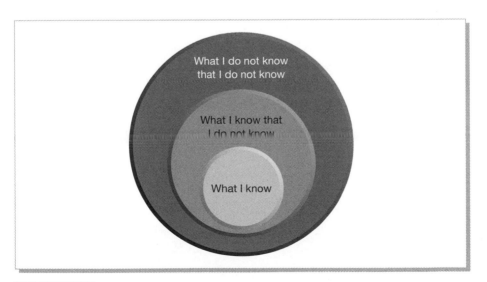

Figure 10.5 **The perceptions of knowledge**

Developing your ability to pick up and capitalise on mega trends

In 2010, Samsung's President Boo-Keun Yoon opened the Consumer Electronic Show in Vegas by speaking about a new trend called digital humanism (as opposed to human digitalism). In his speech he predicted and explained the following concept: digital will soon dominate our experiences and ways of thinking.

In 2012, a plethora of virtual lifestyle apps enabling you to recreate your own reality appeared on the market. One of the most striking proponents of this trend is the company Everfeel. Through 3-D role plays with dialogues between players, it proposes to create an intense and immediate social yet virtual experience in real time. This differs markedly from the dynamic of platforms like Facebook, which focus on sharing past experiences and data.

Trends are shaping markets, consumer behaviours and, ultimately, business strategies. To become an integrated strategic thinker, you need to not only spot trends but also deeply understand their potential impact. You also need to be able to see the less obvious ways in which these trends will have an impact on markets and behaviours.

The financial crisis is a great example of an event that brought with it some very different trends and reaction to them from business. Since 2008, the world has been experiencing an unprecedented financial crisis – from the collapse of Lehman Brothers to the uncertainties about Greece's financial situation and the potential collapse of the European Union. This has had a huge impact on consumers.

The most obvious resulting trend has been austerity and cost-cutting measures. Most consumer businesses have considered lowering their prices as the ultimate adjustment strategy. Only a few companies thought differently and realised that, with austerity, consumers would also be looking to be inspired, to do something to lift them out of the situation. These few also realised that during hard times people need to laugh, to dream, be energised and have fun, so undertook some different strategic positioning activities.

To develop your ability to detect trends, answer the following question.

■ What are the themes I recurrently observe in my environment?

Try a mix of passive and active approaches.

The passive approach – the 'off time' phase

Our brains can take in limitless amounts of information, although we are only conscious of a small percentage of it. Switching off and relaxing helps us absorb and then access all the unconscious knowledge we have stored.

In an 'off time' phase, your mind is left to wander freely, so it can find clues and patterns – essential for trend spotting. Meditation or walking in nature may maximise this effect. Consider regularly adding such activities and times to your schedule. You can also keep a sketchpad or notebook with you to jot down your random thoughts and observations as you go about your day, including drawings or schemes.

Putting aside 20 to 30 minutes at the very end of your day to pause and process your observations is also an effective discipline.

Leonardo da Vinci's sketchbooks are a famous example of this idea. They evidence a wide range of interests and preoccupations and are a mix of deep thoughts and interrogations, innovative breakthroughs and mundane activities. They can be found at the Royal Library at Windsor Castle, the Louvre and the Victoria and Albert Museum.

The active approach – the framework phase

This should complement the passive, off time phase. It consists of setting up specific actions and sessions aimed at gathering and sharing data, followed by analysis of what trends to follow and what actions to take next.

As a preparation stage, the following is a good mix:

■ Subscribe to strategic or business sites, such as *McKinsey Quarterly*, *Harvard Business Review*, WGS, BCG perspectives, Accenture's latest thinking in its podcasts – all of these are good sources of information.

■ Regularly take a wander through bookshops to see what is being written about in various subject areas such as philosophy, theology, sociology or demographics.

- Pay attention to the messages and themes appearing in advertising. This is a good way to do some trend spotting. For example, British Airways' ad featuring the history and innovative spirit of aviation and Burberry's campaign set in the 1940s are indicative of a desire to go back to the stability of the past.

More generally, the work of thought leaders in academic circles is a good place to start to look for trends as they are always at the forefront of any major changes. The preparation stage can be complemented by developing an in-depth knowledge of one particular sector.

Strategic thinking should be a shared and collaborative exercise, so encouraging your team to also do the following will help you to create a more strategic community.

Next comes the analysis stage. At this point, it is useful to identify the trends that are significant, so asking the following questions is a powerful way in which to do this:

- Are changes occurring in multiple areas or environments? For instance, the advent of social media had an impact on both professional and personal lives.

- Are changes having an impact on people's priorities or their perceptions of their roles in society? For instance, a concern about the environment is shifting people towards organic or Fairtrade products.

- Is the trend impacting a particular group, population or type of consumer? For instance, a concern about social justice is being adopted by wealth management institutions.

- Are there signs that the trends are there to last? For instance, environmental concerns are leading to an increasing number of major European cities proposing rented bicycle schemes as an alternative to cars.

- Is there a particularly negative or positive perception of the mega trend? For instance, the development of video games for children led to an increased concern that children were reducing their participation in physical activities.

Coach

At Coach, the luxury handbag maker, it was realised that, during the financial crisis, consumers controlling the purse strings were nevertheless eager to give themselves a lift.

Coach therefore decided to create a new range – the Poppy line. The bags are slightly cheaper than the traditional Coach products, but are more colourful, playful and respond faster to underlying trends. As a result, Coach returned to top-level growth only 18 months after the line's launch, with a rise of 3.2 per cent in sales in the same shops in the second quarter of 2010.

Finally, there is the action phase, which will help unleash the power of your newly discovered mega trends.

In their article, 'Are you ignoring trends that could shake up your business?' (*Harvard Business Review*, July 2010), Elie Ofek and Luc Wathieu propose the following three ways to shape strategies based on a deep understanding of mega trends:

- **Infuse and augment** The purpose is to incorporate into your traditional offerings some of the most pressing needs established by the trend. You are not inventing something new, but adding some elements to create a stronger value proposition.

- **Combine and transcend** This requires the merging or meshing of both the traditional value proposition with all the attributes and potential impact of the mega trend. In this case, the potential impact is creating a new offering or experience that can open completely new markets for the company.

- **Counteract and reaffirm** The purpose here is to build on the positive side of the products versus the perceived negative aspects of the trends.

Figure 10.6 illustrates the three activities you need to grasp to make the most of trends.

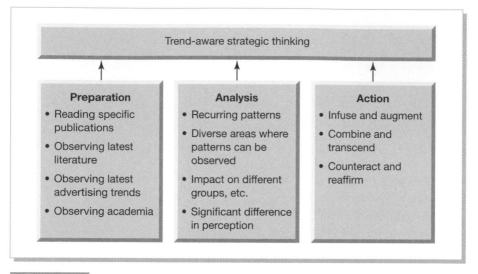

Figure 10.6   The active phase – making the most of trends

Embracing and promoting cognitive diversity

As human beings, we have limited cognitive abilities and these prevent us from assessing or grasping all potential aspects of any business. Bringing together different ways of thinking, different backgrounds and perspectives is a way to overcome this – it is a step towards becoming a truly integrated thinker.

Cognitive diversity – knowing how different people think – is what leaders should look for. Embracing and promoting it requires the following.

Awareness of your patterns and natural biases

See Chapter 3 to remind yourself of techniques and exercises you can try to build your self-awareness. You can complement these by creating a two-columned table with a list of your strengths, weaknesses and attributes on one side and, on the other, the opposite words or phrases. Use this mental picture to proactively look inside or outside your work environment for people who appear to be your complete opposite. Make a specific point of exchange ideas and debating things with them as part of your networking strategy.

In order to help crystallise the above, keep Figure 10.7 in mind.

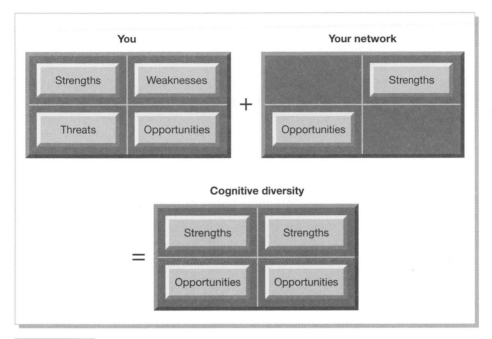

Figure 10.7 SWOT and cognitive diversity

The prioritising of complementarity over excellence

The purpose of a team is to execute and deliver a strategy to realise a vision. From a leader's perspective, this means being clear about what types of resources, competences and attributes it would be most appropriate to gather in order to reach specific objectives. It requires you to proactively go after them using a gap analysis approach, matching what is needed with what you are looking for and filling gaps by trying to find the best candidates for these jobs. The methods and exercises described in Chapter 7 concerning how to build rapport will help with the matching exercise by giving you the information you need to choose wisely.

When you throw the notion of cognitive diversity into the mix, what matters is not only finding the best candidates but finding complementary ones. You might even think of it as actually looking for the 'odd' person. When interacting with your peers, teams and others, systematically look for the person who is different or with whom you do not feel particularly at ease. Try to either recruit him or her to your team or use as a sounding board when engaging in high-level strategic thinking.

You can integrate this dimension into all your exercises in stakeholder mapping and network building.

You might also wish to cascade this approach down to make it part of all recruitment activities. Scott E. Page in his book *The Difference: How the power of diversity creates better groups, firms, schools and societies* (Princeton University Press, 2008), proposed a simple method to ensure cognitive diversity in the hiring process. Draw up a questionnaire that will address the skills you need and, when analysing the results, look for the mix of people who, between them, will give you all the right ones (see Table 10.2).

Table 10.2 Example of using candidates' responses to questionnaires to ensure diversity

Test	Q1	Q2	Q3	Q4	Q5	Q6	Q7	Q8	Total
Candidate 1			X	X	X			X	4
Candidate 2	X	X			X	X	X	X	6
Candidate 3	X	X				X	X	X	5

To fully embrace cognitive diversity and excellence, you would hire Candidates 1 and 2 from these results.

Exercises and action points

Embracing complexity

To be able to embrace complexity you need to virtually deconstruct the way you think. Instead of looking for simplification and shortcuts, you add layers and constraints. This challenging task is well worth the effort you put into it and becomes easier the more you practise. To do this, perform the following activities:

- Draw up mental maps – adding layers, comparing and contrasting them.

- Sit down on a bi-weekly basis for one or two hours to reassess what you have learned in terms of business models, problems, dependencies and so on or what you have been exposed to – new ideas, new products, events. This is a good way to exercise your ability to think in more complex terms and to be at ease with complexity.

■ Integrate a 'strategic pulse' check into your routine – that is, constantly check the adequacy of any given strategic direction. Do this by making regular weekly or bi-weekly rounds and spending time talking with those in different functions or parts of your own organisation. These rounds do not have to be formal – a casual pop down for a coffee or a five-minute conversation is all that is needed. The point is to develop your sensing abilities, keep in touch with what is going on and gather the knowledge you need to be able to respond quickly to changes, before crisis strikes, as well as pick up on trends. You can base these rounds on the following questions:

■ What is going on?

■ What do you see coming up?

■ What has been bothering you lately?

The trend team

Setting up regular discussions to share observations and assess what should be explored further is powerful in its effects. Consider putting together a 'trend team', as Nokia did, calling it the Insights and Foresights team.

The purpose of the team is to gather and analyse consumer or industry shifts in tastes or behaviours at the most diverse level and not necessarily in your industry.

The idea is to meet on a monthly basis to discuss and debate the findings and potentially engage in the action phase, described earlier in this section. It is a good idea to include either your entire team or a core part of your team and rotate them on a regular basis to ensure diversity of thinking and that opinions are regularly challenged.

Summary

Strategic thinking and developing strategies should be at the top of any executive's 'to do' list. Almost all their time should be spent on vision and strategy.

The underlying principles are rather simple when it comes to developing strategic thinking. The first is to build a solid knowledge of strategic tools, the second to always keep abreast of the complexity of your environment by constantly sensing and observing, while the third and final one is to integrate strategic thinking into daily activities – not reserve it for the strategic planning cycle but also include it in less formal situations, such as a weekly catch-up with individuals and your trend team as *all* of these times are important. This will all be helped and accelerated by finding and working with smart people who think differently.

Here's a reminder of some of the key points from this chapter:

- strategy translates vision into tangible steps, focusing on the how, how to, where to and when to

- successful strategic thinking should lead to long-lasting competitive advantages if it is rooted in a deep understanding of your organisation's value chain and observation of its environment

- understanding and adequately using traditional strategic tools will give you a head start and allow you to adapt and develop your own strategic recipes

- the best strategy is derived by assessing, exploring and balancing short v. long term, proactive v. reactive approaches, global v. local, top down and bottom up.

- To grow as an integrated strategic thinker, you need to train yourself to see things from different and opposite perspectives, think in terms of ecosystems – that is, in terms of interdependencies – and be fully aware that you cannot always and entirely predict anything in business.

- Proactively looking for trends and analysing them deeply to go beyond the obvious is also a competitive skill in strategic thinking.

- Embrace cognitive diversity by hiring and adding to a diverse team. This will enable stronger strategies to be developed.

- Looking for diversity will also allow you to identify your natural bias and patterns and increase your level of self-awareness.

11

Boosting your ability to execute

'Vision without execution is hallucination.'

Thomas Edison, American inventor and businessman

This chapter covers:

- the key elements to better decision making
- the best ways to build a high-performance team that is accountable and empowered
- how to lead change.

'Why would they listen?' and the brain v. body dilemma

Mary was a bank clerk in America. She was a very caring and sociable person who had, over the years, developed an informal filing system that enabled her to provide exemplary customer service. When asked why she did not consider pushing her effective system forward to be implemented as best practice, she paused and answered, 'Why would I ever do that? They're not interested in what a teller has to say.' Mary's creativity and empathy was not part of the manual of operating procedures and she did not feel entitled to promote it.

To turn the example above into an analogy, it is like the brain and body being in a state of total disconnect. The brain is sending a message and thinks it has been understood by the body, but the body is executing something quite other.

The brain–body dichotomy analogy can easily be applied to the corporate environment, where top executives decide on strategic issues, create initiatives and then expect the workforce to just execute them. The leadership literature notes this natural dichotomy (see *Execution: The discipline of getting things done* by Larry Bossidy *et al.* for more on this) and actually endorses it as a key recipe to delivery.

Actually, in today's world, this generally leads to a choiceless mentality. A shift in perspective is needed. You could contemplate factoring feedback and ideas from the front line of your organisation into your strategic thinking. You might advocate collaboration and encourage empowerment. If you give your team members and your employees the opportunity to participate and make adequate decisions, you will have a better chance of running a high-performance organisation.

Execution – the ability to work effectively towards and deliver results – is a sought after skill in the leaders of tomorrow. The achievement of tangible results, or, 'closing', is the real acid test. More than any other leadership skills examined in this book, execution is the one that relies on other people – it is never a solitary exercise. It emanates both from the intrinsic personal attributes of the leader, such as the abilities to make decisions and lead change, and, more importantly, the skill to build high-performance teams that feel both empowered and accountable.

Better personal decision making

Decision making is the daily duty of a leader. It should be founded on the awareness that, as human beings, our decision making ability is always imperfect. It is highly influenced by emotions, values and personal goals. To master good decision making skills, you need to develop the ability to look at different alternatives and take into account both analytical data and intuition. It is very rarely an entirely solitary exercise, so developing your ability to leverage your network and team, too, is recommended. It is also important to note that a good level of self-awareness and heightened strategic thinking helps you to develop supreme decision making skills.

Decision making is usually seen as the prerogative of the leader. If you pay attention to what leaders do every day, you will soon realise that their agendas are mainly filled with activities that lead to those points when they need to decide. They are constantly engaged in decision making – in meetings, discussions and networking. The range of types of decisions made can vary from simple – such as hiring or not hiring a person – to very complex – such as entering or exiting a market. They can be immediate – the hiring decision might be for someone to start next week – or they might be for the longer term – defining the new vision or a new strategy for the entire company. However, if you look more closely at decision making you will see that it is more of a process than a singular act. Many different inputs will be considered and weighed, consciously or not.

Embracing your prerogative to make decisions

The leadership role calls for being perfectly at ease with decision making. It will come naturally to some and less naturally to others. There is a handful of key elements to master to fully embrace your prerogative as a leader to decide:

- **self-awareness** – understanding your own internal decision making process
- **decision making style** – whether you are an 'advocate' or an 'enquirer'
- **practice** – build your self-confidence by gaining experience.

Self-awareness

It is important to understand your internal decision making process. You can gauge your natural decision making abilities by reflecting on the following questions:

- How do I usually feel when I have to make a decision?
- How long does it usually take for me make a decision?
- What is the process I regularly follow to reach a decision (including acting on data or acting on impulse)?
- How often do I catch myself rethinking or questioning my decisions?

Your feelings might vary from excitement to fear to ... nothing at all. They may differ from one decision to the other, depending on the impact or the seriousness of the decision you must make. However, they will give you a good indication of your level of comfort with decision making.

If you find you frequently experience feelings of fear or panic, then you will need to work on becoming more comfortable with the process and practise regularly. If you have a tendency to procrastinate or avoid taking decisions, using excuses such as bad timing, lack of information or readiness, this will also give you a good indication of what you need to work on. In some cases, it might be helpful to give yourself strict deadlines to make decisions by or set yourself a target number of decisions to make in a certain period of time.

The decision making process may extend from being a solitary exercise with hardly any input, to a vast consultation process. It will alter significantly depending on the decision you have to make. Being in tune with the different avenues you might take will help you to craft your decision making strategy.

Finally, the core of your decision making process remains the same for both professional and personal situations, so you may consider applying the questioning process to both areas of your life. The only differences will be that there are different actors or sources of inputs – from friends to colleagues or mentors, for instance – and, possibly, the frequency of decision making in each area.

As decision making is firmly rooted in your level of self-awareness and, particularly, your understanding of your values, objectives and mindset, the exercises included in Chapters 3 and 4 should give you additional useful pointers.

Decision making style

Are you an 'advocate' or an 'enquirer'?

In their article 'What you don't know about making decisions' (*Harvard Business Review*, September 2001), David Garvin and Michael Roberto explore two approaches to decision making. One is called advocacy – that is, someone acting with an 'us against them' mindset and only thinking in terms of winning or losing. An advocate acts as a spokesperson. He or she is usually trying to impose his or her viewpoint, merely treating others as opponents who need to be downplayed and converted. He or she will simply ignore minority viewpoints. The advocacy approach is usually viewed as detrimental to achieving the best possible decision, especially in group settings.

The second is referred to as enquiry. This decision making style is based on a more collaborative problem solving approach. The core of the process involves identifying, discussing and assessing the validity of different scenarios. The enquiry style relies on balanced arguments and openness to feedback and criticisms. Everyone is entitled to have a say and, through discussions, the objective is to foster a sense of shared responsibility. This is claimed to be the favoured and most efficient decision making process.

Reflecting on your level of advocacy or enquiry will help you tune into what your natural style is, giving you the ability to switch from one type of decision making style to the other, as you see fit. In principle, enquiry may be the best way to bring people together in the decision-making process, but, in some circumstances, the advocacy style might be what is needed for you or the company. For example, when there is an issue of integrity or the company's reputation is at stake, the advocacy decision making process will probably be required. When you are in a vision building or strategic session, the enquiry process is likely to be more suitable.

Practice

A successful business leader visited an MBA class to enlighten the students. At the end of the talk, a student asked the leader, 'What is the secret of your success?' 'Two words – good decisions.' A second student asked, 'Well, how do you learn to make good decisions?' 'One word – experience.' A third student asked, 'So how do you get the experience?' 'Two words', answered the business leader, 'Bad decisions'.[1]

You can only master decision making by actually starting to make decisions. Practice only makes perfect if time is invested in assessing the impact after the facts and, ultimately, reflecting on what you have learned from both good and bad decision making.

It is largely accepted and supported by different scholars that human beings have limitations when it comes to decision making (see Herbert Simon, Daniel Kahneman and Dan Ariely for more on this). As individuals, our cognitive ability is constrained or conditioned by a mix of

---

[1] Steven Bell (2012) 'Learning to be a better decision maker: Leading from the library', *Library Journal*, 26 April.

factors – the difficulty of assessing every potential angle of a situation (see Chapter 10 for more on this), our natural instinct to listen to or indulge our emotions and so on. We are also programmed to choose the path of least resistance, the way to quicker gratification, and are driven by fear of change or wanting to avoid loss of some kind.

It is therefore important to learn from our bad decision making in order to improve and break recurring patterns. This may be done by reflecting on the following possible causes:

- **Emotion** Did I not listen to my guts? Did I rush into this decision because of some strong emotion, such as desire or fear? Did I make the decision on a whim?

- **Lack of reflection** Did I have all the information I needed to hand? Did I adequately and carefully think through the consequences or impacts of my decision? Did I overlook something?

- **Values** Was I too lazy, self-centred or complacent? Did I just choose the easy option?

Investing time in taking stock and creating a 'not to do' list for decision making can make a significant difference to your future effectiveness.

Improving your analysis skills and developing alternatives

Decision making impacts all facets of the skill set required to become a leader. It has an effect on everything, from gaining credibility to what job or experience to choose, from how to network or build influence to whom to approach as stakeholders or mentors and even to vision building and formulating strategies. What really matters is not being able to *always* make good decisions – by nature we will always be imperfect decision makers – but minimising the number of bad decisions we make.

Try the following, either in sequence or as you see fit, to help keep bad decisions to a minimum.

Gather data

The purpose here is to make sure your decisions are as well informed as possible.

To be informed, you need an adequate amount of data.

The data gathering may take the form of specific trend analysis, financial analysis, past or projected, information on customers, suppliers, the competition …

The fundamental questions to address to ensure you gather the *right* data are the following:

- What do I need to know to get to a certain level of comfort in my decision making?

- Who could help me reach this comfort level and how?

You can do some of the data gathering yourself or question and challenge your team or the person who is asking you to take the decision making role. To develop different perspectives, you can also gather data by bouncing the issue around with those in your network and your mentors. All the exercises and elements described in Chapter 10 can also be useful in helping you decide how to ensure you have all the data you need.

Analysing consequences and scenarios

Gathering data is the first step. The next is to assess the data, interpret it and compare and contrast different pieces of information. Here, the point is to look for interdependencies and the impact and consequences of each potential decision. It is recommended that you specifically focus on the things you can actually control.

The value of analysing consequences and scenarios lies in assessing the impact of your decision on the entire value chain. If you systematically cater for interdependencies, this can only strengthen your decision making process. Use the value maps or mind map referred to in Chapter 10. Use a pros and cons map, decision trees or a voting exercise with your team or even alone. To put things into perspective, it's a good idea to consider the following two questions:

- Which option is going to add the greatest value to the business or organisation?

- Which option serves me best over time?

The world presents us with dilemmas and it is becoming more and more difficult to find obvious solutions. Make sure you acknowledge this in your decision making process. Picturing the consequences of your decision is key.

Embrace discomfort

Do not shy away from decisions that are not the most expedient or the most comfortable. Doing the right thing can often involve some sense of sacrifice or discomfort.

Trusting your intuition

In his book *Blink: The power of thinking without thinking* (Penguin, 2006) Malcolm Gladwell describes how the unconscious mind picks up subtle clues from the environment without you realising it and how this can actually trigger decision making.

In their article 'Good data won't guarantee good decisions' (*Harvard Business Review*, April 2012), Shvetank Shah, Andrew Horne and Jaime Capellá share research that shows data-driven decision making is not always good decision making. So what needs to be added? Intuition is the answer or using both sides of the brain – as indicated in Roger Martin's book *Opposable Mind: Winning through integrative thinking*. Figure 11.1 illustrates the potential range of types of decision makers.

The best decision making is based on a mix of analysis and intuition, which is integrated thinking. If it is relatively easy to develop analytical skills, developing your intuition is a more difficult exercise; some would say it is virtually impossible.

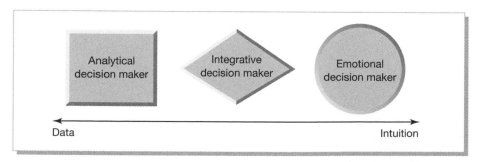

Figure 11.1   The spectrum of decision makers

What is intuition?

In simple terms, intuition is the ability to sense things about a situation and make decisions without involving cognitive activity. It can come from the ability to access all the information you have ever absorbed, consciously or not, that is safely stored in the back of your brain (parietal, occipital, temporal, cerebellum, basail ganglia, hypothalamus).

Intuition can be developed out of these three basic attributes:

- Intellectual knowledge or the capacity to observe, paired with the ability to continually acquire and have access to diverse and wide terms of reference. See Chapters 6, 8, 9 and 10 for exercises to help you.

- Emotional knowledge and awareness. Leaders must be empathetically in tune with their emotions and environment in order to perfect their intuitive decision making abilities. (Chapter 3 looked at this in more detail.)

- The ability to step back and let go, to consciously stop the thinking process, be in the moment and in the flow. Regularly practising meditation can help.

How can you make sure you integrate your intuition into your decision making process?

First and foremost, you will achieve this by pushing away from your mind all the data, trends, opinions or anything else you may have examined or heard. Also, forget any pros and cons lists or other devices before making a decision. Go inside yourself and simply ask either of these questions:

- How does it make you feel?

- What if it was your own money?

Pause and listen to your body and head. If your heart starts to beat faster or if you can hear a nagging inner voice telling you something, or if doubts begin to creep in, then, most probably, the decision is not the right one. Maybe you are missing a critical piece of information or you need to have another look at the data.

Pausing and listening to yourself is particularly useful in crisis mode when decisions need to be made quickly. Using this technique is helpful even before you've gathered all the information you might need to reach a final decision.

So, how do you know if you have made a good or bad decision? Just before you act on it, consider the following two angles:

- **The personal credibility angle** Can I live with the consequences of my decision?

- **The knowledge limitation angle** With what I know today, is there anything I could do differently?

If the answer to the first question is a resounding 'Yes' and the answer to the second question is a strong 'No', then you are probably about to make the best possible decision. If you are not sure, feel free to defer it. At times, releasing yourself from the pressure to make a decision can be the best way to find the most suitable solution.

Identifying and overcoming major obstacles to good decision making

There are some common obstacles to good decision making that will be explored here:

- **Too much information** If you have too many inputs from too many sources, you risk entirely clouding your judgement. In such cases, the best strategy is to pause, empty your head by going for a walk or use meditation to stop it all swirling in your head and regain perspective. As a leader, learning how to say, 'Stop' and taking a step back is important.

- **Too much emotion** If you are too high or too low on your emotional curve, you will not be in the best situation to make a decision. Being in tune with your emotional state is important and, again, having the courage and the ability to defer a decision is important.

- **Too much time** This can lead to both overthinking and procrastination. Make a point of setting adequate amounts of time in which to make decisions. Teach yourself to stop asking questions or for more data to be crunched. Usually, at a certain stage, it becomes apparent that any additional data will only have a marginal effect on the decision.

When faced with two alternatives, if it is not blatantly obvious which is best, it usually means that either they are equally good or equally bad. So, stay tuned and monitor how the situation evolves until the next decision point.

Always try to bear these three points in mind when making decisions:

- It is important to acknowledge that decision making is not an event but a process. It can unfold over weeks, months or years. Elements of your environment will influence your decision making, whether this is the history of the organisation, the different stakeholders or even the power plays. There will also be influences rooted in your personal history and emotions. Acknowledge these pressure points and never rush, but never duck it either.

- Keep in mind that no decision is set in stone. Changing your mind because the situation requires it *is* acceptable. Keeping your decision making loose and fluid is important and yielding the right results is what *really* matters.

- Learning how to make decisions can only come from making bad decisions. It takes courage to make decisions and leaders are courageous creatures. The only commitment you can really make is to try to become the best leader possible. Try and fail and try again to execute.

Figure 11.2 shows the best way to master the art of decision making.

Reflect on the following thought.

There is no good or bad decision, only the decision that you make and you turn into the best one possible. The rest is out of your hands.

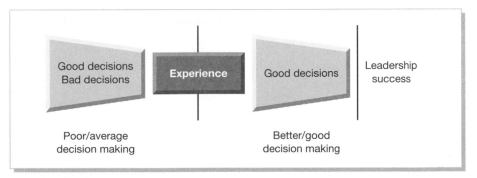

Figure 11.2 From good to great decision making – a learning process

Exercises and action points

The decision making checklist

The aim of this exercise is to help you fully assess your abilities to make decisions. Keep in mind that:

■ the importance of decision making can vary with the circumstances and consequences concerned

■ your emotional state can affect your decision making process.

To help you become more comfortable with making decisions, consider recording, on a daily basis, all the opportunities you have had to do so and assess how many times you have either ducked or embraced the challenge.

The process

Over a period of two to three weeks, systematically record how many times you have been asked to make a decision.

Briefly assess each decision in terms of its complexity and urgency. Also note down whether you felt you were the sole decision maker or not. Record at what time of day the question was asked – morning, afternoon or evening.

Record how much time elapsed between the first mention of the decision to be made and when it was made.

Make a note of the steps you took to reach decisions. For example:

■ discussed with a selected group of people (network, peers or mentors)

■ discussed with your team in a group setting or one on one to bounce ideas around

■ requested more information from a different group or groups

■ asked other colleagues or areas of the organisation for additional support or information

■ took some quiet time to think through or research the topic by yourself.

■ assessed different angles using pros and cons lists, decision trees or other tools.

▶

Also record how and when the decision came to you:

▓ Did you have an 'Aha' moment? If so, how did this happen – as you woke up in the morning, in the shower ...?

▓ Have you noticed if there is a particular time in your day when you are more likely to make decisions?

Your answers here will be particularly useful for spotting patterns and creating your natural decision making roadmap.

The next step is to assess how many of the decisions made turned out to be good ones and how many turned out to be bad. As indicated earlier, it can be beneficial to categorise behaviours that trip you up, such as:

▓ your emotions

▓ a lack of reflection or information

▓ your values.

Once the picture feels complete and you can identify what circumstances and processes turned your decisions into good ones, keep them in mind to replicate them as much as possible.

Are you an enquirer or an advocate?

Discovering whether you are an enquirer or advocate is beneficial on several counts. It enables you to:

▓ define your leadership style

▓ establish rapport with your team

▓ establish rapport with your peers

▓ position yourself in a team of talented individuals or any external circumstances

The above and the decision making checklist can help you to define the building blocks for you to work on, but it is also highly beneficial to have an independent observer give you feedback on the ways in which you tend to lead, participate or make decisions in group meetings.

If you have established a feedback group, consider asking one of its members to attend and observe you at some of your group meetings over a defined period of between two and four weeks. In particular, ask them to answer the following questions.

- What was my natural state at the beginning of the meeting? Did it seem as if I had already made the decision and simply wanted validation? Was I genuinely open to the discussion or argument? Pay specific attention to my speech and body language.

- Could you spot when I switched from enquiry to advocacy (if relevant)?

- At what point could you see that I had made the decision? Note the events that led to that moment, including changes in my body language, who was talking and so on. Did the decision seem to come after long reflection or appear to have been made on a whim?

You can complement this list of questions with anything else you deem necessary. Ask your feedback group member to give you a one-on-one debrief right after the meeting to crystallise what has been learned.

All of the above will be beneficial in terms of identifying not only your style but also who is your biggest influencer and how you manage your emotions. Ultimately, this will help you break unhelpful patterns and lead to you becoming more skilled at decision making.

Ask the same or another member of your feedback group to repeat the exercise three to six months later to measure your progress.

The career choice analogy – intuition and analysis

When it comes to integrating decision making and intuition, the actual or imagined career change decision exercise worked through in Chapter 5 once more serves as a useful benchmark.

How many times have you been through the process of considering changing jobs? Here is the typical scenario:

- You have been contacted by a headhunter.

- You have prepared for the interview.

- You have gathered financial strategy and vision data for your potential future company.

- You have been interviewed, asked all the questions, been to the company's office, met a series of executives you have tried to impress and, in turn, have gained some impressions about them.

- You have talked to mentors and possibly friends and family.

- Now it's decision time.

▶

At this stage, the only questions that are important are:

How do I really feel about this job? The company? The people?

If you go deep inside yourself, to where you can find your dreams, your secrets and your fears, you will probably already have the answers. If, at this very moment, the answer to 'Do I want this job?' is not a resounding 'YES', you already know you will not take the job.

If you run through a similar process any time you need to make a personal decision, you will find yourself embracing an analysis with intuition approach. Other examples might be:

- looking for a new home, stepping inside the door and just knowing that *this* is where you want to live

- for women, it might be looking for your wedding dress and, after seeing many, suddenly finding 'the one'!

Reflect and draw on these experiences to grasp the fine line between an intuitive and an analytical decision making process.

Empowerment, accountability and change: the key concepts for delivering through others

A leader's ability to get results is entirely dependent on whether or not he or she can build a high-performance team and adequately motivate its members.

'Empowerment' is the first key word here. It generally comes from delegating some of your decision making down the line and involving your team in strategic thinking.

'Accountability' is the second key word. It stands for being clear on what will be measured and how by defining and monitoring a set of meaningful metrics. More importantly, accountability also relates to a clear understanding of the consequences of an action and demonstrated consequence management.

Finally, the ability to lead change needs to be acquired, via heightened communication skills and the deliberate crafting of quick wins.

Returning to John Kotter and his definition of leadership, the most important part of a leader's role is to align people, for them to deliver on a vision, make a strategy come to life and get results. The team element is of upmost importance in relation to a delivery strategy, but we are not talking about just any type of team. A leader needs a high-performance team – people who 'get it', will go above and beyond the call of duty and adapt and adjust to any circumstances in order to deliver.

Strengthening your ability to pick the best people

'Play on people's strengths, play on people's "complementarity", inspire them and you will always get the results you need', said Robert Rozek, Chief Financial Officer of Korn Ferry International. What does this mean for anyone aspiring to become a leader?

To put it in black and white, your chances of success will be greatly increased if you have the right team around you. Chapter 7 examined the notion of a team in depth and presented different techniques that are useful when leading a team – knowing them, motivating them and rewarding them. However, picking team members who are going to perform well requires another skill set.

In his interview with *Harvard Business Review*, Kevin Ryan, Founder and CEO of the Gilt Group, summarised what it takes to build a team of people who excel, in three simple steps.

Invest adequate time in your people

Live and breathe the mantra 'People are our most important asset'. Here are some questions that you could ask yourself:

- Do I spend enough time with my human resources person?

- Is he or she critical to the organisation?

- Do I design my vision and strategy in terms of business needs or organisational needs first?

If you answer 'No' to the first two questions and 'business needs' to the third one, you might unconsciously be hindering your organisation's ability to deliver. To bring about change, create a regular routine of contacts with not only your human resources person but also put on your own agenda to constantly scout for talented people inside and outside your organisation. For instance, consider talking about specific projects directly with the team members concerned on a regular basis.

Put together a list of as many people in your organisation as possible and make a point of meeting with all of them in a certain period of time, to specifically assess their potential. It can be easy to do this in a flat structure, but if you are not, establish a realistic cut-off level and reassess on a regular basis. Be very clear that you have the prerogative to call anyone, any time to talk about anything and stick to it.

When it comes to vision and strategy, make a point to always start with the following question:

■ What is the organisation we have or need and how does this impact our vision or strategy?

This will help embed a mentality for employees to excel at what they do into your company's ethos.

Subtract to add

Have the courage to let some poor performers go to find a better match for the position. Commit to making things happen, either by means of internal promotion or going outside if need be.

Make your team accountable for the turnover of its people. As the mantra goes, people join organisations but leave managers. When an excellent person leaves, it impairs the ability of the whole team to deliver. Make sure you always look into the exact reasons why a good person is leaving and do what you can to prevent it happening again.

Create a virtuous circle of excellence

Birds of a feather always flock together. So, excellent people attract and hire other excellent people, whereas not-so-good people usually end up hiring average people. Most people want to work for someone impressive or talented or, simply put, for people they admire and respect.

Your ability to maintain and use both your operational and strategic networks will help with the scouting process (peers, sponsors, competitors, headhunters and so on). Remember that the need for people who excel does not diminish the need for cognitive diversity and 'complementarity' mentioned in Chapter 10. It just provides another angle to bear in mind when building your team. The approach to take can be summed up in the phrase 'excellence in diversity'.

Adopting the notion of 'accountable empowerment'

On 1 July 1916, the British Army lost the battle of the Somme, even though its troops greatly outnumbered those of the German Army. This battle is frequently used as a case study on leadership courses, demonstrating as it does the concept of 'independent thinking obedience'. This can be summarised as the need for a deep understanding of a common and specific objective by all participants in one group, while remaining extremely open and non-proscriptive about how it should be achieved. Each individual feels empowered to adjust his or her decisions and actions in the moment. It gives all the right to react to any information received by observing what is around them, thus maximising the chance of achieving the common objective.

Participants on the leadership courses analyse how the strategy of the German Army was put together, exploring how things were discussed in preparatory meetings, what sort of language was used and how the message was clarified by reformulation and probing. They may even go back further to analyse how the individual training and professional history of the leaders of the group added to the impact on their behaviour and how a certain consistency and cohesiveness of thinking was, at times, critical to achieving the results.

How can you best use the above example to ensure better execution and delivery? Emerging from the story are three salient elements that need to be worked on by any prospective leader:

- being comfortable delegating decision making
- making a point of involving your team in formulating strategies and strategic thinking
- ensuring that there is greater accountability.

Delegating decision making

It is the prerogative of a leader to endorse and embrace the decision making process. However, it can become highly inefficient for the organisation, and somewhat demotivating for the leaders' team, if a decision cannot be made quickly or team members don't feel empowered or enabled to become good decision makers themselves.

To learn how to delegate decision making, remember that not all your decisions are equal, so delegate those you believe others can make. Focus your time and energy instead on taking care of the ones that will create significant change for the organisation. Consider using the matrix shown in Figure 11.3 to help you know what to delegate.

Who you delegate to is also a critical element. So, for the top left and bottom right quadrants in Figure 11.3, consider delegating first to some of your best performers. This will be a good way to test their ability to solve complicated problems and/or work when under time pressure. For decisions falling into the bottom left quadrant, delegate these to train the rest of your team members in decision making.

Decision making is also closely related to time management. To this end Table 11.1 is useful for you to complete, on your own or with your team, to adequately plan your time.

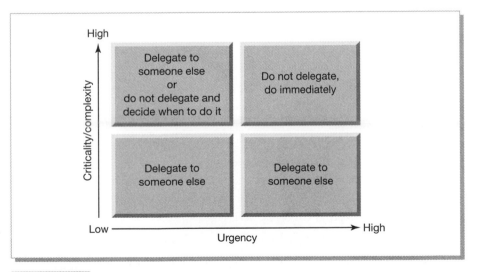

Figure 11.3 Matrix showing when and when not to delegate

Table 11.1 Time management and decision making

	Now	Sooner	Later
Must do critical to the success of the organisation			
Should do important to the success of the organisation			
Nice to do icing on the cake items			

Figures 11.3 and Table 11.1 will allow you to create a clear mental picture of the decision making element of the work you and your team are undertaking. They are also beneficial for managing your time or effort and producing the best results possible. The next steps are to:

- communicate your framework or decision making plans to all your team, peers and others as required

- consider setting up co-creation of objectives sessions with your team (as described in Chapter 7) and discuss the above matrix and table as this helps to establish the ground rules for decision making – when you come in and when your team members have complete freedom – and it will not only position you as a collaborative leader but also contribute to establishing feelings of empowerment for your team.

Be aware also that knowing your team members well will allow you to judge even more effectively what to delegate to them as you will be able to do so based on their strengths and weaknesses.

Involving your team in formulating strategies

As mentioned in Chapter 7, empowerment is a key motivational factor. If you want to produce optimum results, it is critical to not operate solely by means of persuasion but by creating a sense of shared purpose. What is needed is for people to feel that the objective, vision and strategy is theirs. The best way to achieve this is to involve as many as possible in the strategic thinking process as then motivation will follow on from the team's heightened sense of ownership that this creates. Always keep in mind that there are no longer any roles in any organisation where thinking is not required.

Roger L. Martin encapsulates what it takes to deliver results by means of empowerment in article 'The execution trap' (*Harvard Business Review*,

July 2010). He uses the analogy of a white-water river, flowing from the mountain to the sea. Martin explains that in a high-performance organisation, the prerogative of choice cascades from top to bottom. At each level in the organisation, staff can exercise choice. The framework of potential choices is, of course, dictated by the overall objective and what it means for the particular function or business unit. However, every individual is given the opportunity to adjust their courses of action in a way that they think is best fitted to the situation.

There are two main ways to involve your team members in formulating strategies. The first is to adopt a co-creation process for strategic thinking (see Chapter 7). This creates a sense of empowerment as:

- the rationale for a direction or a choice has been shared

- what needs to be done is articulated and debated at the leader and next level down in the organisation at the same time

- the opportunity for the team members to give feedback to the level up and the commitment from that level to act on it or explain why they will not are integrated.

Most companies will have a rhythm of monthly reports and meetings to discuss different financial and operational metrics. You can take this one step further by integrating into these sessions a specific discussion about what is being sensed on the ground regarding what is working or not working in the execution of the strategy.

case study   **Idea Spotlight**

This is WAZOKU's star product. (WAZOKU is a specialist ideas management software company.)

Idea Spotlight is based on online software that can crowdsource business improvement and strategic ideas from employees, customers and business partners.

The beauty of Idea Spotlight is that it uses the same group of people to evaluate and evolve the ideas, so not only do the best ones emerge but also they are quickly brought to the attention of decision makers in the company and can be put into action quickly, too.

The second, and slightly more innovative, way is to use social media and instant communication while formulating strategies as this generates immediate feedback and opinion from a wider group. By encouraging collaboration and ideas from the entire organisation, loyalty, recognition, empowerment and results are all fostered.

In layman's terms, walk the talk and commit for this to happen. It might mean major changes for your organisation, but stick to it and you will soon see results.

Ensuring accountability

Accountability is what transforms delegation and empowerment into tangible results. It is founded on clear expectations, the correct metrics and a clear understanding of the consequences should expectations not be met.

Defining and making your expectations clear to everyone is part of building rapport with your team members. This should be complemented by the co-creation of goals and objectives, at both the strategic and personal levels (see Chapter 7).

When it comes to defining metrics, it is important to integrate the following:

- How does your company create value or make money?
- How does everyone contribute to the value-creation process?

Consider using the value and interdependency maps created in Chapter 10 to define *what* to measure to produce the best results. These represent the basis of your metrics definition, which can be recalibrated as a result of considering the following:

- A mix of sole and shared metrics as these will always foster a greater push towards results. It may seem tough at first to implement shared metrics, as it can create tension and lead to a feeling of unfairness, but this a great way to encourage collaboration.
- Less is more. A lot of organisations engage in a frenzy of metrics and the measurement of anything and everything possible. The truth is, as human beings, we can only focus on a limited number of things at a time. Keep that in mind and consider having no more than a

handful of metrics to follow and focus on. These may be a mix of internal tools (financial and operational) and external ones (assessing competition and customers), as well as a mix of qualitative and quantitative measures.

Table 11.2 shows an example of a comprehensive set of metrics.

Table 11.2 An example of a comprehensive set of metrics

	Sole	*Shared*
Inward-looking metrics	• Forecasting accuracy (Q) • Employee turnover rate (q) • Diversity targets (q) • Sales performance target (Q) • ...	• Cash conversion cycle (Q) • Cost-reduction targets (Q) • Working capital reduction (Q) • Integration of new business (q) • ...
Outward-looking metrics	• Conversion rate prospects/customers (Q) • Customer satisfaction (q) • Year on year contract renewal rate (Q) • ...	• Customer retention (q) • Business performance target v. competition (Q) • Market shares gained (Q) • Employee retention rate v. industry (q) • ...

Q = Quantitative
q = qualitative

You can integrate metrics definitions into your co-creation process to reinforce the message about your expectations, while at the same time creating a sense of joint ownership. For accountability to work, there also needs to be a monitoring process to keep up the momentum or pressure.

Most of the organisation will follow a monthly formal process, but integrating more frequent ad hoc checks and feedback can be effective. (See Chapter 7 for more on this, but the default position should remain a monthly process.)

Finally, the management of consequences is the last element that needs to be addressed when creating a culture of accountability and performance.

Courage is a trait of a leader. When in doubt remember this.

The market is not complacent, investors are not complacent, competitors are not complacent. So why should you be?

In the long term, a lack of the management of consequences when results are not delivered can only hinder the company's profitability. If harsh decisions are not made, the strategy cannot be delivered and competitive advantages are not realised. There is a great deal at stake:

- **the organisational structure**, because those who excel will leave when they see that delivering and not delivering yield the same results

- **the culture**, because a lack of consequences creates a tendency towards procrastination and perpetrates a lack of commitment, where deadlines are discretionary and, ultimately, performance is just a fantasy.

To ingrain that there are consequences the following need to be kept in mind:

- Build your credibility and respect within and outside of your team. It gives you a certain legitimacy to act.

- Be crystal clear about what not delivering means for you and your team members. Under Jack Welch, the practice at General Electric was to get rid of the bottom 10 per cent, in performance terms, of the workforce on a yearly basis. This was a pretty powerful aid to mobilising people's efforts. The management of consequences can be made tangible.

- To foster a trusted and open environment, you have to ensure you position yourself as being there to help and guide, to avoid ruling by fear. Here lies the delicate balance also presented in Chapter 7. Respect and trust matter.

- Lead by example, do what you say and apply a common and universal approach to the delivery of results. Of course, it is important to assess the reasons for not doing so. Is it someone's sole responsibility or is it shared? Is it down to a lack of resources or time? It is important to listen to what people have to say and acknowledge when genuine efforts have been made, but also know when people are making excuses or not being proactive.

The management of consequences clearly emphasises the need for the delivery of results. It puts pressure on everyone to be creative, on the ball and understand what is going on. It calls for people to adjust and react quickly.

As a leader, step back from wanting to be liked when it comes to accountability. It is about building a culture of performance and loyalty to the company, not to you as a person. Accountability starts from the top.

The key qualities for leading change

Leading change is the last element to consider and begs the following question:

- What if the quintessential definition of leadership was to be able to lead change?

As mentioned at the beginning of Part 4, being a leader is about changing the way things have been happening, pushing for something different to happen because of you, because of who you are.

Here, there is a bringing together of all that has been presented to you in the previous pages, to form the skill set you need to lead change.

In his article 'Leading change: Why transformation effort fails' (*Harvard Business Review*, January 2007) John P. Kotter, a professor at the Harvard Business School and authority on the field of change management, describes the process of change in eight easy-to-follow steps.

Create a sense of urgency

Change can only come from questioning the status quo for valid reasons. This could range from losing competitive edge or being in a dire financial situation – Motorola selling its mobility patent capacity to Google to renew its financial performance – to wanting to position your organisation better to meet future market trends or changing dynamics – Shell Downstream launching its strategic review exercise to become a leaner and more agile company.

A sense of urgency is definitely necessary to mobilise others and trigger actions.

How do you create a sense of urgency?

By thinking strategically about your company now and tomorrow by means of vision building (Chapter 9) and strategic thinking (Chapter 10).

By communicating both upwards and downwards in an attempt to connect emotionally with people and describe what it will mean for them (Chapter 9).

By empowering and motivating teams to sustain results (Chapter 7 and this chapter).

Form a powerful guiding coalition

Change needs both powerful endorsements and a critical mass of endorsers and advocates if it is to happy. You need to establish a 'powerhouse' that will work from within to guide the change journey by rising above natural organisational boundaries.

How do you form a powerful guiding coalition?

By developing your abilities to build and lead a team (Chapter 7), but not just any team – a team that has cognitive diversity. It will ensure that you have solid foundations for your change programme (Chapter 10).

By building a strong leadership brand (Chapter 5) and drawing on your credibility as a leader (Chapter 6). By identifying who is needed for the coalition to be successful using stakeholder mapping and networking (Chapter 8) and then using your influencing skills.

Creating a vision

Change needs to be rooted in a clear vision, aimed at achieving a better future and made of big audacious goals. The vision should be inspiring, compelling and realistic – it has to stand the test of time to sustain motivation and effort.

How do you create a vision?

Refer to Chapter 9 for the definition and skill set required for vision building.

To be accepted and tangible, a vision has to translate into tangible steps and relies on honed and developed strategic thinking skills (Chapter 10).

Communicating the vision

Change can only come if a significant number of people in the organisation are willing to embrace it, promote it and work on it. As change can mean sacrifices, uncertainties and lead to fear of the unknown, investing time and effort in adequately communicating the vision is critical to its success.

Frequent communication is key to maintaining momentum and ensuring continued progress. This should use all possible and available media and channels – public speaking, writing about the vision, presenting it and so on.

It is of upmost importance to 'overcommunicate' the vision. So, it is best to position, interpret and make any events or activities align with or support the vision. In other words, live and breathe the change in everything you do – from talking to your team in one-one-one sessions to group or customer meetings.

How do you communicate the vision?

Refresh your memory about Chapter 9 and complement this with Chapter 10 as all the methods described for how to prepare a presentation of your strategy are also valid for communicating the vision.

When it comes to frequency, refer to the sections on keeping your finger on the pulse of your team's motivation and/or devising a motivation and reward schedule.

Empower others to act on the vision

Empowerment is a key factor when leading change. It is necessary to ensure that everyone can take action and make the decision to deliver the vision.

In other words, empowerment is necessary to create an imperative, a call of duty for everyone to pull their weight.

How do you empower others?

By first creating and then fostering a sense of trust, respect and inclusiveness in your team and organisation (see Chapter 7).

By involving others via co-creation in what needs to change (see also Chapter 7).

By clearly articulating accountability and consequences management (see earlier in this chapter and Chapter 8).

By removing all obstacles that could bring the organisation to a standstill and focusing on recruiting people who excel and change agents (see earlier in this chapter and Chapter 8, stakeholder mapping).

Plan for and create short-term wins

Human beings have a relatively short attention span when it comes to change. If positive events do not come about within a 12- to 24-month period from the start of the change journey, it is very difficult to maintain focus and momentum.

Designing, developing and implementing qualitative and quantitative metrics that will act as quick wins is therefore crucial.

Identifying and developing these quick wins springs from a deep understanding of the value equation of your organisation. It also implies that they are aligned with a compelling and realistic vision and a well-defined strategy.

How do you plan for and create short-term wins?

By mastering the value equation of your company (see Chapter 10).

By choosing the right metrics (see earlier in this chapter).

Consolidate improvement and produce more change

Leading change is a slow and fragile journey. Once improvements have started to show, it is even more important to maintain momentum and motivate people to continue their efforts.

Resilience is the name of the game and keeping that going is achieved by leveraging quick wins to accelerate progress.

How do you consolidate improvement and produce more change?

By recognising and rewarding major players in the change journey (see Chapter 7).

By developing the innovative skills of your team to keep them engaged and motivated (see Chapter 9).

Finally, by constantly balancing reactive and proactive behaviours to allow for changes to become part of the core of your organisation (see Chapter 9, especially the section on innovation).

Institutionalise new approaches

This is the last step in a change management process and is about embedding the results of change, and the change process itself, into the very essence of the organisation.

It impacts all aspects of the organisation's system, values, people and processes.

How do you make the new approaches part of how the organisation operates?

By keeping an eye on the mix of your team, identifying, promoting and/or hiring talented people who embed the new paradigm (see Chapter 10).

By making them a key element of your strategy building exercise (see Chapter 10).

By keeping your finger on the pulse of 'the way we do things around here' via your monitoring mechanism (see Chapter 7).

Then, don't forget ...

Change comes from within and needs to be aligned with the needs of your environment. Leading change requires courage and commitment and leaders' personalities, values and drive are essential if they are to successfully complete their change journeys.

Where do these come from? Inherently, they result from having a high degree of self-awareness and self-confidence, which can be achieved when you have found the leader inside you (see Chapters 3, 4 and 5).

Exercises and action points

The quest for talent

Scouting for talented employees should be at the top of any leader's list of priorities. Keep in mind that:

- you will have universally recognised top people who everyone will know about
- you will have hidden gems in your organisation who could become essential to your plans for cognitive diversity.

The process?

First, communicate clearly to your team that talent scouting is on your priority list. Lead by example.

Make sure that any time you address the organisation, you make a point to talk about people and the importance of recruiting the best. Use storytelling to give concrete examples of how people made a difference to the organisation.

In your regular team meetings, always set aside time to discuss the talent pipeline. This may take different forms, such as reviewing the individual development plan or goals and objectives of a particular person or holding a free form discussion about who is emerging or has shown tremendous empathy, drive, progressed and so on in the past month or quarter.

Make a point of organising informal meetings with people to get to know them. You can use the techniques explored in Chapter 7 to do this and assess their potential. Be careful not to switch to interviewing mode – stick to more general questions that will give you a glimpse of what you have defined as your criteria for ideal team members – curiosity, empathy, drive, intellect and so on.

Consider asking everyone in the team to also say who they admire in the organisation (above or below them in the hierarchy) and why. This can feed into your list.

▶

Outside of your team, meet as many people as possible in your company. Always accommodate requests from anyone at any level in the organisation to meet with you.

When addressing groups, always make a point of remembering and then subsequently meeting the few who asked good questions during your presentation.

Talent scouting is just like a fundraising activity – it is a numbers game. The more potential investors (people) you meet and assess, the more likely you are to find the person interested in your deal (the talent) and the more likely you are to raise the funds (build the team of excellent people) you need.

Summary

Enhancing results is about creating an environment in which people feel compelled to take part, lead change, get involved and feel valued for their participation. That environment should be supported by clear metrics and clearly articulated consequence management. Both are truly necessary for creating the framework for excellent performance and establishing a culture of accountability.

Once the culture has shifted and those recruited are mostly people who excel, execution truly becomes part of the essence of the company.

Here's a reminder of some of the key points from this chapter:

- flawless execution is built on mastering decision making ensuring high levels of accountability and understanding how to lead and manage change

- developing decision making skills involves experiencing and learning from making bad decisions; it also involves understanding that decision making is a process that is fed by internal and external factors that you cannot always control

- it is also important to keep in mind that human beings have a limited ability to assess decisions and are emotional creatures; so decision making will always be imperfect

- in order to minimise the making of bad decisions, using a mix of intuition and analysis is key

- intuition can be developed by establishing wide terms of reference, learning how to let go and step back before decision time

- to achieve results, you need to empower your team, which can be achieved by taking a collaborative, co-creation approach to strategy

- for there to be accountability, there needs to be empowerment of members of the team, the delegation of decision making to others, clear communication of expectations, plus solid metrics having been defined and monitored

- the execution of change and accountability are also correlated with the establishment of clear management of consequences and motivation and reward systems

- leading change is the ultimate expression of leadership and requires the fully fledged skill set of a leader, integrating self-awareness, team-building, influence, vision and execution.

Conclusion

What now?

Now is just the beginning. You have the knowledge, you have the tools, you are ready.

Now you need to find your path and leave *your* trail.

Leadership is a journey. It is a never-ending journey that has a purpose – to become a better professional, create more value and have an impact.

Leadership is a journey that involves a process – working from the inside to the outside, from yourself to the world.

Leaders are catalysts for people and ideas. They are the products of their environments and dreams. They are creators of change for themselves and for others. They give to and inspire others to be better and greater.

It is true that not everyone will become a Fortune 500 CEO – most people wouldn't want to anyway! Everyone, though, can hone their leadership skills to both further their careers and make a difference. So, be brave, be authentic, be confident and take the first step.

The leadership reading list

This is a list of the books that every leader or aspiring leader should have on their bookshelves to help them perfect their leadership attributes.

Anderson, Chris (2006) *The Long Tail: Why the future of business is selling less of more*. New York: Hyperion.

Bennis, Warren (2009) *On Becoming a Leader*. New York: Basic Books.

Bossidy, Larry, Charam, Ram and Buck, Charles (2002) *Execution: The discipline of getting things done*. New York: Crown Business.

Buzan, Tony and Barry (1996) *The Mind Map Book: How to use radiant thinking to maximize your brain's untapped potential*. New York: Plume.

Camus, Albert (1955) *The Myth of Sisyphus*. London: Hamish Hamilton.

Carnegie, Dale (2009) *How To Win Friends and Influence People*. London: Simon & Schuster.

Collins, Jim (2001) *Good to Great: Why some companies make the leap and ... others don't*. London: Harper Business.

Covey, Stephen (2004) *The 7 Habits of Highly Effective People*. New York: Free Press.

Franklin, D. and Andrew, John (2012) *Megachange: The world in 2050*. Chichester: The Economist and Wiley.

Drucker, Peter (1992) *Managing for the Future: The 1990s and beyond*. New York: Dutton Adult.

Drucker, Peter (1993) *Managing in Turbulent Times*. London: Harper Business.

Evans, Vaughan (2012) *Key Strategy Tools: The 80+ tools for every manager to build a winning strategy*. Harlow: FT Publishing.

Gladwell, Malcolm (2002) *The Tipping Point: How little things can make a big difference*. New York: Back Bay Books.

Goleman, Daniel (2006) *Emotional Intelligence (10th Anniversary Edition): Why it can matter more than IQ*. New York: Bantam.

Greenleaf, Robert and Spears, Larry (2002) *Servant Leadership: A journey into the Nature of Legitimate Power and Greatness (25th Anniversary Edition)*. Mahwah, NJ: Paulist Press.

Moss Kanter, Rosabeth (1985) *Change Masters*. New York: Free Press.

Kessel, Joseph (1958) *The Horsemen*. Worthing, Sussex: Little Hampton Book Services.

Kafka, Franz (2012) *The Metamorphis*. New York: Tribeca Books.

Kotter, John P. (1996) *Leading Change*. Boston, MA: Harvard Business School Press.

Kotter, John P. and Cohen, Dan S. (2002) *The Heart of Change: Real life stories of how people change their organization*. Boston, MA: Harvard Business School Press.

Lencioni, Patrick (2002) *The Five Dysfunctions of a Team: A leadership fable*. San Francisco, CA: Jossey-Bass.

Machiavelli, Nicolo (2012) *The Prince*. Hollywood, FL: Simon & Brown.

Martin, Roger (2009) *Opposable Mind: Winning through integrative thinking*. Boston, MA: Harvard Business Review Press.

Peters, Tom and Waterman, Robert (2004) *In Search of Excellence: Lessons from America's best-run companies*. London: Collins Business Essentials.

Purkins, John and Royston-Lee, David (2012) *Brand You: Turn your winning talents into a winning formula*. Harlow: Pearson.

Rumelt, Richard (2011) *Good Strategy/Bad Strategy: The difference and why it matters*. London: Profile Books.

Tzu, Sun (Giles, L., trans.) (2009) *The Art of War*. El Paso, TX: El Paso Norte Press.

Zook, Chris (2004) *Beyond the Core: Expand your market without abandoning your roots*. Boston, MA: Harvard Business Review Press.

Zweig, Stéfan (1935) *Joseph Fouché: The portrait of a politician*. Indiana University, IN: Blue Ribbon Books.

Appendices

'Not to know is bad, not to wish to know is worse.'

Nigerian proverb

Appendix 1:
Examples of an individual development plan and goals and objectives

These examples are for your reference. See Chapter 7 for a full explanation of their use.

Individual development plan

Name:

Job title:

Date of completion:

Strengths

Enter the behaviours, skills, knowledge and/or characteristics that position this individual for future success in the Group.

Example: Strong practical focus on results delivery blended with a comprehensive management background and good strategic sense. Ambitious, keen to demonstrate her excellent potential. Has shown real improvement in her leadership skills.

Areas for development

Enter the behaviours, skills, knowledge and/or characteristics that this individual needs to acquire or address for future success in the Group.

Example: Can appear to be risk- or conflict-averse. Would benefit from tempering his obvious drive and commitment in order to allow others to shape solutions and develop joint commitment.

Actions to address development needs

Enter the specific development interventions that are recommended for this staff member during the course of the next 12 to 18 months. Remember that you can also choose a learning event and book it.

Example: Her current role will enable her to leverage her functional leadership, acquire core business knowledge and extend her leadership networks. Exposure to her commercial businesses in the Group. Exposure to large, complex management challenge with bottom line responsibility.

Next job/position options

Enter the position or generic job that may be appropriate for this individual to hold as his or her next assignment. Remember that employee and/or supervisors can also select a specific job from the jobs catalogue.

Example: Vice President Commercial Marketing, zonal role.

Long-term career options

Enter the generic jobs or roles that these indicate.

Example: Strong candidate for CEO of a major Group business. Managerial role with direct bottom line responsibility.

Own views and wishes

Individual views on your current assignment and your preferences for your short- and long-term development. Specific items such as future generic jobs or time in an organisation unit can be selected as additional items in your plan.

Example: In the short term, I want to develop my technical knowledge as a mechanical engineer and my current assignment is allowing me to achieve this. Within the next two years, I will look for an assignment to an operating unit with offshore facilities, then I want exposure to a new project to allow me to move into project management.

Short-term development (preferences for next role and personal development)

Long-term development (preferences for the longer term, five+ years)

Mobility

Fully: You would consider moving to any site or country. You do not have to add further explanation.

Not mobile: You are not able to move from your current location. You may wish to add further explanation. **Example**: Not able to relocate because I look after my elderly parents or only available to work in this office

Mobile with constraints: You would consider relocating, but there are constraints or restrictions involved. Please add a note with further explanation.

Example: Prepared for overseas assignment when children have completed secondary education or would like to work in London, depending on employment opportunities for my partner.

Availability date

The earliest date that you are available for a reassignment. You may specify an end date or indicate that your availability is ongoing by leaving the end date as 31/12/9999. Your actual departure date (negotiated with both organisations) may be later than this date. You may add further explanation.

Goals and objectives
Priorities

1 HSSE performance.

2 Continue on business partnering journey through results delivery (cost, working capital management) and focus on compliance.

3 Deliver migrations agenda.

4 Deliver on weighted average cost of capital project.

5 Deliver on portfolio agenda (exits and joint ventures).

Health, safety, security and the environment

Visible leadership during safety day for aviation.

Airport inspection and participation in toolbox meetings on a periodic basis.

People

Active career management and talent management for aviation community. Drive continuous improvement culture by means of training programme.

Promote and display inclusiveness.

Operational excellence

Support business operational excellence project's LEAN methodology.

Drive/support flawless migrations to shared services centre finance and business.

Maintain FCM compliance in aviation.

Finance differentiators

Strategy, planning and appraisal

Enhance business understanding and drive forecast accuracy mindset.

Actively participate in business-specific formulation of strategy.

Risk management

Champion risk/reward mindset in investment decision to prevent value leakage.

Contract management

- Audit contracting process in sales/JV and supply for aviation.

- Assess strengths and weaknesses and drive corrective actions.

Leadership team contribution

Play an effective role in aviation leadership team in support of aviation VP, ensure finance is equipped to play co-pilot role.

Lead DS finance leadership circle pilot and ensure roll-out in other regions and bigger group.

Appendix 2:
The basics of body language

There follow brief descriptions of some of the basic elements of body language to help you quickly analyse people around you.

Feet and legs
Happy feet

Feet and legs bounce in a happy way.

Feet point upwards, indicating a positive state.

Caution: May signal impatience, restlessness, nerves instead.

Shifting direction/orientating reflex

Feet point towards the things you like and away from things you dislike.

Feet turned away indicate disengagement and a desire to distance oneself from people, objects and so on in the environment.

Shifting feet indicate a desire to leave.

Foot freeze

If someone naturally bounces or wiggles their feet and suddenly stops, it indicates that the person is feeling threatened or stressed.

Foot lock and leave

Interlocking the feet or turning the toes inwards are restraining behaviours. This indicates insecurities, anxiety or feeling threatened. It can appear more natural in women, but maintaining this position for prolonged periods of time is unnatural for both genders.

Knee clasp

Hands on knees with a forward lean of the torso indicates an intention to move or leave.

The leg kick

This is an automatic, subconscious way of combating something unpleasant.

Leg splay

Territorial displays establish dominance. The wider apart the feet, the less comfortable/more dominant the individual.

Leg cross

Standing with crossed legs indicates high levels of comfort.

Bringing legs together dissipates confrontation.

Seated leg cross

When sitting side-by-side, the top leg will point towards the other person if they are on good terms.

If a person does not like the topic companions brings up, he or she will switch the position of the legs so that the thigh becomes a barrier (blocking).

Overall principle: congruence equals harmony.

Torso
Ventral fronting

The ventral front – where the eyes, mouth, chest, breasts, genitals are located – is very sensitive to things and people you like or dislike. People face their ventral fronts towards people or things they like.

Ventral denial

When someone does not like what is being said or the person who is saying it, it is natural to turn the ventral front away or turn so his or her back is facing them.

The torso shield

When it is impractical or socially unacceptable to lean away from someone or something we dislike, the arms or objects may subconsciously be used as barriers. The tighter the grip, the more anxious the person is.

Females may cross their arms over their stomachs or cross one arm across their fronts and grab the opposite arm at the elbow. They may also place their bag on their laps.

Males may suddenly button their jackets, play with their ties, cufflinks or watches and cross their arms.

Torso displays

Splaying or spreading the limbs out is a territorial or dominance display. It is reserved for those in positions of power or authority.

Puffing the chest

This is a signal of asserting dominance. It is used in fight mode.

Baring the torso

Removing an item of clothing, such as jacket, scarf, tie or hat, when unnecessary, indicates a willingness to engage in a fight.

Breathing behaviours and the torso

When under stress, a person will breathe rapidly, the chest expanding and contracting rapidly to oxygenate the body in preparation for a fight.

Arms
Subdued

Restrained, constricted arms indicate negative feelings.

Exuberant

Free, expansive movements (waving, pointing, gesticulating) indicate a positive state of mind.

Arm withdrawal

This occurs when someone is upset, threatened or fearful. It can be observed when two people are arguing.

Restriction of arm movement

Arm freeze, like foot freeze above, can indicate a feeling of distress.

Territorial arm display

This is easy to observe on public transport. It is common to see people vying for extra space by trying to take up as much of the arm rest as possible, at the expense of their neighbours. It can also be observed in boardrooms where one person – usually a dominant one – will spread their papers, pens and so on about and use their elbows to dominate the space. Claiming territory in this manner can have negative effects.

Hooding

This is often seen during business meetings. A seated person will lean back and interlaces his or her hands behind his or her head. A hooding effect takes up a large amount of room so is a sign of wanting to be dominant.

Planting fingertips

If when standing a person leans slightly forwards to plant their fingers, spread apart, on a desk, this is a display of confidence and authority.

Hands
Visible hands

Someone keeping his or her hands visible while talking will be viewed as honest and transparent. It is a natural trustbuilder.

Handshake

Hearty, firm and with a few pumps – a good handshake is critical in creating contacts and a good impression. You can complement it by maintaining good eye contact and smiling.

Aggressive hand gestures

Finger pointing and snapping fingers at someone are both considered highly offensive.

Nervous hands

Stress or being exposed to something very negative can trigger quivering of the hands. However, this can also occur as a reaction to high levels of excitement. Context is key.

Steepling

A signal of the highest level of confidence.

It involves touching the spread fingertips on both hands like a church steeple. Females tend to steeple at waist level, while males tend to do so at chest level, making it more visible and powerful.

When experiencing a rapid change in confidence, the fingers of steepled hands can quickly interlock and become prayer hands – a gesture expressing low confidence. Steeping is an excellent tool for establishing authority in a confident, non-aggressive way.

Thumb displays

Thumbs pointing upwards is always a sign of a high level of confidence. Interlacing the hands, as mentioned above, is usually a sign of a low level of confidence, but this is transformed into the opposite when the thumbs are extended straight up.

People who show their thumbs are generally more aware of their environment, more acute in their thinking and sharper in their observations than those who don't.

When thumbs are stuck in pockets with the fingers hanging out, this indicates low levels of confidence or self-esteem.

Frozen hands

Liars tend to gesture, touch and move their hands and legs less than honest people.

Stroking or rubbing of the hands

A person who is in doubt or under a low level of stress will lightly rub the palms of his or her hands together. If the situation becomes progressively more stressful, the stroking will become more dramatic as a response to this.

Index